Chartres Cathedral

I. Ambulatory

II. North Transept Porch, detail

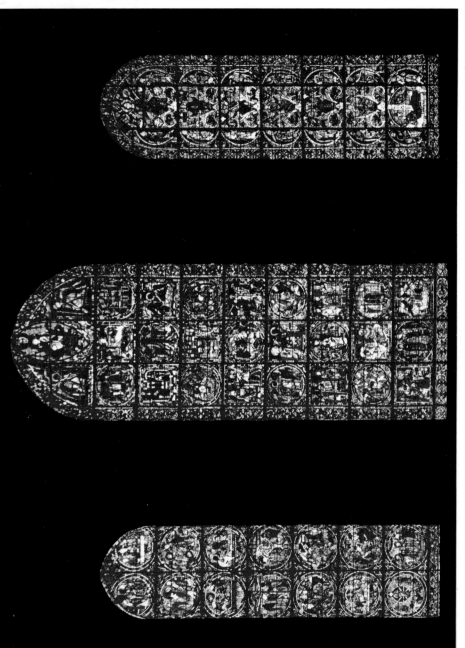

III. West Windows

IV. South Transept Windows

CRITICAL STUDIES IN ART HISTORY

Chartres Cathedral

ROBERT BRANNER

with source material and selected critical writings

125 illustrations, 4 in colour

THAMES AND HUDSON · LONDON

Published in Great Britain in 1969 by Thames and Hudson Ltd., London

500   46002   7

CONTENTS

vi   *Contents*

LIST OF ILLUSTRATIONS

COLOR PLATES

between pages 2 and 3

MONOCHROME ILLUSTRATIONS

PREFACE

The essays brought together here are among the most famous and most penetrating studies of Chartres, one of the best-known Gothic cathedrals. Some of them, such as Vöge's, have never before been translated into English and have therefore been inaccessible to a large part of the American public. Others are merely sections—or even paragraphs—buried in longer works and known only to the cognoscenti and professional historians of art. The differing points of view which the reader will find expressed toward the same monument and, in some cases, toward the same part of that monument prove that the study of Chartres is still in its infancy. It is my hope that the juxtaposition of opinions in this little volume, far from disconcerting the reader, will stimulate him to make discoveries of his own.

Since Chartres has so many diverse aspects, it has seemed best to group the essays in sections, each dealing with a theme or a part of the monument. The Introductory Essay presents a general picture in chronological sequence. The medieval texts are fundamental for assigning precise dates to the monument, but we should not forget that they come from a time when accurate documentation in the modern sense was unknown. The student of medieval art must therefore glean his facts from incidental notes found in documents—such as legal contracts, charters establishing or reforming liturgical practices, and chronicles—that were written with entirely different purposes in mind. Chartres is unusual in having a book recounting the Miracles of the Virgin, that contains a factual description of the fire of 1194 and the reconstruction that followed. Without such a text, it would be almost possible to assume that the rebuilding went unnoticed on the everyday scene at Chartres; as it is, however, we know from the eyewitness account that the creation of the present Cathedral was a matter of paramount concern to everyone. But in the book of Miracles, the historical material was clearly thought to be incidental to the main theme, which was the glorification of the Virgin.

Glorification is still the theme in the seventeenth century, but by that time the physical realities of the monument had come into greater prominence. The feat of constructing a building as large as Chartres inspired awe and became something to rival in the century of the Bourbon kings of France. The period of St. Louis was taken as a model by his descendants, Louis XIII and Louis XIV, who built monuments even larger than Chartres and completed unfinished thirteenth-century cathedrals such as Orléans. Orléans was a symbol of the Bourbon dynasty, but completing it in the Gothic manner involved an archeological study of Gothic methods, a study that was beginning to take root in other European countries at the same time. The difference betwen the late medieval, fantasy-laden approach to Gothic and the modern archeological one is amply conveyed by the contrast between the writings of Sebastien Roulliard (1609) and Vincent Sablon (1671).

The modern student, however, is more interested in Chartres as a work of art than as a historic curiosity, and the remaining essays in the volume fall into this category. It was Henri Focillon, in his lectures at the Sorbonne in the 1920's and 1930's (later published as *Art d'Occident*), who first emphasized the art-historical, as against the archeological, importance of Chartres. With his usual deftness and skill, he sketches the place of Chartres among the cathedrals of the opening years of the thirteenth century. To this Jean Bony has added a brief but stunning analysis of the design of Chartres. Taken together, these two passages are, like Chartres itself, not only a summation of many years of thought but also a point of departure for further speculation. They are supplemented by the technical analysis of the flying buttress by Viollet-le-Duc, the foremost student of Gothic architecture in the nineteenth century, and by Professor John Fitchen's provocative attempt to show how the great Gothic cathedrals may have been erected.

The sculpture of Chartres has attracted much more attention than the architecture, and this is reflected in the presence of two separate sections of essays here. In the first, the older sculpture (on the west façade) is discussed. Although all scholars now admit that Vöge's book of 1894 is the basis for modern studies, it has never been widely disseminated. Those familiar with the recent literature will at once detect flaws in Vöge's arguments—such as that the sculpture of Chartres-West was earlier than that of St.-Denis, or that the façade was originally intended to look the way we now see it. But Vöge's analysis is valuable in another way, for it is a demonstration of method, a way of approaching a monument and of coordinating the multiple impressions we form of it into a single, coherent point of view. Vöge's great sensitivity and imagination are nowhere more in evidence than in this work. Moreover he offers the first sensible explanation of the origin of the statue-column, the fundamental building block of Gothic sculpture. This has been disagreed with—and, worse yet, disregarded —by many more recent writers. But it has never been proven absolutely wrong and may just turn out to be the correct analysis. Alan Priest, on the other hand, takes us further into the intricacies of stylistic analysis in isolating the various masters who worked on Chartres-West. And finally Jacques Vanuxem put a term to certain interpretations of the meaning of these sculptures by explaining the historical context in which they originated.

As for the transepts, Focillon once again gives us a broad picture of the nature of Gothic sculpture at the start of the thirteenth century, while Peter Kidson takes us through the intricate iconographic patterns of the Chartres portals. They supplement one another in clarity of thought and description, forming what I consider to be the best introduction to these magnificent ensembles. Vöge's second essay, in contrast, is a brilliant analysis-in-depth of the work of one sculptor. Although it makes use of a number of abstract concepts (such as "form") that are no longer much used in art history, it is well worth reading since, more than any other essay I know on medieval art, it comes directly to grips with the basic problems of stylistic analysis in sculpture. In its own time, it was an epoch-making work and the intervening years, far from "dating" it, have only served to increase its importance.

Henry Adam's essays on the stained glass, one of the glories of Chartres, are so well known as to need almost no comment. It did not seem right, in an American book intended for the American student, not to include these lines of one of our most noted authors, no matter how often they have been reproduced elsewhere. Maurice Denis' brief statement provides an interesting contrast to Adams' poetico-historical approach.

Chartres has been very well photographed, and I have not thought it necessary to illustrate every point made in the Introductory Essay or to attempt a complete photographic presentation of the Cathedral. Every effort has been made, however, to include a complete illustration of the original essays. Additions to the original texts are indicated by brackets.

ROBERT BRANNER
Columbia University

CHARTRES CATHEDRAL: CHRONOLOGICAL OUTLINE

743: Cathedral burned by Hunald, Duke of Aquitania; reconstructed by Bishop Adventus.

858: Cathedral burned by the Danes; reconstructed by Bishop Gislebert.

962: Cathedral attacked by fire; a new façade built.

1020: Cathedral destroyed by fire; reconstructed by Bishop Fulbert. Crypt ready in 1024; dedication under Bishop Thierry, 1037.

c. 1050–1075: Canon Raimbaud leaves money for a "vestibule" at the western end of the Cathedral.

1092: Dean Abalard gives money for the completion of a tower.

1134: Fire attacks buildings around the Cathedral, especially at the western end. New western end begun with construction of present north tower base, followed about 1144 by the south tower and the sculpted portals; finished about 1155.

1194: Fulbert's basilica destroyed by fire; Gothic church begun. Vaults in place, 1220; canons occupy the choir stalls, 1221; dedicated in 1260.

1323: Capitular hall with chapel of St.-Piat above it begun by Huguet d'Ivry.

1417: Vendôme chapel added to the nave.

1507: North tower spire begun by Jean de Beauce.

1514: Sculptured choir enclosure begun by Jean de Beauce; statutes executed during the course of the sixteenth, seventeenth, and eighteenth centuries.

1763: Choir and sanctuary redecorated in classical style.

THE ILLUSTRATIONS

The author is grateful to all who have provided photographs, in particular to Archives Photographiques, Paris; Courtauld Institute, London; Foto Marburg, Marburg-an-der-Lahn; and to Professor George Zarnecki, of the Courtauld Institute, who took the photographs in figures 24, 32, 36, 61, and 62.

1. Chartres from the southeast

2. Interior

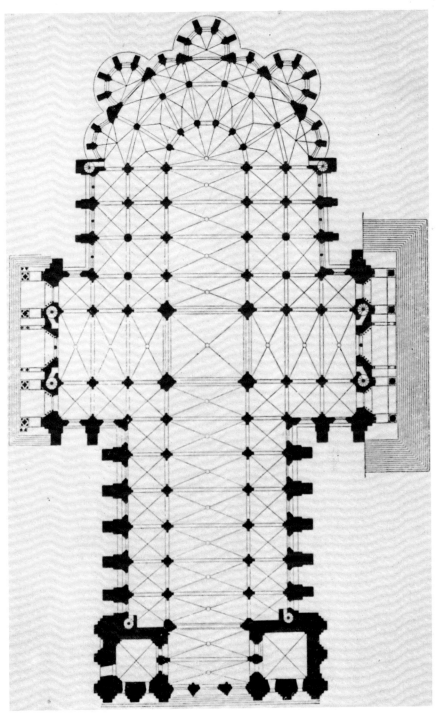

3. Plan of 1194 church

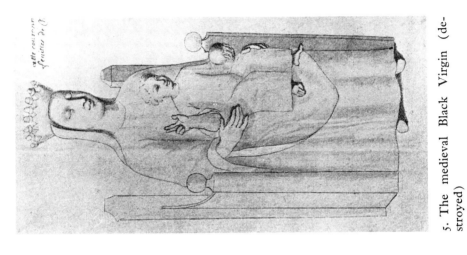

5. The medieval Black Virgin (destroyed)

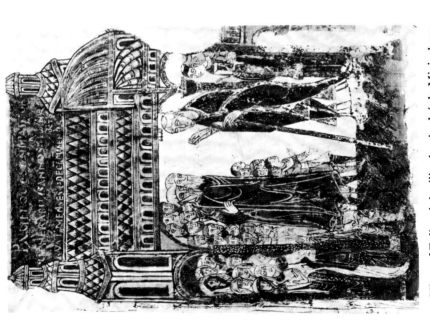

4. View of Fulbert's basilica by André de Mici, about 1030

7. Ebreuil, west tower

6. Plan of Cathedral around 1100 (Branner)

8. Fulbert's crypt

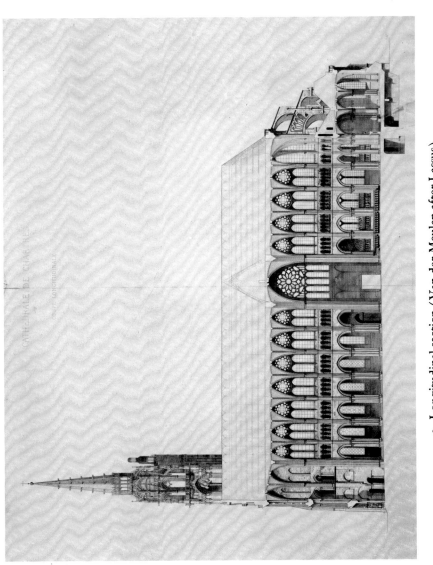

CATHÉDRALE DE CHARTRES

COUPE LONGITUDINALE

9. Longitudinal section (Van der Meulen after Lassus)

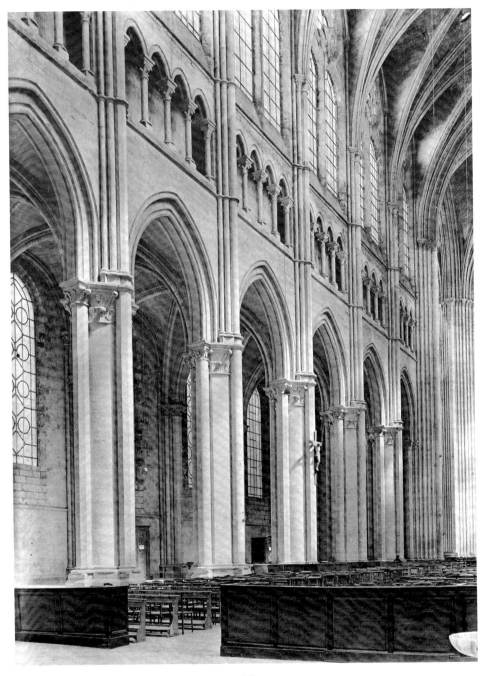

10. Nave

11. Choir

12. Choir aisle

13. Nave aisle

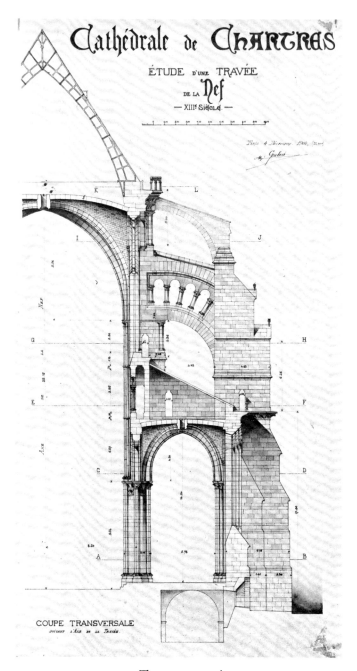

Cathédrale de Chartres

ÉTUDE D'UNE TRAVÉE
DE LA Nef
— XIIIᵉ Siècle —

COUPE TRANSVERSALE
SUIVANT L'AXE DE LA TRAVÉE

14. Transverse section

15. Nave exterior

16. Eastern end

17. Ambulatory

18. Radiating chapel keystone

19. Triforium

20. North tower

21. South tower

22. West façade

23. West portals

24. Central tympanum (West): Second Coming and Last Judgment

25. South tympanum (West): Incarnation

26. North tympanum (West): Ascension

27. St.-Gilles, façade

28. Arles, St.-Trophîme: tympanum

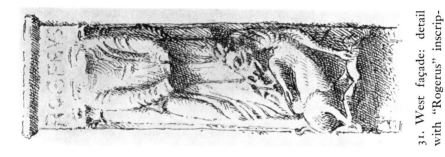

31. West façade: detail with "Rogerus" inscription (Priest)

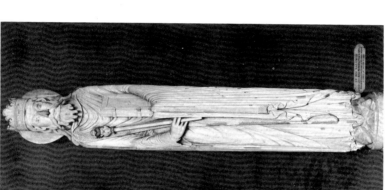

30. Corbeil: King (Louvre)

29. Toulouse, St.-Sernin: Christ

32. North portal archivolts (West): Zodiac and Labors of the Months

33. Central portal archivolts (West): Elders and Angels

34. South portal archivolts (West): Liberal Arts and Angels

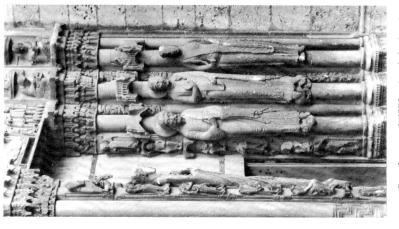

37. South portal (West): right jamb

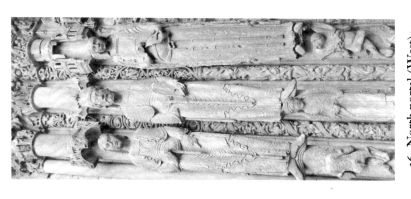

36. North portal (West): left jamb

35. Etampes, Notre-Dame: jamb

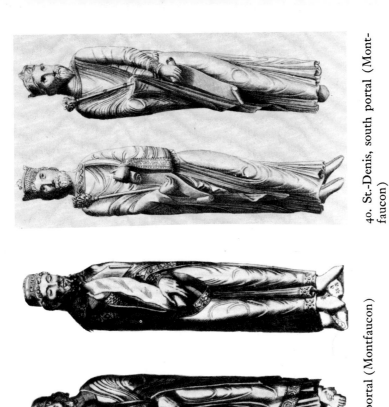

40. St.-Denis, south portal (Montfaucon)

39. St.-Denis, north portal (Montfaucon)

38. Central portal (West): left jamb

41. Etampes, Notre-Dame, tympanum: Ascension

42. Anzy-le-Duc, tympanum: detail

43. South portal (West), capital: Supper at Emmaus

44. St.-Gilles, frieze: detail

45. St.-Gilles, frieze, detail: Last Supper

46. Toulouse, Cathedral cloister, capital (Musée des Augustins)

47. Moissac, lintel, detail: Elders

50. Nesle-la-Reposte, portal (Montfaucon)

49. Toulouse, Cathedral, chapter house: Apostles (Musée des Augustins)

48. West façade: Elder

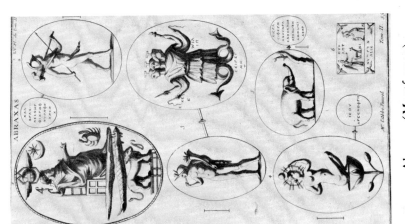

53. Abraxas (Montfaucon)

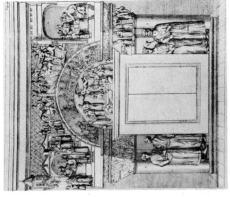

52. Vendôme: Holy Tear (Mabillon)

51. Paris, St.-Germain des Prés, portal (Ruinart)

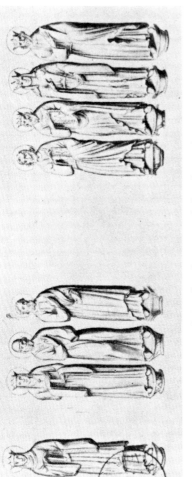

54. West façade statues (Montfaucon)

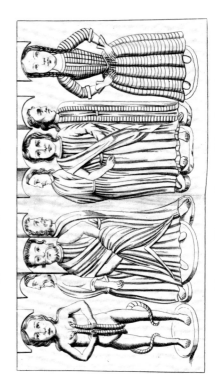

55. Montmorillon: sculpture (Montfaucon)

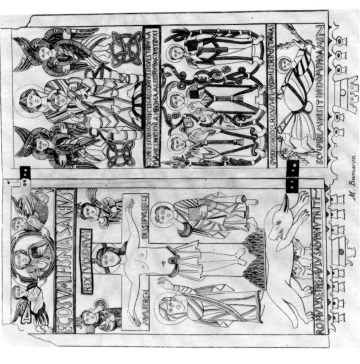

58. Ivory Diptych (Montfaucon)

57. Tomb of Montfau-
con (Lenoir)

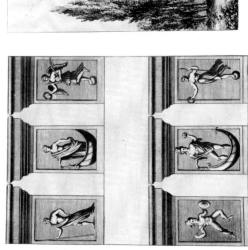

56. Flavigny: ancient sculpture
(Montfaucon)

59. North transept portals and porch

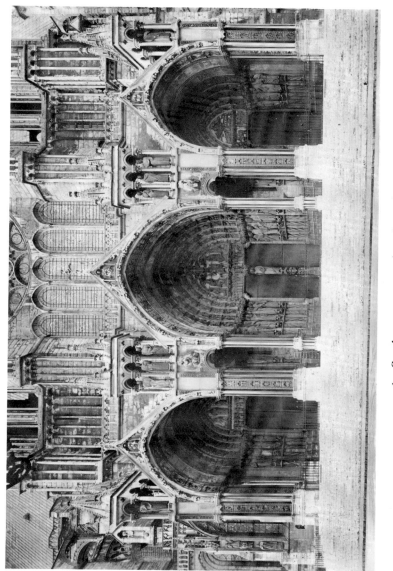

60. South transept portals and porch

61. North transept, central portal, tympanum: Coronation, Dormition, and Assumption of the Virgin

62. North transept, central portal, archivolts: Tree of Jesse

63. North transept, central portal, left jamb: Precursors

64. North transept, central portal, right jamb: Precursors

65. South transept, central portal, tympanum: Last Judgment, Saved and Damned

66. South transept, central portal, archivolts: Angels, Damned, Resurrection

67. South transept, central portal, left jamb: Apostles

68. South transept, central portal, left jamb: Apostles

70. North transept, central portal, left jamb, detail: Melchisideck

69. South transept, left portal, left jamb, detail: St. Theodore

74. South transept, left portal, left jamb: Sts. Theodore, Stephen, Clement, and Lawrence

73. South transept, central portal, trumeau: Beau Dieu

72. North transept, central portal, trumeau: St. Anne

71. North transept, left portal, right jamb: Visitation

76. North transept, right portal, jamb: Balaam, Sheba, and Solomon

75. North transept, right portal

77. North transept, right portal, tympanum: Job and Judgment of Solomon

78. North transept, right portal: King's head

79. North transept, left portal: head of St. Elizabeth

80. North transept, right portal: King's head

83. North transept, right portal: King's head

82. North transept, right portal: detail

81. North transept, right portal: King's head

85. North transept, right portal, archivolt: Samson's lion

84. North transept, right portal, right jamb: Console beneath Judith

86. North transept, right portal, archivolt

87. North transept, right portal, right jamb: detail of Joseph

88. North transept, right portal: Job's wife

89. North transept, right portal, archivolt: "Judith in prayer"

90. North transept, right portal: detail of Solomon's judgment

91. North transept, right portal: detail of Job scene

92. North transept, left portal: detail of tympanum

94. North transept, central portal: detail of Coronation

93. South transept, central portal: detail of Last Judgment

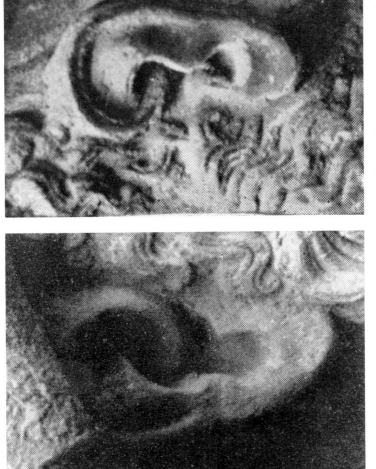

97. Reims, Calixtus portal: detail of ear

96. Reims, Calixtus portal: detail of ear

95. Reims, Calixtus portal, archivolt: bishop

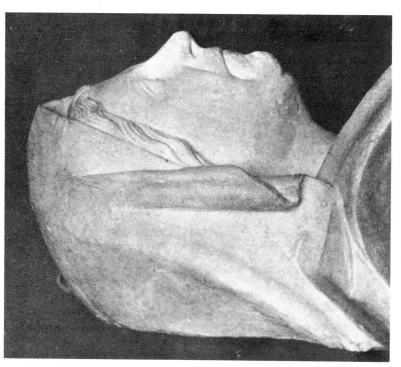

99. Reims, west wall, interior: detail

98. Reims, west wall, interior: detail

101. Reims, Last Judgment portal: St. Paul

100. Remis, Last Judgment portal: St. Peter

103. Reims, Calixtus portal: angel

102. Reims, Calixtus portal: angel

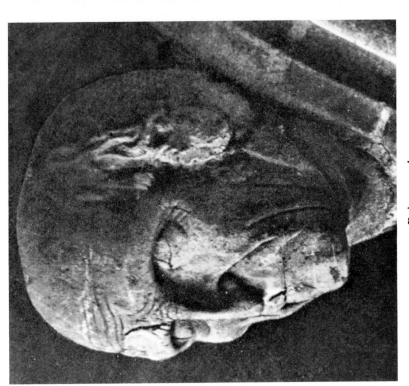

105. Reims: mask

104. Reims, south transept: "Pepin"

l'Eglise de Nôtre dame Veüe par le
dedans à l'entreé de laquelle est le Baron
du Bruëit qui vient offrir à la Vierge le
boulet de Canon dont il a esté frappé sans estre
Blessé

106. Jubé (Nicolas de Larmesin)

107. Jubé: Saved

108. Jubé: Magi before Herod

109. Notre-Dame de la Belle Verrière

110. "Infancy" window: Magi and Flight into Egypt

111. "Infancy" window: Baptism of Christ; Dream of Joseph

112. "Infancy" window: Angel with staff; Twelve Apostles

113. Clearstory windows: Virgin and Child; Robert de Bérou and pilgrims

114. Clearstory windows: Prodigal
Son

115. Chapel of St.-Piat

116. North tower

117. Choir screen: Story of the Birth of the Virgin

CHARTRES CATHEDRAL

To the modern tourist and historian alike, the Cathedral of Chartres is the monument most representative of the Gothic style. It is the only French cathedral to have survived in nearly complete form from the early thirteenth-century, with sculpture decorating every portal, with a full array of stained glass giving the interior a deep, vibrant color, and with architecture which is surprisingly uniform for a medieval church. How fortunate that Chartres also stood at a critical moment in the development of Gothic art! Architecturally and sculpturally, Chartres was not only a culmination of the early Gothic experiments of the twelfth century, but was also the pace-setter for the century that was to follow. It is much more than a mere example of a type, an anonymous member of a class of objects used by the present-day teacher to illustrate historical movements. Chartres was itself a motivating force, a powerful agent of change in the thirteenth century, the first of the so-called High Gothic cathedrals that fixed the future of the Gothic style. Together, these two sides of Chartres—the aesthetic and the historical—give it a unique place in the modern world.

The Cathedral of Our Lady at Chartres rises at the edge of the plain of Beauce, a gently rolling country in the wheat-producing region of France. Its spires, like beacons, can be seen for miles across the yellow fields, drawing the traveler on, promising him comfort and sanctuary. In the city (fig. 1), the towering cathedral was the medieval forerunner of the skyscraper, but, unlike its modern counterpart, it subsumed a number of different functions. It was generally the one building that could hold all the townspeople at once, and therefore sometimes acted as a meeting hall for semireligious events. Moreover, the medieval cathedral was physically integrated into the town. Houses crowded up to its very walls and lean-to's were built right against them. Stalls and stores often abounded here and sometimes the local fair would be held on the *parvis*, the open space lying in front of the façade. At Chartres, the local labor force shaped up in one of the side aisles of the nave. At one moment or another, therefore, the medieval church could serve civic, communal, and commercial purposes. But it was first and foremost a religious building, the seat of the bishop and of the canons of the chapter, his assistants in

pastoral mission. At Chartres, the bishop's palace lay on the north side
of the Cathedral, while, on the other side, the houses of the canons
were grouped around an irregularly shaped courtyard called the
cloister. The Cathedral dominated the town, not only by its physical
form but as the center of spiritual authority as well.

Medieval art was essentially a religious art, not because it was at
the service of the Church, but because the age was a profoundly religious one. The salvation of the soul after death was an event hoped
for and looked forward to and the spiritual life was considered the
highest calling in this world. It was an age of miracles and one in
which men such as St. Bernard and Dante had personally experienced
the revelation of God. It is small wonder, then, that medieval art is
visionary and intense in character, or that a small town like Chartres
should have built an astonishingly large cathedral.

In the Middle Ages, the Church was the greatest patron of the arts,
incessantly calling upon the best artistic talent and providing it with
the wherewithall as well as the incentive to produce one masterpiece
after another. Kings might also commission important and costly
works of art, and, in later times, the bourgeois towns put art into the
service of government and commerce by building townhalls and guild-
halls. But the Church was the only institution that consistently patron-
ized the arts throughout the Middle Ages and, in the twelfth and
thirteenth centuries, it was the only institution capable of concentrat-
ing the diverse energies of all the people—noble, burgher, and peasant
alike—on a single project. Without this concentration, the Gothic
cathedrals could not have been created.

Medieval Chartres considered itself the chief sanctuary of the Virgin
in Western Europe. The source of this eminence was the "tunic of
the Virgin," a piece of cloth thought to have been worn by the Virgin
and given to the Cathedral in the ninth century. The story of how
it came to Chartres has often been recounted, nowhere more charm-
ingly than by Vincent Sablon (see pp. 107–114), and forms a part of
its aura. With this prestigious relic, Chartres became a famous pilgrimage center and the pilgrimage, in turn, was the chief source of the
town's prosperity.

The tunic was kept in the crypt of the Cathedral in what came to
be called a grotto because of its darkness. In the same place were two
other things of importance for the history of the cult at Chartres—
a well and, later, a statue of the Virgin. Water has always been
associated with certain religious acts and the well was probably once
part of a complex of religious buildings dating from Roman or even
Gallic times. The traditional name of *Lieux forts*—the "strong places"
—may have been bestowed on it, because the site lay close to the

Gallo-Roman city wall, the defensive perimeter of late Antique Chartres. In later times, it was altered to *Saints lieux forts*, or, more simply, to *Saints forts*—the "strong saints"—and tales of martyrdom, like that of Modesta, the daughter of the Roman governor, were woven around it (see Sablon, p. 109). The water itself was believed to have curative powers and this served to augment the popularity of the pilgrimage.

The statue of the Virgin also played a role in the general evolution of the cult at Chartres. The wooden statue now in the Cathedral replaced one that probably had been made in the eleventh or twelfth century (fig. 5) and that was destroyed during the French Revolution. Medieval man liked to see an image of the patron saint at the cult site and the statue served this purpose admirably. It came to be considered a sort of holy object and even today, the same charisma is attached to the statue that was carved only a century ago.

The grotto, the well, and the statue later gave rise to an interesting anachronism, for, in the Renaissance, it was felt necessary to prove that the cult of the Virgin had been prefigured by local practices at Chartres long before the advent of Christianity. One of the first modern men to write on the Cathedral, Sebastien Roulliard (see pp. 104–107), supposed that the Druids had had an altar there dedicated to a *virgo paritura*, a virgin who was to give birth. (For a slightly more recent statement of the story, see Sablon p. 108.) The tale, of course, has no historical foundation whatsoever, for the Druids did not use icons and there was no statue at Chartres until the eleventh century. There may, all the same, have been a double source for the Virgin cult at Chartres—one Christian and imported, the other pagan and local. Regardless of what may really have happened in that dimly known time, Christianity was well established at Chartres by the end of the fourth century and throughout the Middle Ages it flourished and found its clearest expression there in the cult of the Virgin.

The present Cathedral of Chartres is largely the work of the late twelfth and early thirteenth centuries, but here and there—notably in the crypt and on the west façade—substantial remains of older monuments are to be found. The history of these early Cathedrals is very imperfectly known, but they are nonetheless important because, in addition to showing that the site had been devoted to religious purposes for centuries, they also serve to explain certain aspects of the Gothic cathedral. A brief résumé is therefore in order.

As far as the oldest Christian building on the site is concerned, only a very general remark can be made. The church probably lay snug up against the late Roman city wall that ran across the area. Locations along city walls were distinctly lower-class and undesirable at that time. But since Christianity was still only a mystery cult of minor importance, the community at Chartres may have been glad to find a site with previous religious associations, as the well suggests. Whatever pagan cult had been there may have moved when the city wall was put up and perhaps that is how the Christians first got the place.

From the time of the Romans to the time of the Carolingians in the ninth century, the architectural history of Chartres Cathedral is a virtual void, punctuated here and there by a text, always frustratingly brief and usually referring to a fire. In 743, for instance, the Cathedral was burned by Hunald, Duke of Aquitania; but it is not known if the church had to be rebuilt from its foundations and, if so, what it may have looked like. In 858, the church was again burned, this time by the Danes, and a new building was begun soon after by Bishop Gislebert. Fragments of this Cathedral have tentatively been identified in the substructures of the present one. It was probably larger than its predecessors, for the apse projected beyond the emplacement of the Roman wall. This indicates that the town of Chartres was beginning to expand outside the fixed Roman perimeter and the larger population, of course, required a larger sanctuary. There was still another fire in 962. The texts tell us that a new façade was then put on the monument, but its design and even its location are unknown. It is only with the Cathedral erected by Bishop Fulbert after 1020 that we reach something tangible.

Fulbert had been a brilliant teacher at Chartres before he became bishop in 1007 and it was he, more than any other individual, who laid the foundations of the famous school that was to flourish at Chartres in the twelfth century. When the Cathedral was destroyed by fire in 1020, he took considerable pains to raise construction funds himself, as we learn from his letters to King Robert of France and to Duke William of Aquitania (see pp. 92–93). The crypt was completed in 1024, but Fulbert died in 1029, before the church above it was finished. The dedication took place under his successor, Thierry, in 1037.

Fulbert's church was nearly as long as the later Gothic Cathedral, and fully as wide (fig. 6). To the east were three large chapels projecting from an ambulatory; the latter joined two side aisles flanking the long nave, which were, in turn, flanked by two towers; and at the west there was a tower. The aisles, ambulatory, and radiating chapels were repeated at the crypt level, indicating that the plan was intended to accommodate large numbers of pilgrims: one could enter the crypt at the western end of one corridor, walk down to the grotto of the Virgin, and come out through the other corridor without disturbing services that were taking place in the church upstairs. Similar patterns of circulation, on two levels or even on one alone, characterized the great pilgrimage churches of the Loire Valley, not far from Chartres, in the late tenth and early eleventh centuries, and Fulbert's basilica clearly was a member of that group.

The form of the church proper is known to us only through a miniature painted by a monk of Chartres named André de Mici (fig. 4). It is particularly important because it was painted in 1030 and shows us the Cathedral before the appearance of new additions in the later eleventh century. The miniature represents the bishop talking to the people, with a side view of the Cathedral rising above them like a proscenium. The view was made without regard for the exact position or orientation of the parts—one of the lateral towers, for instance, was eliminated, probably to give a better view of the body of the church—but we can pick out the major elements quite easily. To the right are the curved roofs of the apse and one of the chapels; behind them is the far or north lateral tower; in the center, the nave and the near aisle are visible, each with a long row of windows; and to the left is the façade tower. The miniature conveys something of the monumentality and massiveness of the building and it is not hard for us to imagine that it cut an impressive figure on the skyline. But it is the surviving crypt that gives us some idea of the magnitude of Fulbert's church (fig. 8). The ambulatory is a bit taller than it is wide and is covered by a series of barrel and groined vaults, one having smooth, semicircular surfaces and the other having pointed ridges or groins that cut across one another. But there are no architectural ornaments at all—no capitals, columns, or decorated window jambs. There were probably some frescoes (the present coat of paint is scarcely a century old), but their form is unknown and they could not have changed the aspect of the architecture significantly. The bare walls and the barren vaults, which, as Sablon said, "recalled the simplicity of our elders," convey an impression of brute strength that is unforgettable. This is pure architecture, like that of the prehistoric Greeks and certain modern masters, in which the aesthetic aspect of the work is formed simply by the combination of basic building blocks, not by the addition of ornament. The church proper must, of course, have had some decoration, as André de Mici's miniature suggests, but its impact probably did not differ markedly from that of the crypt. To the pilgrim, Fulbert's basilica must have seemed not only a safe haven after the uncertain adventures of travel, but also a mighty church, fitting in importance with respect to the cult it housed.

Sometime after the middle of the eleventh century, the western tower of Fulbert's church was enlarged. A canon, named Raimbaud, left most of his estate for the construction of a "vestibule" on the west front, and, in 1092, Abalard, the dean of the chapter, left funds for the construction of a tower, quite possibly completing the work begun by Raimbaud. The new part consisted of a large porch of several bays, open at the sides and vaulted, with a second story containing a chapel.[1] Westworks of this kind originated in the Carolingian period and had become fairly widespread by 1100, so that it is not difficult for us to imagine what the one at Chartres must have looked like (fig. 7).

Fulbert's basilica lasted until 1194, but the late eleventh-century tower was affected by another fire that swept the city in 1134. The Cathedral is famous for the work carried out over the next two decades, for the new west façade is one of the great monuments of early Gothic art. The façade is also evidence that the cult of the Virgin was still strong, because the elaborate sculptural decoration and the large stained glass windows must have been very expensive (fig. 22; the rose window and the north spire were created at a later date). The pilgrimage had continued to attract large numbers of people to Chartres and their donations certainly helped repair and reface the damaged building. But even more than that, in 1144, on the tenth anniversary of the fire, the Cathedral suddenly became the object of a mass exercise in piety and devotion. People of all ranks began to band together to supply the physical labor required to bring the building materials to the site, pulling wagons loaded with wood and stone in what has been called the "cult of carts" (see pp. 93–94). The materials themselves cost virtually nothing and were often donated by their owners, the great landlords. But in the late eleventh and early twelfth centuries, as the new economy based on money continued to supplant the older one based on goods and barter, the old, fixed labor corvées that the peasants owed to the bishop and chapter were replaced by payments in coin. In consequence, labor now had to be purchased. The people, therefore, made a real contribution to the work of the Cathedral. But this must not be confused

[1] See E. Fels, "Die Grabung an der Fassade der Kathedrale von Chartres," *Kunstchronik*, vol. 8, 1955, pp. 149–151.

with the professional talent of the artists and craftsmen who designed the façade and converted the raw materials into what we see today. As a spiritual force, the pilgrims helped call the new work into being and they made it possible financially; but their physical contribution was never more than that of temporary, unskilled laborers. The "cult of carts" was a symbol of the will to adorn the sanctuary of the Virgin with the new and beautiful façade.

The early Gothic portions of the west façade, as we see them today, were not created in one fell swoop, however, and since they have been the subject of intense investigation, this cannot be passed over in total silence. There was one fundamental change of plan in the course of construction. In the original plan, two towers were to be set out in front of Fulbert's church, one opposite each side aisle, and both were to be connected to the long, subterranean corridors leading to the crypt and grotto. Between the towers, there was to be a sort of covered courtyard or portico, open on the west, from which one could either enter the nave of the church or go into one of the towers and from there go down directly to the crypt. The portico was to support a chapel above it, continuing the tradition of the late eleventh-century tower and of Fulbert's building, and the chapel was to have three great stained-glass windows. The entrance from the three-aisled portico into the nave was to be decorated with three sculpted portals, perhaps laid right up against the west wall of Fulbert's church or perhaps on an extension of the latter reaching almost to the eastern side of the towers.

Before the south tower had been carried very high, however, the plan was altered. The sculpture which had been prepared for the east side of the portico was put up at the west side, where we see it today, and the portico was closed off from the elements, becoming a sort of narthex instead. Since there was less space between the towers than on Fulbert's façade, it was necessary to reduce the width of the portals and a number of stones in the lateral tympana, lintels, and archivolts had to be recut in order to make them fit the new emplacement (figs. 25, 26).[2] But the results were spectacular; for the tall, narrow portals were now visually associated with the lancet windows of the chapel to produce a single, harmonious design of great beauty.

Both towers at Chartres were meant to have spires, although the north one was completed only in the sixteenth century (figs. 22, 116). Interestingly enough, the towers originally were probably not meant

---

[2] For instance, the shepherds in the lower right-hand corner of fig. 25 or the wings of the angels in fig. 26. See W. Sauerländer, "Zu den Westportale von Chartres," *Kunstchronik*, vol. 9, 1956, pp. 155–156.

to carry bells, for these would have been hung in a small belfry near the Cathedral, perhaps on a chapel or on another building in the cloister. Gothic towers were not regularly planned as belfries until the early thirteenth century, whereas the two-tower façade was already old in West European architecture by 1100 and was destined to play a leading role in Gothic design. In the twelfth century, however, two different types of façade were current and these are mingled in the present façade of Chartres. In one type, best known in Normandy and the Ile-de-France, each aisle of the church is represented by a portal on the façade—one in each tower base and one in between. This type also has a vertical division of three parts and for this reason it has been called the "harmonic façade." In the other type, known in Alsace, Italy, and Spain (and by one example in Normandy), the tower bases are solid and the space between them holds an open portico of three bays. Chartres, as we see, is thus a fusion of the northern French and the portico traditions. But even in the original plan, Chartres was exceptional, for the breadth of Fulbert's nave meant that the portals could be almost as wide as if they opened onto separate aisles, and the scale of the portico and chapel above was unusually grand.

The south tower of Chartres is a masterpiece of architectural design: the division into two parts is repeated in the arcading of the second story and the whole shape of the tower reappears at tiny scale in the turrets flanking the base of the spire. Architects must have found this tower at Chartres particularly stimulating, for it touched off a whole series of designs in the region in the second half of the twelfth century.

Each tower at Chartres contains two rooms, one above the other, separated by ribbed vaults. Most towers of any real height in the late eleventh century had vaults in their lower parts to strengthen them. Chartres belongs to a group of such monuments found in western France and the Loire Valley, some of them even having ribbed vaults. But unlike the latter, the ribbed vaults in the towers of Chartres (figs. 20, 21) are up-to-date in their technique and seem to be derived, not from western France, but from the Ile-de-France, where Gothic architecture was just beginning to emerge as a style. Anglo-Norman builders had developed (although they did not invent) the ribbed vault and the Ile-de-France builders used this device to implement their vision of an architecture of great voids framed by a skeleton whose members were connected by the very thinnest masonry. The ribbed vault was ideal for this purpose, since it could be made much thinner than either the groined or the barrel vault and hence could span larger spaces and since it could be more easily adapted to spaces of various shapes and numbers of sides. The ribs were erected first and the thin webbing was then laid over them. Moreover, ribbed vaulting made the interior of a Gothic building decidedly harmonious, for the ribs carried the linear effect of the piers across the top of the space to the other side. Of course, only the linearity of pier and vault can be seen in the towers at Chartres, which are not whole churches but semi-independent structures where strength and solidity are paramount. But the presence of modern ribbed vaults there indicates that the architects were in touch with contemporary developments in the Ile-de-France—in touch with what was to become the mainstream of Gothic architecture.

The west portals of Chartres are also close to the fountainhead of Gothic sculpture (see Section 4, pp. 176–185). Here, the key to the new style is the statue-column decorating the jambs of the portals (fig. 23). The statue-column, a new form in medieval art, consists of a figure on a shaft that is set into the architecture. In many ways, the sculpture of the west façade of Chartres is still cast in the older Romanesque mode, as is only natural in an early work of a new and emergent style. The statue-column is still fundamentally a part of the monument, one that cannot easily be removed. And the statutes themselves are somewhat rigid and frontal, with strong overtones of Romanesque iconicism (figs. 36–38). But the position of the statue *in front of* the column had important consequences, for it would shortly begin to move and turn, to activate the jamb as well as the space before it, and to develop the lyricism and the sense of being accessible to us that is latent throughout the decoration of the west façade of Chartres (compare figs. 38 and 71). The exact source of the statue-column is still unknown, although it is now generally agreed that the columns at Chartres, begun about 1145, must be later than those at St.-Denis, where the façade was dedicated in 1140 (despite Vöge's comment, pp. 147–149; figs. 39, 40). But there may well have been more than one source, just as the decoration of Chartres has itself been shown to be varied and to have been carved by a number of different artists (see Priest, p. 149): each man may have brought traditions of his own to bear on the designs of the workshop.

The meaning of the portals at Chartres is complex. Judging from a thirteenth-century text in which they are named the *porta regia* (royal portal), it has sometimes been thought they might have had some direct connection with Louis VII, King of France. This is erroneous in the literal sense because the Latin phrase was widely used in the Middle Ages, to such an extent, indeed, that either word (*porta* or simply *regia*) was often employed alone to signify "portal."[3] Some relation to kingship in general is clear, however, for many of the statue-columns represent kings and queens. In the eighteenth century, it was suggested that they stood for the early medieval dynasties that had ruled France (see Vanuxem, p. 168). It seems more likely now that they were meant to be kings and queens of the Old Testament. But the iconography could also have had more than one level of meaning. According to the medieval "science" of hermeneutics, allegorical and moral meanings could underlie the historical or literal one. Thus just as the columns support the tympana and archivolts, so the kings and queens (including such ancestors of Christ as David and Solomon) support and prefigure the persons and events of the New Testament that are represented above. This kind of alliance or reconciliation fascinated the twelfth century. And in this world of multiple levels, yet another modern interpretation of the statues can be found. According to it, the presence of some priests among the royalty indicates the conjunction of secular and spiritual authority, known as *regnum et sacerdotium*—kingship and priesthood.[4] As the study of Chartres and of medieval iconography continues, however, still other interpretations will undoubtedly be made.

It is the tympana of Chartres that bear the main message of the sculptural program. On the left tympanum, Christ ascends to Heaven while angels announce the event to the seated Apostles (fig. 26); the surrounding archivolts represent the signs of the Zodiac and the Labors of the Months, both cosmic cycles that had been associated with the Ascension before Chartres (fig. 32). In the central portal (fig. 24), Christ is shown surrounded by the symbols of the Evangelists; the twelve Apostles (flanked by Elijah and Enoch, the two Old Testament prophets who also ascended to Heaven) stand below, and the archivolts show the twenty-four Elders of the Apocalypse (fig. 33). The Apostles are usually associated with the Last Judgment and even though the Resurrection of the Dead is not shown here, the tympanum can be said to combine into one the two great themes of early twelfth-century portals—the Second Coming of Christ and the Last Judgment.

The right portal is probably the most significant one of all, for here, as Professor Adolf Katzenellenbogen has shown, dogmatic

[3] See O. Lehmann-Brockhaus, *Schriftquellen zur Kunstgeschichte des 11. und 12. Jahrhunderts für Deutschland, Lothringen und Italien*, Berlin, 1938, under the word, "porta." See also L. Kalinowski, *Drzwi Gnieźnieńskie*, vol. 2, p. 136.

[4] A. Katzenellenbogen, *The Sculptural Programs of Chartres Cathedral*, New York, W. W. Norton and Co., Inc., 1964, pp. 27-36.

themes are expounded and the Virgin takes a leading role. The lowest zone of the tympanum (fig. 25) shows (from left to right) the Annunciation, the Visitation, the Nativity, and the Annunciation to the Shepherds. But the Nativity has been put in the center of the lintel (and the Annunciation to the Shepherds has been stretched, so to speak, to fill up the right side), in order to emphasize it and make it the bottom of a vertical axis running through the tympanum. The Nativity is also designed in such a way that the swaddled Infant lies on top of the manger as if it were an altar; a reference to the Host in the mass is unmistakable. In the next zone, which is the Presentation in the Temple, the Child actually stands on the altar, facing outward rather than turning to either the high priest (left) or the Virgin (right), either of which would be more normal. And finally, at the top, the Virgin holds the Child on her lap and the pair face outward in a stiff pose that suggests an icon. This is the *Sedes Sapientiae*, the Seat of Wisdom. The surrounding archivolts represent the Seven Liberal Arts (fig. 34), the curriculum of the medieval school, and corresponding classical Greek and Roman authors. Thus, the theme of the Incarnation—God-become-man—is presented with great visual clarity in a program that, because of its intricacy and finesse, must have been devised by the theologians of Chartres. The presence of the Liberal Arts on the portal even suggests that these men thought dogma should be taught and defended in a school and it is not irrelevant to recall that, at that very time, the school of Chartres was nearing the height of its fame.

The last—but by no means the least important—Gothic feature of the twelfth-century work at Chartres is the stained glass (see pp. 233–274). In addition to the three great lancets that light the chapel behind the west façade (Color Plate I), one other window has been preserved from that time which, significantly enough, represents the Virgin and Child (fig. 109). Notre-Dame de la Belle Verrière, as it is called, must have been made for a place of honor in the old church, for after the latter was destroyed by fire in 1194, fragments of the window were rescued and reinstalled with thirteenth-century additions in the side aisle of the choir.

It is the west windows, however, that best reveal the new impulse of Gothic. At St.-Denis, the stained-glass maker and the architect collaborated to explore a new and stimulating direction and their success was immediately repeated at Chartres. What the architect wanted was to illuminate the vast open spaces that he took pains to create and his solution was to enlarge the windows. The dim, dungeonlike interior of the Romanesque style was now illuminated by moving, flickering rectangles of warm color. But larger windows not only provided more light, they also reduced the amount of masonry flanking the volumes and replaced it with a translucent screen that literally gave an impression of weightlessness. The window was thus suddenly liberated from the captivity of the wall to become an active force in the complex of architecture while the architecture itself was lightened by the new window. The paintings that had decorated the walls of Romanesque monuments were henceforth banished since stained glass now provided a field for the representation of holy figures and scenes and the stained-glass maker could now, for the first time, design his compositions on a monumental scale. At Chartres, this can be seen in two forms. On the one hand, the central and northern lancets are filled with series of square and round panels (fig. 110–112), each containing a scene from the cycle of the Infancy of Christ and from that of the Passion; although the individual panels preserve the quality of fine, almost miniature, work, the overall effect is prodigious. On the other hand, the third window is a Tree of Jesse, a single, grand composition showing a schematized vine growing from the body of the prophet and holding the ancestors of the Virgin and of Christ in its branches.

The new western complex created at Chartres in the two decades following 1134, therefore, holds an important place in the history of Gothic art. Although it is not a whole church, but merely a "fragment" added to the body of an older building, it contains all the elements fundamental to the development of the style; ribbed vaults, statue-columns, and stained glass. The very combination, in such an early phase of the new style, is proof of the vision of the designers and of their ability to assimilate new ideas rapidly and develop them. It is indeed fortunate that the larger part of this ensemble has been preserved to the present day.

Fulbert's Cathedral burned on June 10, 1194 and a new church— the present one—was begun immediately (see pp. 95–102). The body of the monument was completed by 1221, when the canons first entered the new stalls in the choir, and it was dedicated in 1260, by which time most of the accessory works of sculpture and glass had been completed.

The holocaust of 1194 had a profound effect on everyone (see pp. 95–96). At first, it was thought that the tunic of the Virgin had also perished in the fire, but a cleric found it intact in the crypt and brought it out just as the stunned townspeople were gathering around the smoking ruins. Mourning became jubilation. The people were fired with the desire to rebuild the sanctuary and the spirit soon pervaded the pilgrimage routes. This undoubtedly explains why the monument was finished in the record time of twenty-seven years.

The methods of financing the Gothic Cathedral were traditional but not very efficient. As before, gifts of labor and small sums of cash were made, but these were scarcely enough for the reconstruction. In addition, in an excess of generosity, the bishop and chapter, who were responsible for the enterprise, turned over part of their income to the work for a period of three years; but at the expiration of that time, the funds simply ran out and other sources had to be found. Three years might have been enough to clear away the wreckage and raise the new work above ground in the expectation that once the project was under way the money to complete it would be forthcoming. This is, in fact, what occurred, although it does not seem to have been planned that way. As the author of the *Miracles of the Virgin* tells us, the Virgin herself had to exhibit a miracle in order to start things up again. Some people made gifts for general purposes, while others preferred to specify what their gifts were to be used for. Later on, when the Cathedral was ready for glazing, individuals, families, and even the guilds of the town contributed particular windows, which generally include their "signatures" at the bottom (figs. 114, 113 right). On the whole, however, it is astonishing to see the bishop and chapter undertake what was surely the largest church then within memory, without any sensible appreciation of the difficulties involved and without any budget, however rudimentary. Chartres is vivid testimony of the depth and endurance of faith in an age of great construction.

The chapter of Chartres took its obligations to the Virgin and to the pilgrimage very seriously. It would have been all but impossible to design a church smaller in plan than Fulbert's had been, especially since the crypt of his Cathedral was still largely intact: it was well arranged for mass circulation and could easily be adapted to serve as a foundation for the Gothic church. But there was no physical or programmatic need to make the new Cathedral as tall as it is. That aspect of the design must be attributed to two different factors: one is prestige; and the other is the particular stage of development that Gothic architecture had reached at the end of the twelfth century.

Prestige is the most difficult factor for us to deal with because the Middle Ages does not seem to have discussed the matter except to condemn it—that is, to condemn bishops and abbots who built at a scale far beyond the simple requirements of numbers of people and frequency of services. But Chartres was never condemned for being big, perhaps partly because of its active role in the secular life of the community. On the contrary, it was praised for being imposing and for having "elegant vaults." It is not too much to infer that the bishop and chapter were pleased with such descriptions, which, they felt, showed that they were not wrong in wanting a cathedral that would impress the ever more sophisticated taste of their contemporaries. Indeed, they succeeded only too well, for Chartres has continued to inspire awe down to our own day.

The Gothic Cathedral embraces the site of Fulbert's church almost exactly. A new façade may have been planned at first, but eventually the twelfth-century one was retained and only the portico and chapel (which had protected the sculpture and stained glass from the fire) were removed so that the Gothic nave would open at the portals. A large rose window was simply inserted between the towers (fig. 22). At the eastern end, new walls were thrown up around the crypt chapels to strengthen them and to fill the deep interstices lying between them. The choir, of course, is broader than Fulbert's and leads into a double ambulatory. But the major difference between the two churches was the addition of a great projecting transept.

The transept of Chartres gives the plan a centrifugal look, as if four great arms were thrown from the square crossing in the middle. The transept was also responsible for the look of the church's exterior massing, although this is difficult to appreciate now since it was not completed as planned. Each arm of the transept was originally meant to support two towers similar to those on the west façade, and a broad, but short, lantern tower was to rise at the crossing of the two roofs (fig. 1). This massing of multiple towers was introduced into Gothic in the 1160's, probably at Laon Cathedral, and Chartres went a step further by adding another tower to either side of the choir, bringing the total to nine. Had they all been completed, these towers would have had an extraordinary effect on the skyline, like a many-pronged crown resting on top of the city. More than any other element, they would have emphasized the half-open, half-closed aspect of the Gothic exterior, which was accidented by many different shapes and which was constantly moving as the sun altered the position of the shadows. This was a high point in more than simply the physical way, for after Chartres, the number of towers decreased to six at Reims (1210) and then to two at Amiens (1220), where the transepts were wholly shorn of their tall markers. The transept towers at Chartres also made each terminal into a true façade, and the decoration of the portals with large programs of sculpture was fundamentally only a development of this idea (see Vöge, pp. 207–232).

The interior of Chartres is composed of three stories—the main arcade, the triforium passage, and the clearstory windows (fig. 10). They form the walls of the monument while ribbed vaults form the ceiling. The architect's chief structural concern was how to keep the vaults up and to that end he made use of a new device—the flying buttress (Viollet-le-Duc, pp. 121–122; fig. 15). The flying buttress provided lateral support from the outside. Another device was the heavy arch at the top of the clearstory windows which also appeared on the outside (figs. 14, 15); this arch linked the tops of the supports together down the length of the nave and helped stabilize the wall against the pressure of the roof, just as did the uppermost arch of the flying buttress. And finally, the lowest parts of the vaults were constructed in the *tas-de-charge* technique, in which the first courses are still horizontal, like the piers, although it looks as if they are true arches (Fitchen, p. 124; text fig. 1). The advantage of this technique is that it creates a better bond with the flying buttress, which lies just outside. As in the early twelfth-century work, the ribs were constructed first on some form of wooden centering, such as Professor Fitchen has suggested (text fig. 2), and the webbing then laid across the openings.

The extraordinary quality of Chartres results from its regularity and uniformity, as Henri Focillon points out (Focillon, pp. 115–118). Each bay is a unit, a cell covered by a four-part vault, to which there corresponds a similar but smaller cell in each aisle. The nave, the transept, and the choir are composed of a number of such groups placed side by side, varied only in the hemicycle, where the succession of spaces comes to a grandiose, rhythmic conclusion. The identity of the bay as a cell and as a design on the wall (see Bony, pp. 120–121) is reinforced by the sharp responds which protrude into the space of the nave and which rise from the pavement to the vaults. The horizontal string courses weave in and out across them forming a pattern on the wall surface and giving it texture. The surface itself is broken into zones of solid and void as well as into zones of light and dark by the triforium passage and clearstory. Repetition and agreement are the keys here, for Chartres is possibly the most magnificent example of balance and unity that Gothic was to produce.

The pivotal position of Chartres must be seen in relation to its past and its future. With respect to the twelfth century, it was a conclusion—a culminating point—but not simply a summation. The first aim of early Gothic architects—to create vast spaces surrounded by thin membranes—was pursued and developed throughout the sixty years between 1134 and 1194. Once in command of the ribbed vault, the masters sought ways to increase the size of the monument so as to give greater reality to their vision. Size meant both breadth and height. The first could be had by increasing the number of aisles to five and second by increasing the stories to four, with vaulted tribunes and other devices providing support in the second and third zones. Both aims were achieved in the decades following 1160; at Notre-Dame in Paris and at Laon Cathedral, for example. Laon, which looks forward to Chartres in its rich plastic treatment of the wall, also introduced the triforium passage to Gothic; Paris, where the effect is rather of an extremely thin closure, invented the flying buttress. And in both, an effort was made to "capture" large chunks of space by using six-part vaults, each embracing two bays of the nave.

The architect of Chartres was impelled by some inner urge to create an even bigger structure; not only to conquer more space but also to create a sense of scale that is nothing short of colossal (fig. 2). The triforium passage and the flying buttress were essential to this, for they meant that tribunes were no longer needed: the vaults could now be abutted at exactly the proper place from the outside without encumbering the interior of the edifice. Structurally, therefore, Chartres represented a major simplification, a purgation of those elements which had become unnecessary in the light of new devices. And from the point of view of volumes, of course, six-part vaults (and their counterparts—alternating piers or responds) were no longer necessary[5] because the spaces of Chartres have great real size. The simplicity of the scheme was matched by its flexibility, for the whole edifice could be made larger or smaller and parts could be altered without affecting stability. At Chartres itself, this explains the great height of the monument and is one of the reasons for the astonishing success of the Chartrain formula in succeeding years.

Most important of all, however, is the fact that the Master of Chartres matched his gigantic spaces with enormous piers and shafts and with gigantic bases and capitals. (Color Plate II) The bases of such buildings as Notre-Dame in Paris or of Laon Cathedral are positively minuscule when compared to those of Chartres; throughout the work, wherever one turns, one is faced with elements of an entirely new, monumental order. This accounts for the often noted "will to heaviness" of Chartres. But in reality, heaviness is more fundamental than the mere desire to overbuild a new design so as to avoid the risk of structural failure. In early Gothic art, we have the impression that the monument seems larger than it really is and, in turn, that our own stature has somehow been reduced. This is the visionary nature of the Gothic which was stated quite clearly by the

---

[5] The so-called "alternation" of the piers at Chartres is really only an alternation of octagonal and round surfaces, intended to reduce the monotony of the row, and not a bona fide alternation of compound and columnar piers.

suggestion of vastness in the earliest examples of the style. At Chartres, this is affirmed a hundredfold. And its "reality" is brought home to us by the size of its elements—by the size of the bases we can touch with our hands, by the diameter of the colonnettes on the piers, by many details both near and far. If it is still effective today in an era of unheard-of colossism, how much more impressive it must have been in 1200 to men accustomed to the small scale of the twelfth century!

The impact of Chartres on northern French architecture was profound (see Focillon, pp. 115–120). For thirty years, men experimented with the format and the scale, producing a small group of masterpieces called High Gothic: Soissons, Reims, Amiens, and finally Beauvais (1225). But at the end of this time, colossism had come to an end. This was probably not because the limits of stone construction had been reached—the notion is somewhat romantic and is belied by Cologne Cathedral, which was begun in 1248 and is even taller than Beauvais—but because the urge to create giants was fast passing. We find, instead, a period of refinement and of taste in which sheer size had no place. It is significant in this respect that, instead of finishing the towers at Chartres after 1221, the chapter undertook increasingly complex sculptural programs, all at ground level (Kidson, pp. 194–206). (Color Plate III) But Chartres and its sisters were the fountainhead of the later developments. It was within the format established at Chartres, and upon such factors as the flat, unified bay and the subdivided windows, that Rayonnant architecture of the later thirteenth century was founded.

The transepts of Chartres probably contain the most prodigious wealth of Gothic sculpture of any French Cathedral (Section 5, pp. 186–232). A number of different masters and different workshops contributed to their creation, among them some of the most famous sculptors of the thirteenth century: the Master of the Coronation (figs. 61–64), the Master of the Last Judgment (figs. 65–68) or the Master of the Kings' Heads (pp. 207–232, figs. 75–78, 80–91). Although these men collaborated with the architects, the very nature of their work was fundamentally different. A portal, no matter how complex, can be finished in much less time than a building, and each statue in it poses the same problem anew, so that the sculptor can develop his style with infinitely greater rapidity than the architect. Thus, at Chartres, the grand unity of the edifice is matched by a bewildering variety of sculpture—representing a whole gamut of viewpoints from conservative to avant-garde, or, in Herr Vöge's brilliant essay, from traditional "masters of line" to innovating realists. The very number of portals was not fixed until the limit of six had been reached and, even after that, porches laden with sculpture were added to each transept façade (Kidson, pp. 194–197). Here and there, however, one finds a master who carved in the same classic way that the architecture is classic (fig. 71): observing the human figure anatomically but investing it with a sense of lyricism and style, bringing out the warmth of a human relationship but not ignoring the qualities of the material. Such balance was even more short-lived than it was in High Gothic architecture.

While the portals were still being worked on, the chapter began a monumental screen across the western side of the choir (fig. 106). This was becoming a rather popular idea in the thirteenth century, for it insured the canons' privacy during the service and kept the public at a reasonable distance. In a pilgrimage church such as Chartres, it must have seemed almost essential. Unfortunately dismantled in the eighteenth century, the fragments of the original screen are now preserved in the crypt. They were carved in two phases by two different workshops. One shop worked in the early thirteenth-century style of the portals (fig. 108), but the other, in about 1235, worked in a much more mannered, large-fold style that looked to the future (fig. 107). Nowadays, we turn naturally to Chartres to see Gothic sculpture between 1205 and 1225 and it is surprising to find later work there, especially of such quality. But Gothic sculpture of the 1230's is rare in all parts of France and the later parts of the choir screen at Chartres, therefore, take on an added significance.

With the glazing of the church (Section 6, pp. 233–274), it was ready to be dedicated, an event that took place in 1260. As the statue-column developed from the archaic figures of the west façade to the mature ones of the transepts, stained glass also made astonishing progress. The collaboration between architect and glass maker was not always without its troubles, however, for as the architect enlarged the windows to let in more light, the glass maker deepened the colors of the glass so that the amount of light entering the early thirteenth-century church was about the same as it had been eighty years before.[6] But larger windows provided one extraordinary possibility: the creation of huge single figures in the clearstory (fig. 113). At that distance from the spectator, the small panels of older windows would be hard to distinguish, although they continued to be used occasionally. Great monumental figures were the perfect complement for the serene dignity of the architecture.

With these elements, the Cathedral of Chartres was virtually complete, at least in the interior. Unlike most Gothic cathedrals, the nave

[6] L. Grodecki, "Le vitrail et l'architecture au XII⁰ et XIII⁰ siècles," *Gazette des Beaux-Arts*, ser. 6, vol. 36, 1949, pp. 5–24.

was never disfigured by a string of later chapels; only one, the Chapelle de Vendôme, was added to the south aisle in 1417 (omitted in fig. 3). But in 1323, the chapter commissioned the architect, Huguet d'Ivry, to erect a new meeting hall off the ambulatory, and, by adding a second story, they obtained another chapel connected to the church (the chapel of St.-Piat, fig. 115). This little work is a fair representative of early fourteenth-century style (Rayonnant). Not without solidity, it has hard, metallic-looking ribs and windows with intricate tracery that look as if they had been set ready-made into the jambs.

Intricacy of form and elaborate, lacy effects also characterize the later development of Gothic style, and Chartres has an excellent example of this baroque tendency in the spire of the northwest tower, begun in 1507 by Jean de Beauce (fig. 116). The tower is also characterized by arches made of S-curves, strong contrasts of light and shade, and an "immaterial" quality that masks a very heavy structure. All this is decidedly different from the more regular and orthodox patterns of Huguet d'Ivry. Huguet was still a Rayonnant architect, while Jean de Beauce worked in the flickering, flamelike mode that has come to be called Flamboyant. After finishing the tower, Jean began to build a monumental screen between the choir and the aisles (fig. 117) that was not completed until 1715. The architectural elements show a gradual invasion of the world of Gothic forms by those of the Renaissance, while the sculpture is entirely in the younger style. It is fitting that distinguished examples of these various late Gothic styles should be found in the very place where High Gothic was first created.

DOCUMENTS. ANALYSIS. CRITICISM.

I

MEDIEVAL TEXTS[1]

The architectural history of Chartres in the Middle Ages is outlined in the following documents in which the translators have attempted to preserve the medieval flavor. They range from charters to chronicles and letters. The charters were legal documents and hence are considered most trustworthy, although they generally contain only a terse fact or two relating to the monument. Chronicles are often more informative, but they tend to be less reliable unless they were written by an eye-witness, such as the author of the *Miracles of the Virgin*. Letters are, of course, the best testimony of all, but in the Middle Ages they were rarely dated. The *"Expertise of 1316"* is a report prepared by a group of architects who were asked to inspect the Cathedral and to give expert opinions on what restorations were necessary at that time.

Fulbert's Church

1. The St.-Aignan Chronicle

The third [fire] occurred in the year 1020, the fourteenth year of the episcopate of Lord Fulbert, during the very night of the Nativity of the Blessed Mary [September 8]. In this one, the church was not simply burned, but actually totally destroyed. The same glorious Bishop Fulbert, through his diligence, efforts, and material contributions, rebuilt it from the ground up and, once raised, practically saw it through to a state of wondrous greatness and beauty.[2]

---

[1] Translations from the Latin are by the Reverend Howard Niebling; The *"Expertise" of 1316* was translated from the French by Robert Branner.

[2] *Translationes sancti Aniani*, ed. Clerval, in *Analecta Bollandiana*, vol. 7, 1888, p. 331.

2. Fulbert's Letter to King Robert

Seized inwardly with heartfelt sorrow, now in such great grief of Ours, We let it be known that Our bells, normally signifying joy and gladness, should cease to ring, and We ordered that Our sadness be made public in some way. * * *3

3. Another Letter of Fulbert's to King Robert

If We had at hand all the means as well as the desire to go wandering about, it would concern Your Piety to rebuke Our levity and call Us back to the assiduous task of restoring Our church which was destroyed. But now, since We lack all means of this sort and great need forces assiduity upon Us * * * bear with Us rather, Holy Father, bear with Our foolishness, make up for Our indulgence. * * * A royal farewell!4

4. Another Letter of Fulbert's to King Robert

Added to these misfortunes was the burning of Our church. Because, since I do not have the wherewithal to restore it in a fitting manner, I refuse to allow myself even necessary funds. * * * I am giving much consideration * * * to the possibility of obtaining at any effort, no matter how strenuous, help in restoring the church. * * *5

5. Fulbert's Letter to William V, Duke of Aquitania and Count of Poitou

I would write to you at greater length if I were not preoccupied with many other matters, above all the restoration of Our city and church, which completely burned up recently in a horrible conflagration. * * *6

3 *Sancti Fulberti Carnotensis episcopi epistolae,* in Migne, *Patrologia latina,* vol. 141, *Ep.* 30, cols. 215–216.

4 *Ibid., Ep.* 55, col. 228.

5 *Ibid., Ep.* 57, col. 229.

6 *Ibid., Ep.* 58, cols. 229–230.

6. *Another Letter of Fulbert's to William V*

But there is something that can especially give you comfort, and that is the fact that your riches which you spent for the restoration of the church of the Blessed Mary you will receive back from her not merely intact, but even multiplied. * * * Farewell.[7]

7. *Another Letter of Fulbert's to William V*

I would be happy, beloved Prince, to devoutly attend Your dedication, if the needs of Our church, which must in no wise be neglected, did not detain Me. For, by the grace of God along with your aid, We have completed our crypt and have taken pains to cover it over before the rigors of winter damage it. * * *[8]

The West Façade (1134 ff.)

1. *The Chronicle of Robert de Torigny, Abbot of Mont-Saint-Michel*

In this same year, primarily at Chartres, men began, with their own shoulders, to drag the wagons loaded with stone, wood, grain, and other materials to the workshop of the church, whose towers were then rising. Anyone who has not witnessed this will not see the like in our time. Not only there, but also in nearly the whole of France and Normandy and in many other places, [one saw] everywhere humility and *afflictio*,[9] everywhere penance and the forgiveness of offenses, everywhere mourning and contrition. One might observe women as well as men dragging [wagons] through deep swamps on their knees, beating themselves with whips, numerous wonders occurring everywhere, canticles and hymns being offered to God. On this point there exists a previously unknown letter by Hugh, Archbishop of Rouen, to [Theodore], Bishop of Amiens, examining this matter. One might say that the prophecy was being fulfilled: "The breath of life was in the wheels" [Ezek. 1:20][10]

[7] *Ibid., Ep.* 59, col. 230.
[8] *Ibid., Ep.* 71, col. 236.
[9] The reading of the penitential psalms while prostrate on the ground.
[10] *Chronique de Robert de Torigny*, ed. L. Delisle (Société de l'histoire de France), vol. 1, 1872, p. 238.

2. *Letter of Hugh, Archbishop of Rouen, to Theodore, Bishop of Amiens*

Hugh, priest of Rouen, to the Reverend Father Theodore, Bishop of Amiens: prosper ever in Christ! "Great are the works of the Lord, exquisite in all their delights" [Ps. 110 (111):2]. It was at Chartres that men began humbly to pull wagons and carts for the work of building the church and that their humility began to shine forth even with miracles. This celebrated report spread in all directions and at length stirred up Our own Normandy. Hence, Our own people, with Our blessing, made their way there and fulfilled their vows. Then, throughout Our jurisdiction, they began to come in like manner to their mother church in Our own diocese. Such was their purpose that no one entered their company until he first made his confession and undertook penance, and until those who had previously been at enmity put aside their anger and ill-will and met together in harmony and well-founded peace. Once these conditions have been met, one of their number is appointed leader; under his direction they pull their wagons with their own shoulders in humility and silence, and present their offering, not without discipline and tears. Whenever they come to Us, We demand of them the three aforementioned conditions, namely, confession with penitence, harmony free of all ill-will, and the humility to come along obediently; if they bring these three dispositions, We receive them paternally, absolve them, and bless them. When they come on their journey so disposed, sometimes—and above all in Our churches—oft-repeated miracles occur, even upon their sick whom they bring with them, and they take back completely healed the ones they had brought as invalids. We also allow Our people to go outside Our diocese, but We forbid them to enter among those excommunicated or under interdict. These things have been done in the year of the Incarnate Word 1145. Farewell.[11]

[11] *Epistola Hugonis, Rotomagensis archiepiscopi, ad Theodoricum, Ambianensem episcopum*, in *Recueil des historiens des Gaules*, vol. 14, pp. 318–319, n. a.

The Church of 1194–1260

1. The Miracles of the Virgin

Therefore, in the year 1194 after the Incarnation of the Lord, since the church at Chartres had been devastated on the third of the Ides of June [June 10] by an extraordinary and lamentable fire making it necessary later, after the walls had been broken up and demolished and leveled to the ground, to repair the foundations and then erect a new church.

* * * The inhabitants of Chartres, clerics as well as laymen, whose homes and practically all their furnishings the aforementioned fire had consumed, all deplored the destruction of the church to such an extent that they made absolutely no mention of their own losses; they considered as their chief misfortune, or rather the totality of their misfortune, the fact that they, unhappy wretches, in justice for their own sins, had lost the palace of the Blessed Virgin, the special glory of the city, the showpiece of the entire region, the incomparable house of prayer. * * *

Indeed, when for several days they had not seen the most sacred reliquary of the Blessed Mary, transferred to a more hidden place out of fear of the fire, the population of Chartres was seized with incredible anguish and grief, concluding that it was unworthy to restore the structures of the city or the church, if it had lost such a precious treasure, [which was] indeed the glory of the whole city. At last, on a particular holy day, when the entire populace had assembled by order of the clergy at the spot where the church had stood, the above-mentioned reliquary was brought forth from the crypt. * * * The fact must not be passed over that when, at the time of the fire, the reliquary frequently referred to had been moved by certain persons into the lower crypt (whose entrance the laudable foresight of the ancients had cut near the altar of the Blessed Mary), and they had been shut up there, not daring to go back out because of the fire now raging, they were so preserved from mortal danger under the protection of the Blessed Mary that neither did the rain of burning timbers falling from above shatter the iron door covering the face of the crypt, nor did the drops of melted lead penetrate it, nor the heap of burning coals overhead injure it. * * * And after such a fierce conflagration, when men who were considered already dead from smoke or excessive heat had come back unharmed, all present were filled with such gladness that they rejoiced together, weeping affectionately with them.

* * * When, following the ruin of the walls mentioned above, necessity demanded that a new church be built and the wagons were at last ready to fetch the stone, all beckoned as well as exhorted each other to obey instantly and do without delay whatever they thought necessary for this construction or [whatever] the master workers prescribed. But the gifts or assistance of the laymen would never have been adequate to raise such a structure had not the bishop and the canons contributed so much money, as stated above, for three years from their own revenues. For this became evidence to everyone at the end of the three-year period when all finances suddenly gave out, so that the supervisors had no wages for the workmen, nor did they have in view anything that could be given otherwise. But I recall that at that moment someone said—I know not by what spirit of prophecy—that the purses would fail before the coins needed for the work on the church of Chartres [were obtained]. What is there to add? Since, in view of the utter failure of human resources, it was necessary for the divine to appear, the blessed Mother of God, desiring that a new and incomparable church be erected in which she could perform her miracles, stirred up the power of this son of hers by her merits and prayers. When there was a large gathering of people there, she openly and clearly exhibited a certain new miracle, one unheard of for a long time past, seen by all for the first time. As a result, news of the miracle spread far and wide through the whole of Gaul and made it easier to give credence to succeeding miracles.[12]

2. The "Philippids" of Guillaume le Breton

It happened that not long after this,
the Virgin Mother of God, who teaches by word and deed
   that she is mistress of Chartres,
desiring that the church which she called her very own
   be restored specifically for Him with more praiseworthy
   adornment,
provided Vulcan with a singular opportunity
   and allowed him to rage at will against it,
so that there might occur a salutary burning off of the malady
   under which this house of the Lord lay prostrate,
and this destruction might furnish an excuse for the succeeding
   structure

[12] *Miracula B. Marie Virginis in Carnotensi ecclesia facta* . . . ed. A. Thomas, in *Bibliothèque de l'école des chartes*, vol. 42, 1881, pp. 508 ff.

next to which none in the world gleams so brilliantly this
day.
Springing up anew, now finished in its entirety of cut stone
beneath elegant vaults,
it fears harm from no fire 'til Judgment Day;
and salvation from that fire appears to many
through whose aid the renewed work was brought about.[13]

3. The Necrology of the Cathedral

Likewise [on this day there died] Robert of Blevia, procurator of
this holy church, a man kind and tenderly compassionate toward the
poor, who adorned this church with a silk cope, a dalmatic and a
tunic, two silver pitchers, and an antiphonary for everyday use. In
addition, he donated to the Works a cup, two silver goblets and six
silver spoons, and £25 for the construction of one pillar.[14]

4. The Charter of 1221 Concerning the Rights of the Cantor over the Choir Stalls

B[artholomew], Dean, and the whole body of the Chapter of
Chartres, to all to whom the present writing shall be made known:
greetings in the Lord. Be it known to all that in placing in the choir
of Our church exceptionally formed, newly arranged stalls, We wish
the rights of Our cantor to remain throughout whole and intact.
We have singled out one of these [rights] to be set forth in this letter
as follows. Although the Chapter has the right to install only two
members of Our church, namely, the dean and the cantor, it is the
right of the cantor himself, in virtue of his own rank, to install all
others, personages as well as simple canons and all non-canons, either
at their first installation or when they are transferred from one stall
to another or from one part of the choir to another. Therefore, as
often as the cantor installs anyone in Our choir according to the
custom of Our Church, either for the first time or, as already stated,
by transfer from one stall to another when he is permitted by custom
to do this, he is empowered to assign him, according to his own best

---

[13] *Philippids*, I, iv, ed. H. -F. Delaborde (Société de l'histoire de France),
vol. 2, 1885, pp. 121–122.
[14] In L. Merlet and E. de Lépinois, *Cartulaire de Notre-Dame de Chartres*,
vol. 3, pp. 45–46. The date is February 18, but the year is not indicated.

judgment, among the personages if he be a personage, among the
simple canons if he be a simple canon, among the non-canons if he
be a non-canon, either the first or the last place, or between any two
places, notwithstanding the location or the form of the stalls or anything pertaining to the location or form of same; but without prejudice to the right of any of those persons who hold particular stalls
in choir, namely: the dean, the subdean, the second cantor, the
chancellor, the major archdeacon, the sacristan,[15] and the procurator.
To these, the cantor cannot assign any stalls other than those which
they occupy by right of their own rank, specifically: the subdean
must always be third from the dean, who is the first at the right
of the entrance to the choir; the major archdeacon is always between
them; the procurator is always at the corner of the same part of the
choir. On the other side of the choir, the second cantor is always
second or third from the cantor so that the cantor can, if he wishes,
place one of the other personages between himself and the second
cantor; the corner of the same part of the choir always belongs to
the chancellor; and the last of the higher places always belongs to
the sacristan. Be it also noted that the cantor is perfectly free to
install any personage, if he is not a deacon, in a place other than a
higher one, and then he must assign him the first place before all
the canons. Be it further noted that the cantor cannot place someone who is not a personage of Our church between two independently
installed personages, nor any non-canon between two canons, nor any
canon between two non-canons. In these and all other matters, We in-
tend and grant that the right of the cantor himself, as well as all of
Us, be absolutely preserved. As a memorial and testimonial of this,
We have given to the said cantor of Ours this letter, confirmed by
Our seal. Given in the year of grace one thousand two hundred and
twenty, in the month of January.[16]

5. The Charter of May 26, 1224 Concerning the Moneychangers

Each and every one of Us, personages as well as canons of Chartres,
who had assembled to elect a dean, are agreed that the stalls of the

---

[15] French *chevecier*, that is, keeper of the chevet or eastern end of the
church.
[16] That is, January, 1221. According to the French medieval calendar, the
new year began at Easter. From Merlet, *Cartulaire*, vol. 2, pp. 95–96.

moneychangers, which are customarily in the porch,[17] be set up in the cloister to the south, between the steps of the church and the main tower, so that all the dues from the stalls and the house in which they have been set up and the moneychangers themselves might belong to the Chapter, and that whoever should be elected to the deanship might not lay claim to them, but that they might remain without hindrance, as heretofore, in the possession of the Chapter, in the place where they have been set up this day, in the street which belonged to the archdeacon Milo. Executed in the year of the Lord 1224, the month of May, on the octave of the Lord's Ascension.[18]

6. The Louis IX Foundation of August, 1259

In the name of the holy and undivided Trinity, Amen.

Louis, by the grace of God, King of France.

We make known to all that with regard to the claim to hospitality or *gistum*[19] which We had on the bishop in the episcopal residence at Chartres, and with regard to the other claim to hospitality or *gistum* which We sought from the same bishop at his town of Fresnes: an agreement has been entered upon between Us on Our own behalf and that of Our successors and Our beloved and faithful Matthew, Bishop of Chartres, on his own behalf and that of his successors, with the consent of the Chapter of the church of Chartres, to the effect that We have totally and forever renounced and do renounce all right to *gistum* or such claim to hospitality which We had been able to exact of the said bishop or of his successors; so that neither We nor Our successors can henceforth at any time demand anything from the said bishop or his successors under the title of *gistum* or a claim to hospitality in the aforementioned places or elsewhere. On his part, the same bishop, in consideration of this renunciation and pledge, has promised to Us and committed himself to pay a tax of £ 50 Tournois annually in perpetuum. We have chosen to dispose this in the following manner. Because of the particular devotion which We have to the church of the Blessed Mary of Chartres, in consideration of the divine love and for the salvation of Our soul and those of Our ancestors, We will to establish and

[17] For the interpretation of this word (*capitellis*), see E. Lefèvre-Pontalis in *Mémoires de la société nationale des antiquaires de France*, ser. 7, vol 4, 1905, p. 113.

[18] From Merlet, *Cartulaire*, vol. 2, p. 103.

[19] The king's "droit de gîte," or right to free food and lodging.

found with the afore-mentioned revenue two chaplaincies in the same church. One shall be erected close inside and to the right of the Door of the Cross[20] of the same church, in honor of all the Holy Angels of God; the other, close inside and to the left of the Door of the Cross[21] of the same church, in honor of all the Holy Virgins. Both of the chaplains shall receive annually from the afore-mentioned sum, £ 15 Tournois, on these terms: 100 solidi on the day following the feast of Saint Remigius, another hundred on the day following Candlemas, and another 100 solidi on the day following the Ascension of the Lord. Both of them shall be bound to celebrate mass each day for Us as long as We live, according to the custom of the Church, either personally or through another if they are legitimately impeded. We request also that the mass of the Holy Spirit and that of the holy Mother of God be celebrated rather frequently, and that the collect for Us be said and special prayer offered in all masses. Moreover, on each Saturday they shall celebrate the mass of the glorious Virgin, Queen of Virgins, at the altar of the Holy Virgins, and on each Monday the mass of the Holy Angels at the altar of the Holy Angels, unless some solemn feast occurs on those days whose proper and solemn office they must fulfill instead. After Our death, however, both chaplains shall be bound to celebrate the mass which is said for the departed faithful each day on the afore-mentioned two altars, except that on Saturdays the mass of the Blessed Virgin shall be celebrated at the altar of the Virgins, and on Mondays the mass of the Angels at the altar of the Angels, as set forth above. However, on solemn days on which the Church does not customarily celebrate for the dead, they shall be permitted to celebrate the office which accords with the solemnity of day. * * *[22]

7. The Charter of December, 1259 Concerning the Differences between the Bishop and Chapter

Matthew, by divine dispensation bishop of Chartres, and R[adulph], Dean, and the body of the Chapter of Chartres, to all who shall examine the present letter: greetings in the Lord. We make known to all that since there has been a dispute between Us, Matthew, Bishop of Chartres, on the one hand, and the Venerable Sirs the Dean and Chapter of Chartres, on the other hand, to wit: that We, the Dean,

[20] That is, the north transept portals.
[21] That is, the north transept portals.
[22] From Merlet, *Cartulaire*, vol. 2, pp. 169–170.

and Chapter of Chartres asserted that the Reverend Father Matthew, Bishop, and any bishop who at any time is and has been bishop of Chartres, is bound, by the usage and approved custom of the church of Chartres, to pay the expenses of all goldsmiths and silversmiths who at any time are working or have worked and will in the future work on the reliquary or about the reliquary of the Blessed Mary, and on the frontal or about the frontal which is before the main altar of the church of Chartres, and on the retable or about the retable or tablets of the main altar, and about those things which pertain to the main altar of the churches of Chartres, while We, Matthew, Bishop of Chartres, assert the contrary; and that the dispute also revolves around the arrears or expenses encountered relative to the aforementioned by reason of the passage of time; finally, We, the Bishop and Dean of said Chapter, have jointly given assurance concerning all and each of the above-mentioned matters to the Venerable Sirs John, Archdeacon of Chartres, and Arnulph de Berjouville, Canon of Chartres, promising in good faith that We, Matthew, Bishop of Chartres, and We, the Dean and Chapter of Chartres, will observe without fail and cause to be observed whatever the above-named archdeacon and Arnulph shall pronounce and ordain with regard to the aforementioned matters. With regard to the arrears, moreover, We have left to the above-named John, Archdeacon, and Arnulph, by reason of the passage of time, to pronounce and ordain as they will.

Now We, John, Archdeacon, and Arnulph, Canon, of Chartres, having diligently inquired into the truth about all afore-mentioned matters from persons worthy of credence, pronounce and ordain that the Reverend Father Matthew, by the grace of God Bishop of Chartres, and any bishop who will at any time be bishop of Chartres, shall henceforth pay and be bound to pay all expenses in food and drink, to all goldsmiths and silversmiths who at any time are working and have worked as well as those who shall in the future work on the châsse or holy reliquary of the Blessed Mary of Chartres, and on the frontal which is and will be before the main altar of the church of Chartres, and on the retable or tablets which are and will be upon the main altar of the church of Chartres at the back of the same altar. But with regard to the arrears We ordain, on probable grounds, that the Reverend Father Matthew, the said Bishop of Chartres, shall be bound to pay nothing for what has already been done, by reason of the passage of time.

In witness and confirmation whereof We, Matthew, Bishop of Chartres, and We, Radulph, Dean, and the Chapter at Chartres, and also We, John, Archdeacon of Chartres, and Arnulph, Canon of Chartres, have affixed our seals to the present act and rescript. Executed in the year of the Lord one thousand two hundred and fifty-nine, in the month of December.[23]

The "Expertise" of 1316

In the year of the Lord 1316, on the Thursday after the feast of the Nativity of the Blessed Virgin, Holy Mary, a report on the defects of the church was made by the masters who were appointed to look into the said defects by the chapter, as follows:

My lords, we say to you that the four arches which help carry the vault are good and strong, and that the piers which carry the arches [are] good, and that the keystone which carries the summit[24] [of the vault is] good and strong; and it would not be necessary to remove more than half of your vault, at the place[s] where one will see what is needed. And we have noted that the scaffolding would move from above the tracery of the glass;[25] and this scaffolding can be used to help cover your rood screen and the people who will pass beneath it, and to hold the other scaffolds to be constructed in the vault, which one can see will be required and needed.

Here are the defects which are in the church of Notre-Dame at Chartres, seen by Master Pierre de Chelles, Master of the Works of Paris; Master Nicolas des Chaumes, Master of the Works of our lord, the King; and Master Jacques de Longjumeau, Master Carpenter and officer of Paris, in the presence of Master Jean de Reate, canon of Chartres, originally from Italy; Master Simon, Carpenter; and Master Berthaud, officer of the aforementioned work, upon the order of the dean.

First: we have seen the vault of the crossing; repairs are necessary there; and if they are not undertaken very shortly, there could be great danger.

Item: we have seen the flying buttresses which abut the vaults; they need pointing up, and if this is not done at once, much damage may ensue.

Item: there are two piers which support the towers which need repairs.

[23] *Ibid.*, vol. 2, pp. 172–174.
[24] French *la clef qui porte la clef*; literally "the keystone that carries the keystone."
[25] French *enmerllement*; probably the assemblage of stones in the window tracery.

Item: repairs are needed on the porch piers and a plank should be provided in each side opening to carry what lies above; and, on the outside, one of the jambs will be moved above the dado on the corner pier and the other jamb will be moved above a reworking of the fabric of the church; and the plank will have a support so as to reduce the strain; and this will be done with all the ties that are needed.

Item: we have seen and devised for Master Berthaud how he will [re]make the statue of the Magdalene where it now is, without moving it.

Item: we have looked at the great tower[26] and see that it has real need of important repairs; for one of its sides is cracked and creviced and one of the turrets is broken and coming apart.

Item: the needs of the front portals follow—the coverings are broken and in pieces; wherefore it would be good to put an iron tenon in each to help hold them up, and it should be well-seated so as to remove the danger.

Item: for the advantage of the church, we have noticed that the first scaffolding will be moveable from above the tracery of the windows so that the vault of the crossing may be redone.

Item: for the advantage of the church, we have noticed that the post that carries the little angel[27] is all rotten and cannot join the other pier of the nave of the minster, for the pier of the minster is broken on the upper side of the assemblage of the beam; and if they want to work well, [the masters] will put two trusses with those which are on the chevet and will put the little angel on the second of these trusses; and the larger part of the beam, which is on the afore-mentioned ridge, could be put inside.

Item: the belfry, where the little saints are,[28] is insufficient, for it is very old, as is the one where the large saints are; repairs to them are necessary at once.

Item: the roof of the minster needs four new tenons, [to replace those] which now are rotted at one end; they can be repaired, if you do not want to replace them, in the manner which we explained to your masters.[29]

[26] The south tower.
[27] The statue at the point of the roof covering the hemicycle.
[28] The bells, which were usually given saints' names.
[29] From *Congrès archéologique*, Chartres, 1900, pp. 312–320.

2

OLDER HISTORIES OF CHARTRES[1]

SEBASTIEN ROULLIARD

from *Parthénie, ou Histoire de la très auguste église de Chartres*, (Paris)—[1609]

This is one of the first modern descriptions of the Cathedral. Roulliard is famous for having canonized the story of the Druidic origins of the church; a better version of this tale is included below (Sablon, p. 107). But his description of the monument is worth reading because of its objectivity, which is in sharp contrast to the medieval "descriptions." The selection of a few main points of interest, the rather rambling "itinerary," and the inclusion of the dimensions of the building set the pattern for popular guidebooks to the Cathedral that is still in use today.

[The church of Chartres] is built in a magnificent manner on a hill which is the highest point of the town; its structure is made of hard ashlar, raised high and held up by flying buttresses of several stories, enriched with twin galleries, upper and lower, going completely around the building, garbed with great towers, partly square and partly round, platforms, pyramids, columns, aediculae, niches, and statues which are so exquisitely and distinctively sculptured that, at the mere sight of them, all the Polycleites of yore would throw down their chisels and all the Vitruviuses of the past would seize upon this masterpiece as the model for their own architecture.[2]

Its roof covering is all of lead, the carpentry outstanding and admirable; the roof is commonly called the "forest," as much because of

---

[1] Translated by Robert Branner [Ed.]
[2] Polycleitus and Vitruvius were among the best known sculptors and architects of classical Antiquity [Ed.].

the prodigious multitude and quantity of wood as, perhaps, in com-
memoration of the fact that the forest or body of wood of the Druids
formerly stood on the site.

There are three principal entrances to the church, each accompanied
by two side portals. The first and main entrance is called the Royal
Portal, because the king passes through it when he is received into
the church; it faces west. Outside it, there used to be a large stair-
case which is now hidden below ground, because the church cloister
has since been reconstructed [around it], so that only four or five
steps can be seen. The second entrance faces south; the third, north.

All of these portals are enriched with stories which are artfully
delineated and sculpted. They are also embellished with an endless
number of tall columns on which is placed such a quantity of statues
of more-than-human size and of such admirable workmanship that
some seem to disappear from sight because of the others—one scarcely
knows at which one to pause or of which to have the highest opinion.

The entrances on the north and south are still decorated with great
and splendid porches held by admirable bases and columns; they are
vaulted high and enriched by the images and stories that are im-
planted upon them with outstanding ingenuity. The porches are as
long as the transept [including the aisles] is broad; to get up into them,
large staircases are provided whose excellence can be seen even though
the earth hides more than half of them for the afore-mentioned reason.

The inner length of the church, from the Royal Portal to the chapel
of St.-Piat, which is behind the choirscreen on the [south] side, is
69 toises.[3] The nave, from the entrance and main door of the choir
beneath the pulpit to the Royal Portal, is 36 *toises* and one foot long,
and 8 *toises* wide internally.[4] The aisles of the nave, which are single,
are each 4½ *toises* wide. The transept is 31½ *toises* long and 7 *toises*
wide. The transept aisles are each 4 *toises* wide.

The choir, from the pulpit to the altar which is behind the main
and principal one, is 20 *toises* long; and from the main altar to the
pulpit is 17 *toises*; the width is 8 *toises*. In the choir, to the sides of
the main altar and the two portals aligned with it, are six chambers
or cabinets ingeniously placed between the columns or piers which
surround it. In one of these cabinets are locked several holy reliquaries.
The other five serve the clerical and lay guards of the church, who
sleep there when on duty. Behind the main altar is another, above
which (and beneath one of the arches of the choir) are several saints'
bodies in divers reliquaries.

---

[3] A *toise* measured a little over 6 feet in length [Ed.].
[4] Dimensions taken from the inner faces of the masonry are still one of
the standard methods of measuring a building [Ed.].

All around the afore-mentioned choir, nave, and transept, there are high passages through which one can walk entirely around the church and see inside.[5] From them, one can also easily go on top of the aisle vaults of the church. The vaults of the choir and nave are equally high from the pavement; it is 19 *toises* to the keystones. The vaults of all the aisles are also equally high from the pavement and the keys are at 10 *toises*.

Around the choir, between the columns and arches which form the choir screen, are four excellent chapels intended for the preservation of several holy reliquaries. * * * The choir screen is made of very white, polished stone, cut and chiseled with exquisite workmanship, enriched with statues, faces, hieroglyphs, and other contrivances. And on this enclosure, together with several representations of the miracles of the holy tunic or shirt of the Virgin, are represented the stories of the life or acts of Our Lady, and the mysteries of our redemption, in a kind of sculpting that is naïve but well done.

Having made this circuit and having come to the door of the choir to go out into the nave, [we find] two cut-stone staircases which go up on either side of the pulpit which is 11 *toises* long by 7 *toises* 9 inches wide. The latter is artistically made in cut stone, with divers scenes, flowers, and panels, and is held by monolithic columns so thin and delicate that the best architects of [our] time would hardly dare promise to do better. At the two ends of the pulpit are cupboards with doors in which the lay guards sleep to serve the church and protect it, like their colleagues [in the choir]. * * *

In front of the pulpit, to the north, is a statue of Our Lady. The statue is seated on a high throne that has been placed on a round column of very hard stone and is surrounded by copper columns and bars. A century or so ago, the late Master Vastin de Fugerets, during his lifetime a canon of the church, had the image put up so that it would be freely exposed to the veneration of the people without disturbing the divine service in the choir. There are such crowds around it, and the devotion is so great, that the stone column holding up the statue has a hole in it made by the kisses of the devoted, Catholic people! [This is believable, for] Cicero writes in one of his Verrine orations that the statue of Hercules, adored in Sicily, had the knees worn off by kisses. * * *

Opposite the statue, to the south, on the arcade nearest the pulpit, is the organ of the church, made with such industry, such rare artifice, and of such well-proportioned size and such ample width, that despite the great noise made by people in the church, especially

[5] The triforium passage [Ed.].

on the feasts of the Virgin, its harmony can easily be heard. Since I am in the upper parts, I would like to add that the windows of the church, which make it very light, are many in number and betray great age, for they are of very thick glass and are painted with flowers and with the stories and miracles that were done by the intercession of that holy Virgin. * * *

VINCENT SABLON

from *Histoire de l'auguste et vénérable église de Chartres*, (Chartres)—[1671]

> Sablon repudiated Roulliard's history of Chartres but gave further support to the story of the Druidic origins of the church, particularly by his rational argument. His book also emphasized two concepts still popular among historians of the Middle Ages—the continuity of institutions from one era to another, and the great antiquity of religious sites.

[The Druids] were idol worshippers and adored Teutates, Hesus, Belenus, and Taramis. Their religion was very close to superstition and they were so attached to their own ceremonies that they held all others in low esteem. The people could not make sacrifice without them, and since they particularly claimed to be able to divine and foretell the future, they were consulted far and wide. They normally lived in forests because of the mistletoe, which was the main object of their cult, and although they were widespread in France and were [also] found in Brittany and Germany, they were especially populous in the area of Chartres. It was there, according to Caesar, that they held their reunions and their general assemblies at certain times of the year. They celebrated their rites in caves and underground places because they believed that they were descended from the gods of Hell; and since Chartres—called *Antricum* in Latin by Ptolemy, because it was full of caves, caverns, grottos, and places hollowed in the rocks—was largely built underground, the Druids made it the center of their cult and consecrated an altar to a virgin who was to give birth, *Virgo paritura*. Before His incarnation in the Word, God spoke particularly to three sorts of divines—the Magi, the Sibyls, and the Druids. The Magi were skilled in astrology and, having foreseen that the God of Heaven would one day be born on earth, they looked forward to His appearance with extreme impatience; God told them of it by a special dream and by an extraordinary star. The Sibyls received the gift of prophecy in recompense for their virginity and penetrated the deepest mysteries of the Christian religion. The Druids, who were in touch with the Egyptians, the Phoenicians, and the Jews, and who had read their books, learned through a prophetic spirit rather than through a fortuitous prediction that a virgin would one day bear a child for the welfare and happiness of the world. In several places, they put up altars to her with the inscription *Virgini pariturae*, and in this way they laid the foundations of the devotion to the Virgin and of this superb temple which the Christians have dedicated to her glory and which today is the masterpiece of art, the astonishment of nature, and the residence of sanctity and grace. * * *

The altar erected by the Druids in honor of the holy virgin in the city of Chartres, long before the coming of the Son of God, remained in the same state until the shadows of paganism were dissipated by the light of the Gospel. I will not raise here the questions as to whether Sts. Savinianus and Potentianus were the first apostles of this region, whether they passed through Chartres before going to Sens, whether they sent Sts. Edoaldus and Altinus to cultivate the faith they had planted, or whether St. Aventinus was the first bishop of the city.

I will only say that it is certain the faith was preached there shortly after the death of Jesus Christ and the separation of the apostles and that those who were sent into these regions to announce the Gospel made much progress and found in the relationship of the Druidic ceremonies to our own a marvelous means by which they could convert the people. There were three main ceremonies: the cult of the virgin-who-was-to-give-birth; the oblation of bread and wine that was regular in their rites; and the adoration of the Tau [T]. These were but three preparations for the faith of the principal mysteries of the Christian religion: the Incarnation of the Word; the sacrifice of the Eucharist; and the death of Jesus Christ on the cross. And if St. Paul, seeing an altar dedicated to an unknown god at Athens, used it as an excuse to preach the coming of Jesus Christ to the Greeks, then one cannot doubt that the altar of the virgin was a very forceful argument for these early missionaries to convince the people of Chartres of the truths of the [Christian] faith. In fact, they preached with such success that they shortly converted a large number of the people of Chartres to Christ. Seeing the fulfillment of their predictions, the Druids left the shadows to follow the Truth; their caves and caverns were converted into oratories, and the Christians assembled in this subterranean spot dedicated to the Virgin and celebrated a divine service there daily. Quirinus, the governor of the town under the [Roman] emperor, Claudius, learned of these things and persecuted the new faithful; noting the time at which they met in their "holy chapel," he sent soldiers there who ran a number of them through with the sword and tumbled the bodies into a well underneath the virgin's altar. Because of the power and constancy of these first Christians in suffering martyrdom, this well is still called the well of the "strong saints" [*saints forts*]. The tyrant's rage grew still greater against them as well as against his own flesh and blood when he learned that they had introduced into their sect his only daughter, Modeste, and had baptized her; he caused a horrible massacre [of Christians] and put his daughter through every suffering of which inhumanity is capable, finally having her body thrown into the well with the other martyrs. He imprisoned the heads of the new Church; but while he was meditating its complete destruction, God allowed a quick death to carry this tyrant off and made an exemplary punishment of it. The blood of these martyrs was the seed of the Christians; the murder of so many innocent people made the chapel the more venerable and frequented. Divine offices continued to be celebrated there; the Christians went to them assiduously; and this sacred place was, for two centuries, the haven and refuge of the persecuted Church from the violence of tyrants.

As the number of Christians grew from day to day and this subterranean church required more space, several oratories were made in the town. Finally it was decided to build a church above the holy grotto, one capable of holding all the people. This was not difficult in a city which was among the largest in Gaul, and which was the regular residence of kings and sovereign pontiffs. The temple was beautiful and magnificent, as one can tell by the grottos built in that period and preserved down to the present. The devotion to the holy Virgin was so great that people came on pilgrimage to Chartres from the ends of the earth. * * * The church remained in this state of peace and tranquillity down to the reign of Charles the Bald and to the time when Frobold, the forty-second bishop of Chartres, held the chair. Then Hastings, chief of the Norman Danes, feigning that he had abandoned his hostility toward the inhabitants [of the town] and that he wanted to be baptized (as if he burned with an ardent desire to become a Christian), took advantage of the naïveté of this good bishop, his canons, and townsmen, who in good faith let him and his soldiers into the city; as soon as Hastings and his men were inside, they made rivers of blood and tears flow, they burned everything down pitilessly, and they put to the sword whatever the flames spared. It is said that the lead roofing on the church poured by the bucketful down the streets. * * *

This subterranean place is covered with strong vaults and is light in nearly every part because it has a number of windows through which the sun shoots its shafts, so that the grotto is never musty or humid and does not smell. There are thirteen chapels among which the most beautiful are those touched by the sun. The first and principal chapel is the one of the Virgin, consecrated by St. Potentianus at the altar where the ancient Druids' idol used to be. This chapel, which until recently had a simplicity recalling that of our elders, is now the richest and most ornate in the world. Its walls are covered with marble; its rail is of the same material; around the altar there is only gold, jasper, and painting; and the place where the people go to pray to the holy Virgin is ornamented with beautiful paintings which cover the walls as well as the vault from top to bottom. Behind this chapel there is a kind of hiding place and next to it is the well of the *Saints forts*. It is at this altar, which is called Notre-Dame-sous-Terre, that the people of Chartres and the pilgrims pay their greatest devotion. It would not be out of place here to describe the Virgin which our ancient Druids put up on this altar. She is seated on a throne holding her Son in her arms. She is black or Moorish in color, as are nearly all the images of the Virgin in Chartres, and the Druids are thought to have given her this color because she came from a country more exposed to the sun than ours. The real color of her skin is not known, but one can imagine it from what Solomon, in a prophetic spirit, said—that she was dark but not lacking in beauty [Cant. 1:4]. Nicephoras, however, says he saw several paintings made from nature by St. Luke, in which the color of her skin was the color of wheat—which is probably to say that when wheat is ripe it tends to be brownish or a chestnut color. * * *

Chapter XII. How the holy tunic of Our Lady came to Chartres and how it miraculously saved the town several times

According to Nicephoras, the holy Virgin, feeling herself close to death, told the apostles to give her clothes to an honest widow who had always served her from the time her Son had returned to His Father. While this holy clothing was in Palestine, it worked several miracles, which is the reason why the people into whose hands it fell treated it with the greatest care and had beautiful reliquaries made for it. With the passing of time, the clothes went through many hands and it happened that the holy tunic fell to the lot of a Jewess. Candidus and Galbius Patrick, two brothers from Constantinople, were staying with her on their return from Jerusalem, where they had been on pilgrimage to the holy places. They found out that the holy tunic of the Virgin was preserved in a reliquary the size and shape of which they carefully noted. They remained some time with the woman, who begged them in all goodness to relax a bit so as to be fresher for the continuation of their trip. While they were with her, they took the opportunity to steal the reliquary from the Jewess. To accomplish this, they had another reliquary made like the original one and exchanged the two, taking away the one they passionately wanted. Joyous at possessing this great treasure, they set out at once for Constantinople and came to the suburb of Blacherna, having resolved to hide their rich prize so that no one would know about it. But they did not keep it long, for the tunic made itself known by several miracles. And the emperor took it away from the men and built for it a temple surmounted by a dome of artistic workmanship. This reliquary was called the protector of the empire. It always remained in that city until Charlemagne, returning from Jerusalem, passed through Constantinople, where, at that time, were to be found the Emperor Nicephoras and his wife, Irene, who shared the empire with him, and some also say Aaron, King of Persia. These magnificent princes opened their treasury to Charlemagne and offered him several rare and inestimable things, among which was the holy tunic; he refused them all except for the tunic and some other reliquaries * * * and he had them taken to Aachen in Germany.

This whole story is ingeniously represented in the great stained-glass window of the chapel of St.-John the Baptist behind the choir of the great church at Aachen. One can still see painted there the three princes, with a number of open chests near them and with the holy tunic. Charles the Bald, grandson of Charlemagne, had the precious relic taken to France and gave it to the church of Chartres. Nicolle-Gilles described it in his *Life of Charles the Bald*; the titles of the church always include it; and an old French poem from the time of St. Louis [1226–1270], on the miracles of the Virgin, mentions it in these lines translated from the Latin poem of 1262 by Jean le Marchand:

> Then they took the holy tunic
> From the Mother of God, who departed—
> A noble gift once at Constantinople.
> At Chartres, a great king of France,
> Called Charles the Bald from infancy,
> Gave it to [the Church of] Chartres,
> Which is still thought to have it.

> The Lady who wore it
> When she bore the Son of God
> Thought it would be put
> At Chartres, in her main church,
> And that it would be preserved
> In the place of which she is called the Lady.

These lines refer to the miracle which took place through [the powers of] the holy tunic shortly after it was taken to Chartres and to the miraculous delivery of the people of Chartres from the siege of the Normans. The story, according to the annals of France and the chronicles of Chartres, is as follows.

Around the year 908, when Charles the Simple was King of France and Gaucelin Bishop of Chartres, Raoul, Duke of Normandy, sacked and pillaged a number of towns and provinces of France. He then laid siege to Chartres with a cruel and angry army at a time when there were only bishop and townsmen to defend the city [but no viscount or army]. The [inhabitants of Chartres] had no hope of outside aid because France was desolated and its prince overcome by miseries; his "simpleness" could be taken for cowardice more than anything else.

The bishop, seeing that no human aid could be found for the people, had recourse to divine assistance. He exhorted the populace to cast their eyes toward heaven and to entrust themselves to God in their princess and tutelary lady. He took the tunic, raised it like a banner, went bravely out against the enemy, and, as if the Virgin had in these happy moments given battle near this banner amid legions of angels and archangels, he spread such fear and awe among Raoul and his men that they turned 'round like stupid, senseless beings, threw themselves upon one another in disorder and fled in such a way that the fields of the Porte de Dreux, where they had set up their camp, has always since been called the Field of Flight. Here is how our poet, indeed venerable because of his age, describes it:

> The people of Chartres took the tunic
> And placed it on the crenelations of the walls
> Instead of standard or banner.
> When the opposing forces saw it,
> They began to make fun of it
> And to laugh and joke amongst themselves.
> They brought out bricks and fired them like arrows,
> And bows, and mangonels, and crossbows.
> But God, Who saw their disbelief,
> Showed His divine vengeance.

He blinded them so that they lost
Their sight and could not see;
When the men of Chartres realized
What a miracle
The Lady of Chartres had done for them,
They were full of joy,
And got ready to issue forth,
And put on their armor;
Donned their hawberks and laced their helmets,
Together with their bishop, Gaucelin,
Who carried the holy tunic
For defense and for guarantee,
Together with another banner
Which was with the Virgin's tunic;
And all issued forth from Chartres
With great vigor and a great noise
And went toward the camp of the pagans.
They made great slaughter
However they wished;
There were so many dead
That the earth was strewn with them;
So many headless were there.

This signal victory, won by the holy tunic, is represented in low relief in the choir of the church. At the time of St. Fulbert, the Virgin performed another miracle through the tunic. The church caught fire the day before the [feast of the] Nativity of the Virgin and the holocaust came on so suddenly that the flames seemed to appear everywhere at once and no one knew from whence this misfortune could have come. There were some men of Chartres, so zealous and so devoted to the Virgin that they threw themselves straight into the fire to carry out the reliquary containing the tunic. They were, in fact, resolved to die rather than to lose so precious a treasure. They carried it on their shoulders through fire and flame and, coming out safe and sound, they put the reliquary away in the grotto. Straight afterward the high bell fell down and melted, together with the lead of the church roof. The only sound to be heard was one of disorder and ruin, of great stones and piers falling; those who had taken refuge in the grotto had no way of getting out nor any hope of rejoining the living, since everything threatened them with death. The fire spread to the very doors of the grotto and the people saw themselves dying of hunger or becoming food for the flames.

Reduced to this state of helplessness, they implored the aid of the Virgin, whose tunic they had with them, and presently a singular thing happened to them. As if the flames feared her voice, they stopped at the very portals of her sacred cave! The Virgin gave her desolate flock such force and vigor (for being without food or water they were filled instead with her grace), that they all seemed to become invincible athletes. In this way she preserved her tunic and kept it safe and sound from the violence of the flames.

When the fire was out, Bishop Fulbert, the chapter, and the clergy, with most of the citizens of Chartres, ran to open up the grotto, thinking they should find the poor people dead from hunger, unconscious with fear, or burned up; but above all, they feared the loss of their holy relic. But God—Who never afflicts His own so much but reserves more pity for them than they deserve—and His holy mother—who took care to preserve for these people what they held most dear—astonished bishop, clergy, and populace when they saw these people safe and sound, as if coming out of an earthly paradise rather than a grotto surrounded by the horrors of death. What made them tremble with a pleasure that was all the greater because their fear had nearly made them despair was the agreeable sight of their holy reliquary untouched by the conflagration.

Then they sang hymns and canticles with tears and joy. The bishop and the dean put the holy reliquary on their shoulders to carry it in solemn procession so that everyone would have greater fervor and zeal in thanking God for His Grace, and to sing canticles in honor of the Virgin in their happiness at having saved what they thought was lost. Here is how our Old French poet describes it:

> When everyone was together,
> The holy reliquary was brought
> Out of the grotto to
> Where the people were.
> Thus, bishop and dean,
> One ahead, the other behind,
> Carried it on their shoulders.
> There was great devotion
> When the reliquary came into view—
> Cleric and layman alike grew glad. * * *
> One can scarcely describe
> The great joy of everyone;
> They gave thanks to God
> And to His glorious lady
> Who had saved the gem
> And the glory of their city.

3

THE ARCHITECTURE

The analysis (as distinct from the simple description) of medieval monuments is a fairly recent development in the history of art. It involves such things as the program or social function of the building; the structure; the massing and the volumes, or the inner and outer composition; and the lighting. In the following selections, to which my Introductory Essay is a supplement, Henri Focillon discusses Chartres as a member of the High Gothic group of cathedrals of the early thirteenth century; Jean Bony analyses its design; and Viollet-le-Duc and John Fitchen discuss certain technical procedures.

HENRI FOCILLON
[The Classic Phase of Gothic Architecture—1938][1]

Lying as it does on the fringes of Beauce, on the edge of the sharp descent down from the plateau, Chartres is both a town of the plains, ringed round with a wide horizon of cornfields, and a town of the uplands, where the roofs climb up steep slopes and along alleyways flanked by gables [fig. 1]. To the east, the land on which the church stands is intersected by a fault, so that the apse dominates the void; westwards, the plateau falls gently away. The cathedral, like a fortress, overlooks and controls the town. From the channels of the Eure which flow round garden-islets at the foot of the escarpment, it seems to draw the town upwards, as if to extend into the clouds its bridges, its mills, its tree-lined boulevard, its fortified gateway, and its churches —Saint-André, Saint-Pierre and Saint-Aignan. These sites and scenes

[1] From Focillon, *The Art of the West in the Middle Ages*, edited and introduced by Jean Bony, published by Phaidon Press London, and Phaidon Publishers Inc., New York, vol. 2, 1963, pp. 34–38; originally published as *Art d'Occident*, Paris, 1938 [Ed.].

among which Gothic thought developed were incorporated into it.
There, in the closing years of the twelfth century, it conceived and
began its masterpiece, and, from the principles which had been tested
by the architects of the preceding period, it evolved a new form of
architecture.

Work was begun in 1194, immediately after the burning of Fulbert's
basilica.[2] The site was limited on the east by the geological fault and
on the west by a façade, which the fire had partially spared, com-
prising a pair of towers and, between them, the Royal Portal, which
had been moved forward somewhat earlier.[3] For this reason, the
church is relatively short, with an extensive choir taking up one-third
of the length at the expense of the nave. The old foundations were
utilized, at the cost of a certain irregularity in the disposition of the
piers of the choirs, which terminates in an ambulatory with radiating
chapels. The development of the transept was unrestricted, and each
of its arms is conceived as a monumental unit, terminated by a
façade whose triple portal is sheltered beneath a porch.[4] In addition
to the towers of the west front and the spire over the crossing, there
are also two towers flanking each transept arm. Laon * * * provided
the model for this composition, as well as for the external passage
of the chapels. The technical data are as follows: sexpartite vaulting
is replaced by quadripartite, which ensures a unified distribution of
parts, since one bay of the aisle now corresponds to one of the nave;
the supports are conceived as an articulated system, whose members
rise in tiers, according to function, from the pavement up to the vault;
the flying buttress is envisaged and designed, not as a reinforcement,
but as an integral element of the structure; the tribune is suppressed
for the benefit of the aisles; and for the benefit of the clerestory the
wall extending from the triforium up to the formeret is removed

----

[2] The fire of 10th June 1194 spared, in addition to the eleventh-century
crypt, the two towers built in the middle of the twelfth century and the
Royal Portal. The main structure and vaults of the new cathedral, begun
by Bishop Renaud de Mouçon, were completed in 1220. The lateral porches
belong for the most part to the second third of the thirteenth century.
Among later additions, the Saint-Piat chapel dates from the first half of
the fourteenth century, and the Vendôme chapel from 1417. The spire
of the north tower was built in 1506 by Jean Texier.
* [3] The Royal Portal is now considered to have been moved forward when
work had hardly begun, c. 1150 at the latest: see M. Aubert, "Le portail
royal et la façade occidentale de la cathédrale de Chartres: Essai sur la
date de leur exécution," *Bulletin monumental*, vol. 100, 1941, pp. 177–218.
* [4] On the successive stages in the design of the transept façades, see L.
Grodecki, "The Transept Portals of Chartres Cathedral; the Date of their
Construction according to Archaeological Data," *Art Bulletin*, vol. 33, 1951,
pp. 156–164.

between each pair of piers, so that light falls, not through narrow and deep-set windows, but through immense sheets of glass opening to the sky. Note that each of these expedients is a function of the others and reacts upon all of them. The unity of the bay demands unity of abutment and puts an end to that undulation of forces which is characteristic of churches with alternating supports. The double flights of flying buttresses, strutted with colonnettes, prop the critical points against which, at regular intervals, the thrusts are delivered, and permit the annulment of the upper wall, which becomes no more than a connecting web, or mere useless weight. They also deprive the tribunes of their function in the equilibrium of the church, so that the lateral vessels may be heightened without subdivision into storeys.

In this way the skeleton church was defined—a combination of active forces, in which the cohesion of the parts is ensured by their interaction, by the theorem of functions, by the structure of the specialized members, and even by the type of masonry. The twelfth century has already shown us almost all the elements of the system established in various types of church, of which one, of great beauty, was still Romanesque in composition—the church with tribunes. The architect of Chartres was both follower and innovator; we can no longer overlook the contribution of Saint-Vincent at Laon, but what he took from elsewhere he recreated. The elements of the solution remained the same, but he demanded more from them and his reasoning was more closely knit. The measure of his originality is perhaps given by his unchallenged domination of contemporary art. The thirteenth century began with Chartres, and the *Rayonnant* style which, in the second half of the same period and in the following century, seems at first sight to introduce new forms, in fact did no more than extend the reasoning and carry it forward to dangerous extremes of refinement.[5] Chartres, as compared with the line of great cathedrals which it inaugurated, had the advantage of youth—not as abstract priority, but the vital quality of a style, in full command of its resources, making its first appearance. By its retention of the twelfth-century work in the old towers and the Royal Portal, it indicated the stock from which it sprang. It abandoned the alternation of supports, yet retained a vestige of it in the piers, which are alternately cylindrical and polygonal. The flights of flying buttresses,

---

* [5] On the logic of Gothic architecture, see the important essay by E. Panofsky, *Gothic Architecture and Scholasticism*, Latrobe (Pennsylvania), 1951, where the analysis of the forms and methods of mediaeval logic brings a new light on the subject. [Note: Also available in paperback, New York, 1967—Ed.]

linked by squat columns, are of quadrant form. The archivolts of the
clerestory windows are still semicircular. Finally the walls, cut from
the rough shell-bearing limestone of the Berchère quarries, are no
fragile partitions, but monumental masses. When one considers in
addition that the tradition of the Royal Portal workshops continued
to inspire the earliest sculptors of the transept doorways, it is apparent that Chartres, which in its youthful vigour took a long step
beyond the twelfth century, nevertheless retained the charm and
grandeur of the old ways.

The study of the great cathedrals of the thirteenth century com-
prises fewer varieties than that of twelfth-century cathedrals. There
are fewer essential differences between Chartres, Reims, and Amiens
than there are between Sens and Paris, or even Paris and Laon. A
classic mode of thought in architecture is as stable as a beautiful
language, which, once established, has no need of neologisms. Reims,[6]
whose history was intimately associated with that of the monarchy,
from the Hincmars and the Adalberos onwards, gave the cathedral
of the coronation a nave of ten bays, but its transept has neither
the monumental development of Chartres, nor the porches which
there give exceptional relief and colour to the subsidiary façades.
The eastern parts are seated on massive concretions which serve as
a basis for the vertical development of the structure. On this for-
midable masonry rests an architecture whose elegance appears in the
design of the windows, the profiles of the mouldings, the more open

[6] One year after the fire which, on 6th May 1210, had destroyed the old
Carolingian cathedral of Reims, Archbishop Aubri de Humbert laid the
first stone of the new church. The choir was completed in 1241, as were
also, no doubt, the transept and the first two bays of the nave. This
section was the work of Jean d'Orbais and his successor, Jean le Loup.
These masters were followed by Gaucher de Reims (about 1247) and Bernard de Soisson (from about 1255 to the end of the century). The west
doors were begun by the middle of the thirteenth century, and the towers
were in course of construction in 1299—they were finished in 1427. At the
beginning of the sixteenth century the restoration of the transept gables
was put in hand; these had been damaged by a fire in 1481. See L. Demaison's studies, "La cathédrale de Reims, son histoire, ses dates de construction," *Bulletin monumental*, 1902, and "La cathédrale de Reims,"
Congrès archéologique de Reims, 1911. * The chronology of Reims Cathedral
is difficult to establish in all its details. Important remarks were made by
H. Deneux, "Des modifications apportées à la cathédrale au cours de sa construction du XIII⁵ au XV⁵ siècles," in *Bulletin monumental*, vol. 106, 1948,
pp. 121–140; but the most penetrating analysis of all the problems involved is
found in three recent articles by R. Branner in *Speculum*, XXXVI, 1961,
pp. 23–37; *Zeitschrift für Kunstgeschichte*, vol. 24, 1961, pp. 220–241; and
Journal of the Society of Architectural Historians, vol. 21, 1962, pp. 18–25.

and audacious form of the flying buttresses, and even in the pinnacles surmounting the main buttresses, which are contrived as niches containing figures of angels, and topped by little spires. The façade provides a gorgeous development of a theme which was renounced, with an exquisite sense of fitness and for the better co-ordination of the parts, by the Chartres architects, who allowed the Royal Portal to retain its full emphasis and pierced only a rose in the sober wall above the earlier triplet of windows. In Paris, despite the importance of the galleries and the enormous diameter of the rose, the wall preserves its severe strength and its character of a broadly modelled mass. The Reims architects composed a skeletal, highly-coloured *décor*, sustained by an armature of buttresses, hollowed out below with deep door-splays surmounted by openwork gables, overrun even in the upper storeys by an admirable sculpture, and enlivened with arches and colonnettes. The design is related to, but more elegant than, that of Amiens, where the volume and depth of the portals are so stressed that they seem almost to be porches, separate from the main building.

But Amiens[7] is above all a masterpiece of structure. The nave is the purest and most perfect expression of the Gothic system, with an absolute quality, an inerrant logic, which is rendered clearer and colder by the even light falling through uncoloured windows. Nowhere better than here can one grasp that harmonious progression of the supports, by which, as they ascend, new colonnettes are constantly added to sustain the springing of new arches. A horizontal string-course runs beneath the triforium-sill, and its ornamentation introduces into this elegant, severe order a slight movement and a just measure of relief. In details of this sort we see how sensitive the style is. Even in its strictest expression, this architecture is not exclusively intellectual. The nave of Amiens, running counter to the normal practice of commencing the church from the east end, is older than the choir. But no abrupt transition marks our passage from one age to another. Amiens shows us how homogeneous this art was in its successive variations, and the details which we notice in the

---

[7] The old cathedral at Amiens had been destroyed in 1218. Two years later the new building was begun, under Bishop Évrard de Fouilloy. The nave was completed in 1236, the radiating chapels in 1247. In 1258, work was interrupted by a fire. The choir was completed before 1270. From 1220 to 1288, Robert de Luzarches, Thomas de Cormont, and his son Renaud, were successively masters of the works. The series of chapels between the buttresses was begun before 1292; the two latest were built for Cardinal de Lagrange, during his episcopate (1373–75). The north tower was begun about 1366; the south tower is the work of the early fifteenth century.* P. Frankl, "A French Gothic Cathedral: Amiens," *Art in America,* vol. 35, 1947, assesses the significance of the building.

choir suggest a change of programme rather than a new style. This
is true of the glazed triforium, tending to merge with the clerestory,
a characteristic feature of *Rayonnant* architecture. We see here an
early stage of the development which was to end with the complete
absorption of the triforium, but all this could have been foreseen from
the day when the architect of Chartres dispensed with the upper
walls, and began to speculate concerning the void as his predecessors
had speculated concerning the solid. The immense windows of the
Amiens chapels, cages of glass sustained by piers and projecting buttresses, are a direct consequence of the same principle. * * *

JEAN BONY
[The Nave—1957–58]¹

Chartres * * * is a bold simplification [of twelfth-century design].
During the war and just after, when the stained-glass had been removed and Chartres was once again reduced to pure architecture, one
could almost have heard the Chartres master explaining his ideas,
stressing the need for clear thinking, for simple and radical solutions,
and, above all, the idea that a new situation had been created by the
invention of the flying-buttress a few years before, and that a complete reappraisal was now necessary. This logical mode of reasoning
was easy to follow, the solution proposed was simple and convincing,
and Chartres became almost at once the classic type of Gothic
elevations. In fact, the whole history of French Gothic in the thirteenth century, and even after, could almost be reduced to the development and metamorphoses of the Chartres type.² * * *

Chartres meant, of course, a number of different things: it meant
a vast programme for a great pilgrimage church taking form in a
highly articulated plain; it meant a new degree of technical achievement in width and height, and a new composition of the inner space.
If the usual comparison of the elevations of Chartres and Laon is
made, one finds a reduction in the number of stories and a completely
different setting out of the elevation, in larger and taller panels. But
what counts essentially in this new style of architecture [fig. 10] are
the four following points. First, the gigantic size of the clerestory,

---

¹ From Jean Bony, "The Resistance to Chartres in Early Thirteenth-
Century Architecture," *Journal of the British Archaeological Association*,
ser. 3, vols. 20–21, 1957–58, pp. 35–40, *passim* [Ed.].
² This would give an oversimplified view of the evolution of Ile-de-France
Gothic and the tendency of modern research has been to stress the importance of less conventional lines of development.

the very large windows. We all know that they were made possible only by the flying buttress, which meant that the high vault could be carried upward far above the lateral volumes; but at least it can be said that every building in which the windows are on that scale belongs to the Chartres group. On the other hand, when the windows remain short and do not come down below the level of the upper capitals, this means a refusal of the Chartres idea. The second point which affects the character of the building is the vigorous accentuation of the vertical direction in the piers, and no doubt this was meant to express the force of gravity. Heavy projecting shafts stress the axes of the piers right up to the main arcade and they are continued above by voluminous groups of shafts, which cut the inner space into narrow vertical slices and give to the whole edifice its particular spatial expression. This contrasts with the longitudinal insistence of the earlier galleried churches, and even of Bourges, where the pattern is one of continuity. The third feature is the absence of detached shafts, of applied monoliths used *en délit*—to take this convenient French term, meaning against the direction of the quarry-bed. At Chartres the whole structure is built in regular courses of masonry; it has a perfect unity of texture, nothing is detachable. This again contrasts with the habits of twelfth-century architects who loved the sharp linear effect of applied monoliths. The fourth and last essential feature is the flatness of the elevation. The triforium alone has a certain depth, but otherwise the whole of the elevation forms one flat vertical plane, which continues the plane of the triforium arcading, without any hollows or recesses, as if it were just a thin sheet of glass and stone. This is all the more noteworthy at Chartres, because the structure of the upper walls is rather thick; but the effect of depth is kept on the outside. The Rayonnant elevation of Saint-Denis, with its effect of spiderwork surface, was possible only because Chartres had established that original flatness of the limit. * * *

E. E. VIOLLET-LE-DUC
[The Flying Buttress—1875][1]

FLYING BUTTRESS. These are exterior arches that are intended by their position to counteract the thrust of the ribbed vaults. They spring from buttresses, their summit touching the point where the thrusts of the transverse arches and of the diagonal ribs converge. * * * The system of flying buttresses * * * is the most frank and

---

[1] From E. E. Viollet-le-Duc, *Dictionnaire raisonné* . . ., vol. I, Paris, 1875, pp. 60 ff., *passim*. Translated by Robert Branner [Ed.].

energetic expression of the medieval manner of construction. Prior to their appearance in Gothic churches, there was a great deal of fumbling; from the moment flying buttresses were clearly marked in buildings, the development of the structure of churches set out with vigor in a new direction. To want a Gothic church without flying buttresses is to want a boat without a rudder; for church as well as for boat, it is a question of being or not being. * * *

It was only at the end of the twelfth century that the flying buttress came to the fore in the religious architecture of northern France; it appeared in central France and in the Midi only as an importation toward the end of the thirteenth century, when the ribbed-vault style that was already advanced in the Ile-de-France, Champagne, and Burgundy, spread throughout western Europe. * * *

The method of opposing that thrust of the vault by double flying buttresses (with two superimposed flyers, as at Amiens or Soissons) did not always seem sufficiently strong to the builders of the thirteenth century; they thought of solidifying the two arches by a series of spokes which join them together and of giving them the resistance of a solid wall, while at the same time allowing them great lightness. The Cathedral of Chartres is an admirable example of this sort of flying buttress [fig. 15]. The construction of this building shows remarkable strength in all its parts. The vaults are unusually thick (about 14 inches); the materials—heavy, rough, compact—do not readily lend themselves to the delicacy of Gothic architecture of the first half of the thirteenth century. In order to counteract the thrust of these heavy vaults of no less than 45 foot span, it was necessary to establish vigorous, solidly based abutments; thus [fig.14], one can see that the whole system of arches penetrates the buttresses, as it were in a channel; that all the joints of the stonework are normal to the curves; and that, finally, it is a completely oblique construction intended to resist weight that also pushes obliquely. * * *

JOHN FITCHEN
[Vault Construction and Scaffolding—1961]¹

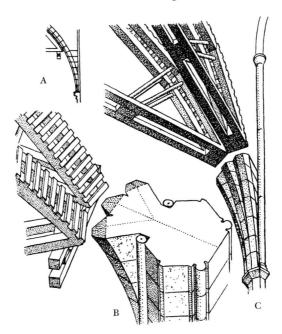

Text illus. 1. Convergence of the Rib Frames at the Top of
the *Tas-de-Charge* (Fitchen)

1. *Convergence of the Rib Frames at the Top of the* Tas-de-Charge

The small detail at A shows a *tas-de-charge* of seven courses, each
with horizontal bed. Radial joints begin for the rib voussoirs at the
top of this series of corbels, and   is at this level that the centering
frames are set. In B and C the ribs are simplified to bevelled instead
of moulded profiles. The ends of the centering frames for a diagonal
and a transverse rib are seen from above in B, from below in C. The
pair of frames has a common end support on a wedged-up sill, in B.
This view also shows the large single block—the highest of the
tas-de-charge courses—which was sometimes used to transmit the
vault's lateral pressures directly to the half arch of the flying buttress.

¹ From John F. Fitchen, III, *The Construction of Gothic Cathedrals*,
Oxford, 1961, reproduced by kind permission of the author [Ed.].

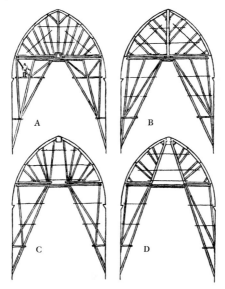

Text illus. 2. Four Diagrammatic Schemes of Framing and Undergirding the Half-Frames of the Gothic
Ribbed-Vault Centering (Fitchen)

2. *Four Diagrammatic Schemes of Framing and Undergirding the Half-Frames of Gothic Ribbed Vault Centering*

For the falsework assemblage of undergirding gantries, A to D
indicate successively less massive timber-work, since support for the
rib centerings are needed progressively less close to mid-span, and
the major struts lean out over the void at less of an angle with the
vertical. These gantries provide a working platform at about the level
of the top of the *tas-de-charge*, on which the centering frames could
be maneuvered and wedged up. * * * The centering frames shown
here apply to the intersecting diagonals as well as to the transverse
ribs. In A, a large bracketed crown insert is separately wedged up
from below. B involves a central tree-like column from which struts
incline like branches to all four half-frames. C shows two half-frames
of fanning struts, with a single separator block at the crown. D relates
centering frames to gantry more rationally by aligning major elements
of both portions of the falsework, so that the compressive stresses may
be carried down directly to the triforium passageway level. In all
four schemes, major timbers and struts are indicated by double lines,
secondary ties and braces by single lines.

4

THE SCULPTURE OF THE WEST FAÇADE

Vöge was the first historian to look at the west façade of Chartres as a coherent work of art. He was also the first to recognize the profound importance of the statue-column for Gothic sculpture and to give a reasonable explanation of its origin. His stylistic analysis of the sculpture also provided the foundation upon which more recent art historians have built.

WILHELM VÖGE

from *The Beginnings of the Monumental Style in the Middle Ages*—[1894][1]

The Royal Portal of the Cathedral of Chartres and its Composition

The west portal of the Cathedral of Chartres, with its triple opening and its extravagant riches of reliefs and statuary, is striking for the unity and completeness of its composition [fig. 23].

This is also true of the iconography. We see in the right tympanum the Christ Child on His mother's knees together with scenes of the Infancy [fig. 25], on the left the Ascension [fig. 26],[2] and in the center Christ in Majesty [fig. 24]: the beginning, ending, and crown-

---

[1] Selections from W. Vöge, *Die Anfänge des Monumentalen Stiles in Mittelalter*, Strasbourg, 1894, translated by Alice Fischer and Gertrude Steuer. Only the essential footnotes have been translated, and no attempt has been made to produce Vöge's style in English [Ed.].

[2] I shall prove below that this scene must be interpreted as an Ascension.

ing fulfillment of His mission. Could one possibly sum up more felicitously the life of the Redeemer? Is it intentional that here, at the entrance to the church, the memory of Christ's sufferings is tactfully avoided?³ Only in the innermost sanctuary does the worshipper face the anguished figure of the Crucified.

On the projecting jambs of the portals we see a continuous row of life-size statues—originally twenty-four⁴—representing the Ancestors of Christ, men and women mostly in royal attire [figs. 36–38]. Thus the victorious career of the Hero is elucidated by the story of His royal descent. This is epic in truly medieval manner.

The statues lean against the same number of columns. Above them, the capitals are brought together in a continuous frieze, unfolding once again, but on a smaller scale, a cycle of the Gospels. Like densely woven wreaths, the projecting, staggered archivolts of the three portals surround the three tympana with their figures and scenes.

Here, again, there exists an unmistakably deliberate order. The enthroned Christ and the Apostles are surrounded by the Elders of the Apocalypse and a row of angels [fig. 33]. The representations of human activities are placed around the tympana of the lateral portals —at the left, the Labors of the Months and signs of the Zodiac [fig. 32]; at the right, the Liberal Arts with their personifications [fig. 34]. This parallelism is not unintentional. I believe that the artist linked the two cycles (the Labors of the Months and the Liberal Arts) to one another. He himself naïvely furnishes the evidence for this: two scenes belonging to the cycle on the north,⁵ for which no

---

³ There is no Crucifixion pictured on the capital frieze; see Bulteau, *Monographie de la Cathédrale de Chartres*, Chartres, 1888, vol. 2, p. 36 ff.

⁴ Only nineteen partly mutilated figures are extant; for the drawing of the portals made for Roger de Gaignières (see Henri Bouchon, *Inventaire des dessins exécutés pour Roger de Gaignières*, Paris, 1891, vol. 2, p. 198 and p. 395; these drawings were included in the *Grande topographie de la France* of the *Cabinet des Estampes* at Paris, Département d'Eure-et-Loir) show it already in this state, but the now headless statue at the right, next to the left lateral doorway, has a bearded head without a crown. This might represent the original state.

⁵ These are two signs of the Zodiac. The theme of the Labours of the Months reappears once more among the twelve statuettes decorating the pilasters which separate the portals; among others there is a butcher, an armorer, and a merchant (?); a cyclical unity between the representations is absent; close by them are figures of Prophets or Apostles. Bulteau (*op. cit.*, vol. 2, p. 70) assumed that they represent donors, "be it in the person of their patron saint or in the representation of their trade." This seems rather doubtful to me; it may be that we deal here with the purely decorative use of all sorts of motifs which happened to be on hand. This is true also of the related scenes decorating the door posts, where we find a pell-mell of prophets, angels, a musician, a man with scepter, and so on.

space was left, appear on the south. This should not be interpreted as error of execution; it was planned beforehand.

Thus, we deal here with a planned and unified iconographic whole, revealing, in the execution, traces of a youthful groping that had not yet learned to master all difficulties.

In analyzing the composition from the artistic point of view, we find the same spirit.

There is a very peculiar and difficult problem here: a commanding central portal and two smaller side portals were to be united into a compact compositional ensemble within a relatively tight space.[6] There was, first of all, the problem of tying together the three portals with strongly accentuated horizontals; but it was also important to emphasize the central portal by means of a larger opening and a correspondingly larger scale of elements. It seems the artist did not quite realize that these requirements, based on factual data, are in contradiction with one another. He tried to do justice to both.

He made the central doorway much wider, but decided to make the side doorways as high as the central one. This way he achieved an equal height for all the capitals and could set a continuous cornice above them. In addition, all the columns were placed on equally high bases. In between and above the horizontals that run across the entire façade, we see different vertical designs on central and lateral portals. Compare the tympana! [Figs. 24–26.] The one on the central portal, though higher, is divided into only two parts. On the lateral doorways, however, a second sculpted register is placed between the lintel and the tympanum proper, thus reducing the size of the tympanum and of the figures, so that they are smaller than the figures of the enthroned Christ in the center. At this point, a study of the large statues in the embrasures becomes especially interesting. On the side portals between statues and capitals, the artist interposed canopies decorated with small architectural motifs, with the purpose of camouflaging the long shafts of the columns. As in the tympana, on the embrasures also the proportions are intentionally reduced in order to point up the secondary importance of the side parts. Nevertheless, the difficulty referred to above was not yet overcome. It is too bad that statues of different heights on the central and lateral portals have

---

[6] The breadth of the portal was originally determined by the width of the older church. Originally the portals were placed to the rear, as far in as the back of the towers. Only after the fire of 1194 were they moved to their present location. The central portal corresponded to the nave and the lateral ones to the aisles; the new thirteenth-century nave is as wide as nave and aisles combined in the former church. Thus, all three portals now open into the nave. [For more recent discussions of this matter, see the Introduction.—Ed.]

been placed in a continuous row. Just at the most visible points, where the projecting buttresses separate the three portals, statues of considerably differing height stand side by side.[7] Apparently the sculptor miscalculated the narrowness of the available space; doesn't the artist here again reveal rather than conceal his intention through this naive solution? Be this as it may, we have here, iconographically and artistically, a design calculated to produce total unity.

Such a composition was certainly planned by one individual, but several "hands" are distinguishable. To the far right and the far left, on the outer jambs of the side portals [figs. 36, 37], the statues are sculpted by a different hand from the one that made the coherent central group [fig. 38]. This easily explains a number of incongruities in style and arrangement. At this point, it is the latter which interests us. On the central portal, we have a gradation in the size of the statues, which become shorter as they approach the recessed doorway. This is so conspicuous on the north side of the portal that there can be no doubt the artist was aiming at a decorative effect there. Had he wanted to compensate for the receding jambs; by using perspective, he would have reversed the order, that is, he would have placed the tallest figures farthest away from the eye of the beholder. In putting the shortest statue there, he intended to stress the depth of the portal. In addition, he placed the most distant figures on higher bases. This, too, was not arbitrary; the evidence may be found at the left side of the door, where a piece of about two hand widths in height has been added to the base, obviously confirming the artist's intention of placing the statue at this height. What we have here is an artificial raising of the focal point. Only when this delicate matter has been grasped, can the beholder appreciate the unique aesthetic effect of this portal. It floats like magic around the figures, forcing the eyes into the depths, then raising them as if they were pulled upwards, gliding along the figures, to fall upon the image of Christ Enthroned and upon half-dark vaults of the nave behind.[8] The composition of the side portals is not so successful [fig. 23]. The

---

[7] This is less conspicuous now, because one of the statues in question is missing on the right side, and one on the left is mutilated.

[8] Chartres lacks a trumeau; there never was one and the effect is particularly impressive with open doors. I cannot share Viollet-le-Duc's enthusiasm for the motif of the trumeau; with closed doors the effect is quite satisfactory; but when they are open, which is the case on all festive occasions, the post obstructs the view. One cannot help but feel that this motif was invented purely for technical reasons. On the other hand, the post appears too narrow and too weak for the load of the tympanum and the lintel. That the Middle Ages chose this element out of necessity shows the numerous devices which were tried out during the Romanesque period.

obvious reason is that someone else collaborated with the Master of the central portal. Proof for this can be found on the extreme right and left embrasures, which must be ascribed to another artist on stylistic grounds. There is no reduction in the size of the figures closer to the doorway. They are simply arranged symmetrically; that is to say, the statue in the center is more or less visibly emphasized by being set somewhat higher (compare the tips of the feet). The figure is also distinguished by having a more richly sculpted base and is also the largest in size (on the right side) or has, at least, the largest head (on the left). We notice, on the other hand, that the figures on the jambs adjoining the central portal, which are also stylistically related to its sculpture, follow the same principle of arrangement as the latter;[9] the one nearest to the beholder is again the largest one. It is set apart by a more elaborate and higher base (and canopy). Here, too, the figure next to the door is placed highest.

One is justified in asking whether the medieval artist should really be credited with so much finesse in decorative planning. Is the undeniable attraction of this composition entirely calculated? It would not be an error to assume that the varying length of the figures was simply due to the more or less uneven size of the blocks[10] assigned to the sculptor. It apparently never occurred to these old masters that a particularly beautiful block could be shortened by a head-length or so in order to obtain an even-sized group of figures. Don't the statues themselves prove this assumption? In all instances, the halos reach the very top of the block, while the tips of the feet strain to touch the lower edge. There is hardly room left for a short, aphoristic image on the base. Occasionally, the long robes of the women even extend over it. Doesn't this explain the one violation of the principle governing the grouping of the statues? I have in mind the over-elongated female statue to the right of the central portal [fig. 23]. The figure is adroitly enough fitted into the group, but while the head remains on a level with the rest of the statues, its feet extend further down than do the ones of its outer neighbor. With fine artistic consideration, the master created a grouping with the given sizes. Whether guided by sound artistic instinct or by experimentation, he arrived at this perspective gradation, so uniquely satisfactory that a sensitive beholder can hardly miss it.

[9] The bad state of preservation of the group in question allows only an approximate evaluation.

[10] The height of the statue and the size of the block always coincide in the works of the Head Master. In the case of two other statues, even the canopies above the heads were cut from the same block. The following stylistic analysis will completely justify this opinion.

Provençal Influences on the Sculpture of Northern France and the Growth of an Original Northern Style

The first problem that must be dealt with is the specific style of the statues.[11] Their strange rigidity has always been perplexing and has always been the source of all errors connected with them. Their style suggests the idea of great antiquity, and they were named after the Merovingian kings, the oldest dynasty. While browsing in Montfaucon's *Monumens de la monarchie françoise* [figs. 39, 40, 50], the reasoning behind this opinion became clear to me: it stems from the free, painterly style of the authentic portraits of the Carolingians. Compared with the broadly and softly modeled portraits of Charles the Bald or Lothar which we see in manuscripts, these statue-columns certainly appear to be personages of a much earlier generation.[12]

Joined for their entire length to columns[13] and perched on fragile consoles, these figures seem to be suspended between heaven and earth. Shaftlike themselves, with narrow shoulders, females as well as males chestless, limbs hidden under the folds of the garments, gesturing only with their forearms, their heads high and their chins pulled in, these figures look like creatures from another world, a world less perfect maybe, but not without law. What reinforces this impression is their lack of a lively rapport with the beholder and with one another. No hand is stretched out, no head is turned, no attribute reveals a human experience. With a scepter, a book, or a scroll in their hands, they seem to be vegetating beings rather than living ones.[14]

[11] In the following, I shall consider mainly the statues of the Head Master.

[12] It is strange to see that the old theory has not yet lost its credibility. Hermann Weiss tried, even in the second edition of his *History of Costume*, to use these figures as examples of Merovingian dress. Here and there one still finds a tendency to date these figures earlier. Buhot de Kersers dates the related statues of Bourges in the ninth and tenth centuries.

[13] See Lübke's good description in his *Plastik*, vol. 1, pt. 3, p. 426. But I cannot agree with his interpretation of them as being "submissive servants." The figures are solemn and majestic. This was also the opinion of Viollet-le-Duc, Rigollot (*Histoire des arts du dessin*, Paris, 1863, vol. 2, p. 74 ff.), and others. It is also wrong to say that the heads of the figures are lowered. It is their chins which are retracted. A new terminology has even been invented in order to do justice to this style. Pottier speaks of "dressed columns," Langlois calls the drapery "bunches of asparagus," Viollet-le-Duc describes the figures as "swaddled in their garments like mummies in their bandages" (*Dictionnaire*, vol. 8, p. 118), and somewhere else he speaks of folds like "organ pipes" and so on.

[14] Lebeuf remarks someplace: "these figures were, in the minds of their

Moreover, the statues are structurally functionless.[15] By no means do they serve architectural needs; they seem to have retreated there for protection. Lübke says, "You can see how the sculpture obtrudes upon the architecture." This architecture is nothing but a simulated scaffold placed in front of the wall, for all the columns could be safely removed without endangering the upper structure.[16] I shall not attempt to say how far the singular relationship of the two art forms can be justified theoretically; the unique style of the sculpture can only be comprehended in its close union with the architecture, and surely the whole offers an impression of harmony and beauty. The style is, without a doubt, justifiable in connection with this composition. Despite their abnormal proportions and rigidity, the figures, wherever we find them, achieve a convincing life of their own. And the almost menacing power of this style! As if it were following a very strict canon!

Some German scholars felt that this creation was a matter of conscious artistic effort, but they have not proved it.[17] How could they decipher the secrets of this creation without knowing its sources? It is not possible through aesthetic and technical analysis alone to bring into accurate focus an accomplishment of the past and to make it shine as brilliantly as it did on the first day. It is also not sufficient to compare the work with other creations of the same time. It is imperative to search out the works of art which directly influenced it. Only after we have determined the sources will we be able to tell how the Chartrain masters proceeded and will we be able to separate in their work the original accomplishment from the heritage of tradition. Only then will their originality become recognizable and the tradition come into its own. Even if we assumed that the Chartrain sculptors had never seen a similar iconographic cycle or an older representation of Christ's genealogy, who would still dare to

---

sculptors, nothing but symbols" (*Histoire de l'académie royale des inscriptions*, vol. 23, Paris, 1756), an expression suggested by the style.

[15] Those who spoke about these and similar statues as caryatids were wrong; see, among others, E. Hucher, *Etudes sur l'histoire et les monuments du département de la Sarthe*, Le Mans and Paris, 1856, p. 41 ff., "exactly like Greek caryatids"; see also, among others. Charles Herbert Moore, *Development and Character of Gothic Architecture*, London, 1890, p. 254.

[16] The load of the archivolts is directly absorbed by the wall. See the technical analysis of the medieval column portal in Viollet-le-Duc, *Dictionnaire*, vol. 7, p. 406.

[17] Robert Vischer, Lübke, and Moore, too; quotations will be cited elsewhere.

believe that their sculpture was also created out of a void? "One must always, in art, find a point of departure."[18] An original style does not appear out of nowhere.

Up to now, no one has ever tried to trace the style of Chartres back to its sources. There are some hints and suppositions in the scholarly literature, but only Louis Gonse formulated a precise statement:[19] "The accomplishment of the façade of Chartres . . . , by its superiority, brings into prominence a group of works . . . a school . . . whose deep roots are probably connected with the famous Romanesque School of Aquitaine (Toulouse, Moissac) with a good measure of Burgundian or better Cluniac influence (Vézelay, Charlieu, Avallon) added to it. It looks as if this School developed around Paris, passing first through the admirable lateral portals of Bourges, which form the link between the southern types and the School of Chartres." For him, as we can see, the School of Languedoc, with its centers in Toulouse and Moissac, is the original source of this artistic trend. He traces the approximate route it traveled and also supposes an additional influence coming from Burgundy. I do not like to contradict this fine scholar of Gothic, but things are not so simple. Some kind of relations to these two Schools is not entirely out of the question and as for Toulouse, I believe that I can throw more light on it. At any rate, I would like to call attention to the one school which is not mentioned and which should have been given first consideration: the School of Provence. I shall prove that the essence of Chartrain art comes without a doubt from Provence, that it is the richly decorated west portal of St.-Trophîme at Arles with which our composition at Chartres has the most in common. Because of the very noticeable disparity in styles, this connection has heretofore been overlooked. Is it permissible at all to look for direct stylistic and technical relationships? Should we not assume that the nature and manner of the technical and stylistic execution is *a priori* our artists' own? A deep gulf always and everywhere necessarily separates the creative accomplishment from the past. Won't the abyss close if we find out what circumstances and forces prompted the growth of the new out of the old? Let us turn at once to the comparison and take a broad, general look at both compositions—that of Chartres and that of Arles.[20] The tympanum of St.-Trophîme, just as the central portal of Chartres, shows Christ in Majesty surrounded by the symbols of

---

[18] Viollet-le-Duc, *Dictionnaire*, vol. 8, p. 182.

[19] *Loc. cit.*, p. 414; also Schnaase, *Geschichte der bildenden Künste*, Düsseldorf, 1872, vol. 5, pt. 2, p. 567.

[20] I stress here only what is important for the comparison with Chartres.

the Evangelists [fig. 28].[21] It is framed with a double row of angels
in half-figure. On the lintel are seated the Twelve Apostles. The
tympanum proper is separated from the lintel by a band of acanthus
leaves and this is carried over, on the right and the left, to the walls
which are decorated with life-sized statues, Apostles and saints, all in
high relief. The figures are separated from one another by ornamental pilasters. Above them are two bands of reliefs: the upper one
is as wide as the lintel and is also connected to it iconographically;
the lower and narrower one is decorated with biblical scenes.

And now to Chartres. Here again is Christ with the Tetramorph,
framed by angels in half-figure; the Apostles are shown on the lintel
[fig. 24]. The embrasures are decorated with life-sized figures, but
here they are strangely transformed. In place of those rougher figures
in high relief that are technically reminiscent of ancient steles, we
find the medieval statue-column which is worked with much greater
care. It is worth noting that we find again at Chartres the ornamental
element which separates the statues from one another. But this under-
goes a change similar to that of the sculpture. Instead of the ornamental pilaster, there is a column covered by a vine. Even the frieze
with the Gospel scenes is not missing at Chartres! Here, too, they are
placed above the large figures. They have, if I may say so, shared the
fate of the latter! The high reliefs of St.-Trophîme were transformed
into statues columns and the frieze with the biblical scenes was transposed to the capitals of the columns. In place of a continuous relief,
we have at Chartres an uninterrupted row of historiated capitals.

Above the capitals we discover another old friend. The cornicelike
slab above them shows the same acanthus-leaf motif as the cornice
over the reliefs at Arles.

Right here and now, I would like to point to another splendid
façade in Provence, namely to that of St.-Gilles [fig. 27],[22] which is
closely related to Arles. Here we find a portal with three doorways,

[21] Departement des Bouches-du-Rhône; see Henry Revoil, *Architecture
romane du midi de la France*, vol. 2, Paris, 1873, p. 33 ff. and pls. XLI-LVI;
Iconographie du portail de Saint-Trophîme, Honoré Clair, in *Congrés
archéologique de France* (XLIIIe session; Séances générales, tenues à Arles
en 1876), Paris, 1877, p. 607 ff.; see also, from the older literature: Prosper
Merimée, *Notes d'un voyage au midi de la France*, Paris, 1835, pp. 288 ff.
and Jean-Julien Estrangin, *Etudes archéologiques, historiques et statistiques
sur Arles*, Aix, 1838, p. 202 ff.; see also a notice of Charles Linas in the
Revue des sociétes savantes, 1875, vol. 1, p. 194.
[22] See Revoil, *op. cit.*, p. 47 ff., illustrations and details of the façade pl.
LIX ff. Illustrations also in the *Archives de la commission des monuments
historiques*, vol. 2, and Baldus, *Les monuments principaux de la France*,
Paris, 1875. For more literature, I mention Mérimée, *op. cit.* p. 336 ff.;
Quicherat, *Mélanges de'archéologie et d'histoire* (edited by Robert de

as at Chartres. And, as at Chartres, we see the history of Christ on the three tympana: a Christ in Majesty fills the central tympanum, an enthroned Virgin with the Child is in one of the side ones, and in the other is a Crucifixion instead of an Ascension. On the walls, once again, there is a continuous row of life-sized figures and above their heads a frieze of biblical scenes. At St.-Gilles also, as at Chartres, we notice the continuous, fluted plinth.

Nothing is more likely than that the rich iconographic program came to the artists of Chartres from another school. This assumption is suggested by the peculiarly powerful union of the sculpted decoration and with the architectonic framework. A school which employed the structural system that served as model for the Chartres portals obviously did not at first consider the principle of a portal decorated with figural sculpture. At Chartres, a sort of simulated scaffolding masks the entire expanse of the wall. Column crowds column, and colonnettes are squeezed between the larger shafts. Corresponding to the latter, there rise rows of projecting archivolts. Here, despite the narrow space, the medieval columnar doorway[23] found a classical formulation. The lateral portals press against the central doorway; there remains between them only enough space for a narrow pilaster which, in turn, is crowded by columns. In short, we find here a succession of projections and recessions of the wall, a crammed contiguity of structural parts. Such a façade was not originally intended to be decorated with figures and scenes.

But on the shores of the Rhône, as we have already seen, there was a school of sculpture which, according to the two most important remaining monuments, had developed an extensive system of sculptural decoration showing remarkable relationships with the work at Chartres in nearly all essential features. In Provence, this sculptural decor seems entirely at home. There is neither contradiction nor friction between the architectural and the decorative elements. The representational sculpture, except for some figural motifs on the capitals and bases of the columns, unfolds here in totally neutral

---

Lasteyrie), vol. 2, Paris, 1886, p. 177, 179, and the new edition of Vic et Vaissète, *Histoire générale de Languedoc*, vol. 4, p. 514 ff. [See now R. Hamann, *Die Abteikirche von St. Gilles*, Berlin, 1955.—Ed.]

[23] Regarding the type, see Viollet-le-Duc, *Dictionnaire*, vol. 7, p. 406; Rudolf Adami, *Architektonik des muhamedanischen und romanischen Stils*, Hannover, 1887, p. 318. Here the writer completely expounds the idea that the medieval portal represents an artificial widening of the doorways which usually are neither especially wide nor high. At the same time, it emphasizes aesthetically the purpose of the portal, namely to serve as an entrance for the worshipers.

places that have no structural function for the eye. Cases in point are the sculpture on the tympana, the figures making up the broad, friezelike bands, and the high reliefs placed in the architectural framework of the walls. It should be noted that the archivolts of St.-Gilles are without sculptural decoration and that the angels surrounding the portal at Arles only fill a space but do not function as a frame. One is tempted to say that this lavish architecture was designed for the sake of the sculptural decoration.

Considering these facts, the assumption that the principal roots of Chartrain art lie in Provence seems quite justified. Let somebody find in Languedoc or in Burgundy such complete coherent sculptural programs, compositions that show in one ensemble the continuous row of life-sized figures,[24] the frieze with biblical scenes, and the typical motifs on the tympanum: Christ surrounded by the Tetramorph with the row of Apostles, and the enthroned Virgin.

All this is still not proof, as I said earlier. In case there should really be some connections between the façades of Provence and the School of Chartres, these relations would have to be verified in detail. Then we could say that the royal figures of Chartres are derived from the Apostles of Arles. Indeed, at first sight the disparity between these statue columns and the Apostles is great. A link seems to be completely missing here. Were they not always described as the representatives of two entirely different trends, as it were, opposite poles of the plastic arts in the twelfth century? Let us consider what Henry Revoil says about the statues of both Provençal façades:[25] "It is not surprising to find the influence of Roman sculpture in the statuary of these two buildings, since it was right there before the eyes of the sculptors who made this part of the decoration. But when in our minds' eye we go to the Cathedral at Chartres, where the west façade repeats the same architectural program (?!) it is at first hard to understand why the statues there are so different from those of St.-Gilles and St.-Trophîme, since they were all made at the same time." Here Revoil appeals to the *deus ex machina*, namely Byzantium, in order to explain the differences of style: "The reason is that they were conceived under a totally different influence. At Chartres, indeed, one could believe the figures were the work of Etruscan or Greek sculptors, so thin are the folds of these elongated statues and so visibly do they bear the stamp of that elegant type. There is sufficient material here for a complete archeological dissertation. Let

[24] The characteristic façades of Burgundy do not have them at all (Autun, Charlieu) or have them in a totally different arrangement (Vézelay).

[25] *L'architecture romane du midi de la France*, vol. 2, p. 64.

it suffice to point to Byzantine influences carried by the crusaders, who were much more numerous in the northern provinces and who returned home with eastern artists who had studied Greek statuary."

Revoil completely overlooks the originality of the Chartres composition! He considers it to have the same architectural elevation as the façades in Provence. But where, in the twelfth century, could one find two more different portals? The portal at Arles comes straight from the Roman temple. * * * The columns are still unattached and stand in front of the wall. They therefore allow a more natural sculptural decoration of the wall surface. The columniated portal at Chartres is a composition of an entirely different kind and origin. The uniqueness of the accomplishment at Chartres rests on the aim of these artists to apply the same scheme of sculptural decoration under totally different conditions. While trying to transfer it to their façade, they were forced to change all its elements. The life-sized figures of the embrasures had to somehow be organically linked with the columns. If they were unwilling to forego the frieze, they had to put it around the capitals. The archivolts, populated with scenes and figures, were then a natural outgrowth of this design. In short, a direct linkage of the figural decoration to the structural elements was intended as a principle from the beginning, and thus this work, as we can see, stands in the sharpest contrast to the one in the south. That the Chartrain masters had the daring to carry out their plan consistently is in itself indubitable proof of their [northern] French origin. Such a complete change of decorative principle could not remain without profoundly influencing the style of the figures. The transformation of the latter goes hand in hand with the transformation of the decorative program. With truly astonishing consistency, * * * the figural concept of the artists of Chartres was created out of technical and architectural conditions. The Chartrain style is no less French than the Chartrain composition! There is no direct connection with Byzantine or Greek works.[26] This School stands, if I may say so, on the shoulders of a native predecessor and its sources water native soil. What distinguishes the Chartrain *oeuvre* from the

[26] Revoil's almost grotesque assumption, that the Chartres sculpture was the work of oriental masters trained in the study of Greek sculpture, is also found in Eméric-David's *Histoire de la sculpture française*, p. 47: "The verity and, we could also say, the grand style of the heads, the richness and elegance of the attire, the embroidery with which they are decorated, the small pleated folds of the tunics and the good quality of drapery pattern may lead us to doubt whether such unique merits should be credited to Latin chisels. . . . If this were not Greek sculpture, we have to suppose that Gallo-Greek schools were formed in France either in the tenth or the eleventh centuries."

one in Provence, is the adroitness and finesse of the northern French hand, the originality of the northern French mind, and the seriousness of the first study of nature. It is the spirit of the French genius which transformed the reliefs at Arles into the kings of Chartres. * * *

The world of forms of the south underwent a profound and total change in the region of the Seine. The magician who wrought this miracle was the French genius. It breathed new life into these forms and integrated them logically into medieval architecture. I would like to illustrate the stylistic change with the statues of the Head Master of Chartres.[27] What could be more attractive than this performance?

In order to express the quality of this sylistic metamorphosis in words, I would like to use a figure of speech and say that the Master of Chartres used a concave mirror when he redesigned the sculpture of the southern school, because the figures seem so consistently transfigured into long, thin images [figs. 23, 38]. Attire and drapery also take part in this transformation; it reminds us of an organic growth. Nine folds can be counted on the right thigh of the Saint James at Arles,[28] as well as on the king with the book at Chartres. But on the latter they are distributed over a larger surface. The cloak, as it were, has been stretched out. Thus, in spite of the increased proportions, there is no multiplication of details. On the contrary: the complex tripartite costume is more often than not reduced to a simple formula: a long tunic and a cloak. The parts cutting across the body, such as the stolelike ends of the cloaks, are simply tucked in. Absent, too, are the folds of the hem, gay and windblown, which join the body of the garment like spirals to the left and right and lend the figure a certain picturesque breadth. This results in more continuous folds, pleats rising more steeply, and a sharply accentuated silhouette. There develops a style of costume completely conforming to the bodily proportions.

The figures at Chartres [as compared to those of Arles] have narrow shoulders and are strangely angular. The joints are more abruptly bent and the gestures more accentuated, giving the impression of being arranged rhythmically. Since the dress follows the movement of the limbs more consistently, the structure and mechanism of the body become more visible under the garment. While at Arles the figures look as if they were covered with rugs, at Chartres the robes are tightly wrapped around the bodies. The fabrics seem more finely woven; they have lost their dull weight. The intrinsic nature of these bodies—their somewhat youthful angularity—is also reflected

[27] And the works of his atelier.
[28] To the right of the portal.

in the motifs of the dress. Compare the neckline of the chasubles: At Arles, they are simple cut-outs for the head; at Chartres, they are turned over like a collar.

The Chartrain artists are closer to nature and inject new life into the traditional images.

The heads are the best example. The schematically separated strands of hair become wavy, flowing masses of curls. Hair and beards no longer look like glued-on wigs. The faces seem to have removed their masks. It is not the physiognomy,[29] the "portrait likeness," that is new, as we have already indicated, but this characteristic, vigorous beauty,[30] the understanding of the lawful order of the human form, the youthful vitality which, as it were, is flowing from the Master's chisels. How the facial expression has changed under their hands! The sullenness and the pensiveness of old age are things of the past, having been replaced with the tautness of manly energy, the flawless beauty of masculinity, and the laughter of youth.

The same is true of the bodies.[31] In spite of their tectonic construction, the figures are not conspicuously distorted, the limbs are not twisted as they occasionally are at Arles.[32] The modeling of chest and belly is flat but not wooden or misunderstood. It is simply rendered in lower relief. Hands and feet are lifelike and softly rounded. In order to understand the advance, we must compare the statues of Chartres with the lifeless, flat forms on the façade at Arles.

Here, all is combined to envelop the work with the appeal of youth and originality. Does the artistic composition not bespeak youthful daring? And how new and lively is the technique! Here are garments with delicately ornamented borders, women's hair artfully braided— as if combed by a female hand—lacing and delicately worked jewels, competing in loving care with the creations of the minor arts.

How youthful, too, is the gravity with which these sculptors create the new style and how methodically they carve the form in accordance with technical and tectonic conditions; how well they relate the single parts of the whole composition! A unified decorative effect of the whole was the aim of these artists and they achieved it with the beginner's consistency. This is the premise on which sculpture

[29] Contrary to Viollet-le-Duc, who saw Gallic head types here, Lübke says: "Here, like the first smile of Spring, the Germanic (!) physiognomy greets us with its good-natured, plain features. Up to now, medieval art retained the head form of antiquity, though debased to extreme dullness."

[30] Is it astonishing that this typical beauty bears French features?

[31] Compare Moore's excellent remarks in *Development and Character of Gothic Architecture*, London, 1890, pp. 252 ff.

[32] Most of all, compare Christ in the tympanum and the figure of St. Peter (right arm) in the cloister, etc.

is admitted here. In northern France, as we have seen, figural decoration entered into a union with structural members. A primary and most important rule was imperatively forced upon the sculptors if they wanted to avoid endangering the total effect: no matter how the individual statues were designed, they were never allowed to obscure the architectural organism. The artists knew perfectly well that the elements of structure must always remain visible and present behind the screen of figural decoration. They proceeded deductively. First they sketched out the rough architectural form, and then they determined the scale of all the sculptural parts.

We would know nothing about it were we not able to reconstruct the rough form. This is possible by determining the shape and size of the original blocks from which the statues and scenes were carved. We come to the following conclusion: all the jamb figures are cut from blocks of the same size and shape—a pier 6 feet high with a 14 inch square base. This pier is placed diagonally against the wall; the outer planes correspond to the projecting rectangular bases below and the impost of the capitals above. On the lateral portals the canopies inserted between the statues and the capitals are cut from diagonally set cubes corresponding exactly to the statue-blocks. The same principle governs all parts of the composition: nowhere is the form of the block altered to accommodate a particular figural motif. All figures and scenes in the archivolts are cut from rectangular voussoirs. If we attempted to construct the portal anew with these blocks, imaging them to extend upward and downward, we arrive not only at a completely harmonious architectural composition but actually at the simplest and therefore the most ideal basic form of this type of portal. The sculptor's task consisted of integrating his configurations into the stereometric body. The unity of the entire composition was assured from the beginning, no matter how the artist proceeded. It is characteristic of the northern French masters that they did not feel confined by this extraordinary constraint but made it the point of departure for their new stylistic creation. The strictures had no inhibiting effect—on the contrary, they were a discipline and a stimulation. The masters made a virtue out of necessity! In their attempt to evoke human beings out of the stones, they laid the foundation for an original style.

Nothing is more interesting than looking into the artists' workshops and watching the emergence of their figures from the raw, tectonic form.

Since figure and column were always linked together, only the front section of the block was available for the statue and the artist made fullest use of its entire bulk. Narrow as the stone is, it did allow the sculptor to loosen the forearm from the body, to let attributes project freely, and to model the head in the round. The body, however, remains flat and the shoulders, although disengaged from the shaft, still look something like the wings of a stage set. A free projection of the feet could not be considered. With feet extended downward, the figures seem to float. The angularity and sharp edges of the figures, with their steep, abruptly sloping silhouette, point back to their stereometric origin. The peculiar sternness and the rhythmic motion spring directly from the original tectonic premises. Since the sculptor had to limit himself to the outer part of the block, all the figures are standing erect and solemn, side by side.[33] Because the width had to be the same at the elbow and the shoulder, the upper arms cling firmly to the body and the forearms are pushed outward. Certain "routines" developed almost naturally. When the figure held an attribute in its hand, for example a book, it was supported preferably by one hand on the top and by the other on the bottom, because the arms could not be crossed in front of the body. This motif occurs frequently at Chartres but is rarely found at Arles. We seldom find what would be most natural, an open book facing the observer. The book is usually placed vertically on edge with an oblique slant. Arm and attribute try, in some measure, to retain contact with the original form of the block. Very often, the arm holding a scepter or a scroll hangs deep down, bending sharply forward at the wrist only. It is especially noteworthy that the edge of the book, often slightly opened at a narrow angle, lines up vertically with the center of the statue and so coincides with the frontal edge of the block [fig. 30]. This is not a matter of stylistic whim, but a design consistent with artistic logic.[34] The great elongation of the figures derives from the changed scale of the architecture. This, alone, propels them upward. Nothing is so obvious as this direct influence of the architecture on their proportions.[35] We have already shown that the

---

[33] An exception is the statue with the crossed legs on the right side of the left lateral portal.

[34] Compare the jamb statues with a trumeau figure, for example, St. Etienne, at the central portal of Sens, with his large Gospel book. Here the book is shown in its full width to the beholder. The central post, invented to support the lintel, cannot naturally be placed diagonally, for it would neither provide the necessary flat surface for the doors nor line up with the jambs. The figures which we find on trumeaux and which in earlier times were carved directly out of the block can develop more broadly than the sculpture on the blocks of the jambs, which are placed diagonally. A striking illustration, for instance, is the sculpture of the portal of Villeneuve-l'Archevêque in the Yonne Department.

[35] See Schnaase, *Geschichte der bildenden Künste*, vol. 5, pt. 2, p. 576. The same concept is also found in Lübke's *Plastik*. Lübke points repeatedly

new size of the bodies led to the logical transformation of the details.[36]

At this point, let us once more define clearly the roles of the interweaving factors. When the sculptural decoration of the northern French portal was linked with elements of the architectural structure, it had to yield to more stringent and severe tectonic rules. But this alone does not account for the change of style; northern and southern French sculpture differ from one another only in degree but not in principle. Not for this reason alone is it subject to a new law of form.

What is decisive is the totally novel and original manner in which the Chartrain artists used the tectonic constraint as the basis of their work. This gave birth to the new style. Let us add at once that style never results from external influences but is born out of artistic spirit. Whatever the sources, the influences, the conditions may be, one can still maintain that style springs from the artist's head fully armed. The statuary of the portal at Arles is also wall sculpture, but the master there was considerably less constrained. He took advantage

---

to the fact that figures of entirely different proportions appear on different architectural parts of the same composition. He calls our attention, for instance, to the short and stocky Apostles on the lintel of the south portal of Le Mans. He notes the same of the figures on the biblical frieze at the west portal of Chartres. From this he concludes "that the sculpture of the time had neither rules for the proportions of the human body nor any understanding of its relationships." However, this is no longer true for the great masters of this School. The Head Master of Chartres undoubtedly followed a strict canon of proportions. His Apostles on the lintel as well as his figure of Christ in the tympanum have the same proportions as the jamb figures. If the tiny figures of the biblical frieze are stout, it matters little because they are by a different hand.

Schnaase's and Lübke's opinions are found in the older French literature; see among others, Romelot, *Description historique et monumentale de l'église patriarcale de Bourges,* Bourges, 1824, p. 65; A. Aufauve and Charles Fichot, *Les monuments de Seine-et-Marne,* Paris, 1858 (concerning St.-Loup-de-Naud); Batissier, *Histoire de l'art monumental,* Paris, 1860, p. 504; and Charles Herbert Moore, *Development and Character of Gothic Architecture,* London, 1890, p. 253 ("Their exaggerated elongation (is) largely of definite architectural purpose").

The gauntness and the seeming ascetism of the sculpture very often led to erroneous interpretations. Cherzé (*Congrès archéologique de France,* 1869, p. 28) says about the sculpture of the porch of St.-Ours at Loches "that the artists intended to convey the idea of pre-eminence of the holy personnages by their exaggerated size"; similarly, Bulteau says (*Monographie,* vol. 2, p. 68): "there was a wish to show spiritualized figures glorified in heaven." Compare de Launay's remarks in Léon Hublin's *La cathédrale du Mans,* Le Mans, 1888, p. 15.

[36] An accurate interpretation of the art of Chartres is found in Pottier's text to Willemin's *Monumens français inédits* ("the first spurt of a truly

of his freedom, for instance, by placing among the statues of Apostles[37] a scene depicting the stoning of St. Stephen. But all in all, he, too, had to reckon with the given space. In studying the cloister at Arles, we find that random plastic decoration is a common practice on big Provençal façades, but it should by no means be considered a universal characteristic of sculpture in Provence.[38] Tectonic demands also existed at Arles, but they proved to be primarily negative and restrictive instead of challenging and formative. A study of the figure of Christ in the tympanum at Arles is an excellent illustration of the point I wish to make.

   The Christ figure is cut from a long, narrow block [fig. 28]. The artist evidently overestimated the size of the figure in relation to the block. It extends over the top and the bottom of the tympanum edge and is not sufficiently developed in width. Therefore, the artist resorts to such perspective means as foreshortening the arm. But in

---

national school"); see also Rigollot's *Essai historique sur les arts du dessin en Picardie*, Amiens, 1840. Rigollot rightly relates the flowering of sculpture with the rapid growth of native architecture: "we believe that it gave the artists an opportunity to create completely original works and that the invention which they showed in developing a new architecture—which then took on a special character—was also noticeable in the work of the sculptors." These words were coined for the statues of the School of Chartres.

It must be said, however, that German scholars in general were mostly right in their evaluation of the art of Chartres. See Lübke's *Geschichte der Plastik*, vol. 1, pt. 3, pp. 425 ff. Here, in reference to the School of Chartres, he says, among other things, that the architecture is of such overwhelming strength that the sculpture had to submit to its controlling demands. See also Schnaase's excellent remarks in *Geschichte der bildenden Künste*, vol. 5, pt. 2, pp. 566 f., and the previously mentioned essay by Robert Vischer, *Zur Kritik mittelalterlicher Kunst*, printed in his *Kunsthistorische Studien*, 1886; see also Charles Herbert Moore, pp. 253 f.: "Within the limits fixed by his conditions the artist has managed abundantly to show his skill as a lifelike and graceful designer"; "the restraint of the figure is apparently self-imposed in obedience to the demands of its architectural position" (p. 255).

[37] Compare also to the Apostles on the portal of St.-Gilles, their more relaxed posture, the painterly motifs of the garments.

[38] The piers—clearly structural elements—are here decorated with reliefs and statues. To be sure, they are broad and wall-like. The statues placed on the corners, for example the figure of St.-Trophîme, are flanked by pilasters on each side. Thus, they give the impression of space fillers in spite of the capitals placed behind their heads. They are standing, so to speak, in front of a "column" sunken into the wall. The same can be said of the statues in front of the broad side on the pier. They stand in front of a pilaster whose capital supports the cornice around the pier, although they appear to be standing in front of the wall.

relation to the thickness of the block, the relief is too high. Conse-
quently, [its] left arm is distorted and [its] right one raised un-
naturally high.

At Chartres, the spatial setting was less favorable (though much
better than that in the jambs), because the tympanum is also the
place where the sculpture is placed on a large, flat surface [fig. 24].
However, as a result of the compact composition, the tympanum is
much narrower here than at Arles. Nevertheless, the Chartres Master
succeeded in fitting his design so completely into the frame that the
representation seems to unfold freely and harmoniously. The mandorla
is steeper, almost lancetlike; the figure of Christ in Glory, rendered
on a smaller scale, conforms perfectly to the available space. The
sculpture does not even touch the edges of the tympanum. To avoid
empty spots above and below the sculptor added a footstool and extended the halo to the apex of the tympanum. Furthermore, he
deviated from the regular arrangement of blocks. The central one,
with Christ and the mandorla, is relatively wider, thus permitting
the figure to develop comfortably to the right and left. Instead of an
affected pose, we find a noble and relaxed bearing and measured,
natural proportions. The artist also accommodated himself easily to
the thickness of the block. At Arles, the figure is carved almost in
the round but is seated on a throne which can be seen, as it were,
only in a kind of planimetric presentation; at Chartres, the artist suc-
ceeds in bringing the seat and the footstool forward by tilting them
downward, thus increasing the effect of the entire work. At Arles,
the thighs are foreshortened; here, they are sculpturally rounded.
This artistic device is further justified in the context of the entire
composition. We previously described how the sculptor achieved an
artificially raised focal point through the perspective grouping of the
jamb statues. Using the same method on the tympanum, he completes
the illusion by making the figure of Christ appear to look down on
us.[39] It seems evident that this unified, carefully calculated design
was intended by the Master whose artistic wisdom we have often
noticed on other occasions. How sensitive he is to the purity of the
architecture! How well the figures and wings fit into it![40] The whole
forms the yardstick for the order and size of the parts. The spirit
guiding the Master at the creation of the statue-columns is also present

[39] The tympanum is also the work of the Head Master of Chartres.

[40] The Master of the portal of Arles lacks this sense. The heads of the
figures extend over the cornice and some details even spread over the bases.
See the relief representing the stoning of St. Stephen. The wings and feet
of the symbols of the Evangelists extend over the ornamental border of the
tympanum.

in this relief. The position of the lower animals, with their heads on the outer sides of the tympanum, was obviously dictated by the limited space. By turning their heads upward toward the Redeemer, the Master fitted them naturally into the field. Through this design, the figures achieve a proud bearing: the legs stride more vigorously and the wings spread solemnly to both sides.

The relationship between the two Schools immediately becomes clear when we compare them to a similar representation from another School [fig. 29].[41] No commentary seems necessary. The work at Toulouse is a stranger to the others. Among the numerous examples of our School, the Christ of Chartres is the one which comes closest to the figure of Arles. I refer, among other similarities, to the organpipe folds of the cloak, which are retained at Chartres, and to the broad, beltlike drapery motif below the chest. In the rendition of the heads, I see another noticeable correspondence—one which indicates the adoption of particular facial features. The left eyebrow is raised higher than the right one, the former bending sharply and the latter tapering off in a low curve. The relationship between the head types is further noticeable when one compares general features—for example, in the cut of the eyes or in the modeling of the cheeks and beards. An occasional look at the relief of Toulouse will be helpful!

During our examination, we have gained a twofold insight. First, we encountered extensive affinities between the two large Schools, clearly distinctive some of the time and rather vague and loose at other times, but, all in all, irrefutable. Secondly, we experienced the uniqueness of Chartrain art in its very special beauty. A comparison with the art of Provence reinforces this singular achievement. And behind the statues and stones appear their makers, living people at work, disclosing the depth of their souls. Their instincts and intentions, their aesthetics and ideals, the coherence and purity of their sense of style, their youth and sophistication, their earnestness and zeal, their daring and driving toward the novel, their felicitous use of traditional elements are all revealed. The *porta regia* of Chartres still stands as splendid as it was in the glory of its first day.

The two conclusions of our inquiry support one another. We are able to comprehend the creativeness of Chartrain art only after we

[41] The relief now in the ambulatory of St.-Sernin at Toulouse probably formed the central group of a tympanum. One of the two recently found tympana in the Cathedral of Valence (Drôme) can, perhaps, throw light on the original composition. I would like to stress that the grouping of the figures in both tympana is different in that it does not fill the entire field. We see the same thing at Moissac and Cadenac. This leads to the conclusion that this arrangement is peculiar to Languedoc.

have looked at its sources. Now that we are certain that the style and technique of the masters of Chartres were entirely their own, we can understand why such a deep gulf separates their work from their sources and our last doubts about the relationship of the two groups vanish.[42]

St.-Denis, the Point of Entry of Influences from Toulouse and Moissac

Although it is not possible to establish a direct derivation from Toulouse for the sculpture of Chartres, there were, in all likelihood, some connections. Artists from Toulouse, among them Gilabertus, apparently did work in northern French workshops. They may initially have been called northern because of their skill and the reputation of their School, but they certainly did not occupy leading positions at Chartres itself. However, they must have exerted some influence and received some new ideas. In fact, traces of their activity can be found at Chartres, but not in the work of the Head Master, as I have shown earlier.

We find, for example, on the three last statues on the right side [fig. 37],[43] several technical peculiarities which may point to a hand[44] from Toulouse. I would particularly like to mention in this connection the semicircular folds on the chest, which are so characteristic of the Apostles at Toulouse, as well as the double outline of the pleats[45] and the fine indentation of the borders. On the figure of the king, the wide sleeve is turned over to form a steplike drapery motif which we find quite often in similar places on the Apostles of Toulouse. In addition, I would like to call attention to the emphasis given to the modeling of the knees. This is not only found on Gilabertus' large figures, but also and even more strikingly on the capitals in the cloister at Toulouse. These sculptures are attributed either to Gilabertus himself or to his School.

The cornices of the portal at Chartres[46] are decorated with acanthus leaves and, in some parts,[47] the stylistic interpretation of the

----

[42] Revoil remarked that the two statues in the cloister of Montmajour are related to Chartrain sculpture. I must admit that I fail to see any relationship.

[43] To the right of the south portal.

[44] See the following passage about the Head Master of Chartres.

[45] See especially the king's cloak.

[46] The cornicelike, continuous imposts of the capitals.

[47] The cornice, although evenly ornamented, was carved by different hands.

antique foliage comes very close to the typical Toulousain manner.[48] Furthermore, in the Museum at Chartres, there is a fragment of a Romanesque tympanum[49] which depicts a figure of Christ in Glory as on the central portal of the Cathedral. The halo is decorated with radiating and scalloped motifs, a treatment characteristic of Gilabertus and his workshop.[50]

Such points as I have made are not significant for the development of the school of Chartres. Did not Toulouse leave a more important heritage to Chartres? While studying the sculpture of Chartres, I was surprised to find that the portraitlike heads, so typical of the Head Master, disappear very quickly from his School, although the style of his figures generally remains the basis of the School's work. Subsequently, a new facial type emerges. This occurs for the first time in the work of the Master of the Two Madonnas and is very pronounced. The characteristic features of this type are the strong brows slanted outward, the bulging eyes, the projecting forehead, and the hair brushed down onto the face.[51] A comparison of this Master's work with the Apostles of Toulouse leaves, I am certain, no doubt about the origin of the type [see fig. 49]. * * *

It seems that the three statues on the portal of Chartres just mentioned were carved by the Master (or workshop) that sculpted the eight figures which once decorated the central portal of the Abbey Church at St.-Denis.[52] Is it possible that the influence of Languedoc was stronger there, where this Master or a member of his atelier was in a leading position?

At St.-Denis, the statues on the left portal [fig. 39][53] are less tectonically formed than, for example, the figures of the Head Master of Chartres. Almost all of them have their legs crossed as if they were

[48] The parts in question are on the left side of the central portal of Chartres.

[49] Registered by the Société archéologique d'Eure-et-Loire as a fragment of a figure of Christ, but it is undoubtedly a piece from a tympanum; the Christ shown is naked and covered only with a cloak; it therefore must be the central figure of a Last Judgment as we know it from St.-Denis.

[50] They can be seen on the Apostles and on the capitals in the cloister. Such halos exist on works belonging to the School of Chartres, for instance on the portal of St.-Maurice at Angers and also on the south portal at Bourges.

[51] See also the heads of the statues on the west portal of St.-Loup-de-Naud.

[52] We know these statues only in the drawings and engravings of Montfaucon.

[53] B. Montfaucon, *Monumens de la monarchie françoise*, pl. XVI.

dancing.[54] The thighs are fuller, the knees are again "coquettishly" marked, and even the double outline of the folds reappears. In short, they come remarkably close to the works of Gilabertus and his shop. A comparison with his second pair of Apostles makes this very obvious, but the resemblance can even be recognized on the smaller figures of the capitals in the cloister at Toulouse [fig. 46]. The relationship is also evident on the borders of the cloaks. Apart from the cloverleaf motif that is frequently used on the capitals, we find at St.-Denis those wide borders encrusted with precious stones, which we have seen on Gilabertus' Apostles [figs. 40 and 47].

And one more surprise awaits us on the right portal of St.-Denis; namely that the heads show a strong resemblance to the ones on the portal of Moissac [fig. 47]. The foreheads are broad and the projecting cheekbones sharply edged; the faces are triangular, eyes and noses are similarly cut; the curls are treated as ornament, and the beards are schematically and harshly set off [figs. 39 and 40]. There are, again, similarities in the borders: for example, the bands with the large, appliqued circles are frequently used on the portal at Moissac. Still more affinities can be seen in the motif of the drapery: here, also, we note the double outline of the fold;[55] and the cloth is often pulled tightly around the thigh, resulting in long folds that extend below the knee and that look as if a loop were thrown around it. All this points to the same source.

It is known that Abbot Suger, under whom the façade of St.-Denis was built, called workmen and artists from all parts of the country.[56] References to their origin are missing in his writings and only once does he speak in passing about goldsmiths coming from Lorraine.[57] Our stylistic analysis leaves no doubt that masters from Toulouse and Moissac must have been among his sculptors. St.-Denis was the center of influence from Languedoc.

The Master who created the statues on the right portal of St.-Denis probably came from Moissac. From the stylistic point of view, he quite obviously went beyond the accomplishments of this School on its home ground. Strained gestures and exaggerated shapes and proportions are avoided here and the garment becomes simpler and more natural. It seems that the artists from Languedoc, while working in the Royal Domain and in Beauce, entered into a new phase of their

[54] This can be found only once in the work of the Head Master of Chartres.

[55] For example the Christ of Moissac.

[56] See E. Panofsky, *Abbot Suger*, Princeton, 1946, ch. 24, p. 42; ch. 27, pp. 46–48; ch. 34, pp. 72–76 [Ed.].

[57] *Ibid.*, ch. 32, pp. 56–60 [Ed.].

development.⁵⁸ They had to face new tasks and they came under the disciplining influence of Chartres.

Among the works of the School of northern France, the portal of St.-Denis and its masters are overshadowed by the overwhelming greatness of Chartres. Only in rare instances can we prove the influence of their sculpture on other works of this group. But the fact that the west portal of Senlis—one of the important monuments built during the transition from the restricted style of the twelfth century to the freer style of the thirteenth century—is indeed related to St.-Denis gives to this sculpture a significant place in the entire development. * * *

ALAN PRIEST

The Masters of the West Façade at Chartres—[1923]*

> Priest continued and refined the analysis of Vöge. His essay, following in the footsteps of another American art historian, Arthur Kingsley Porter, marks the first important venture into the history of Gothic sculpture made on this side of the Atlantic.

As great monuments of art recede farther and farther into the past all the little details of iconography and construction, too commonplace for contemporary record, become precious to the student who seeks to understand the creation of the monument. Nearly eight centuries of a civilization which changes with ever increasing violence and rapidity separate the moment from the building of the west façade of the cathedral of Our Lady of Chartres. It is difficult for the Twentieth century to understand the religious mysticism which found its purest expression at Chartres; it is even more difficult for the Twentieth century to reconstruct the physical development of the art which is the vehicle of expression.

Yet such reconstruction has been admirably begun by Herr Vöge. His work has been continued and a little corrected. The recently published folios of M. Houvet¹ are the occasion for a further advance.

⁵⁸ There are hardly any statue columns in the School of Languedoc. We do find something similar in Valcabrère (Haute-Garonne), but the attempt was not successful. The sculpture in the cloister of St.-Bertrand de Comminges and of Valcabrère form a closely related group; they are certainly by one and the same master.

* This essay first appeared in *Art Studies*, vol. 1, 1923, and is reproduced here through the kind permission of the author [Ed.].

¹ In seven folios, published separately, M. Etienne Houvet, Guardien de la Cathédrale, Chartres, 1920. I am grateful to M. Houvet for permission to reproduce several plates from the volume on the west façade.

The volume on the west façade consists of pictures of almost every detail which make possible a more careful comparative study than has hitherto been made. The first business of such a study is the disentanglement of the various hands at work on the façade. The discussion of the headmaster and his several assistants involves the consideration and possible solution of several of the problems which the façade presents.

I. The Headmaster of Chartres

The best work at Chartres is that of the headmaster. To him belong the tympanum, the lintel, and all the jamb figures of the central portal, the portal of the Christ in Glory [figs. 23, 24]. To him also belong the jamb figures of the inner sides of the adjoining bays, and the sundial on the south west corner.[2] The rest of the sculpture of the west façade is the work of assistants dominated by the impassioned spirit of the headmaster, a man who made of the Christ of the Apocalyptic vision a figure not to inspire terror but to inspire confidence. There is no strain of warning, no hint of the *Dies Irae* at Chartres; there is rather the tranquil assurance of the ascension-tide *Salutis Humanae Sator*.

The headmaster understood and used his medium as few sculptors have ever done; never for an instant does he forget that he is working in stone, even in his most sensitive modelling he suggests the block from which he carved. And by the deliberate neglect of imitation he achieves the illusion of life which realism ever fails to achieve, not an empty counterfeit of life superimposed on the stone, but the abstract idea of life emerging from it.

The sculptor's style is delicate and strong, a repetition of fine vertical lines varied by the parabolic curves of caught up draperies and by the lines which define the hems of the garments, lines sometimes rhythmic, sometimes irregular and exquisitely nervous. The heads are well balanced and fine in detail. The most subtle of modelling has gone into the high foreheads, the firm cheeks and the tender half-smiling mouths; the most skillful of cutting into the delicate noses and honest eyes. The attitude is one of proud humility. The attenuation of the body increases the majesty of the figures.

[2] The attribution of work to the headmaster of Chartres follows that of Herr Vöge whose analysis of Chartres is the foundation for later work and to whom I shall often refer. See *Die Anfänge des monumentalen Stiles im Mittelalter*, Dr. Wilhelm Vöge, Heitz und Mündel, Strassburg, 1894. [Note: Passages from this work appear in Priest, p. 149—Ed.]

There is an intimate relation between the work of the headmaster of Chartres and the lost jamb figures of St.-Denis. Comparison of the two churches is extremely hazardous because the sculpture which still exists at St.-Denis has been changed by restoration and the jamb figures themselves are known only through the drawings of Mont-faucon. These drawings were made in the Eighteenth century, and they were not made because of the intrinsic beauty of the jamb sculptures but because Montfaucon supposed the figures to be por-traits of the Merovingian kings.

If these drawings could be accepted as evidence at all they could be used to help reëstablish Herr Vöge's early assumption that St.-Denis is a derivative of Chartres. The jamb figures of St.-Denis are generally accepted as earlier than those of Chartres because the façade of St.-Denis is dated 1137–1140, and the date which is at present accepted for the beginning of the façade of Chartres is 1145. It is, however, not impossible that the jamb figures at St.-Denis were added at a later date. The neglect of the Abbot Suger to mention the sculpture of St.-Denis in his meticulous records of the church remains inexplicable. The Montfaucon drawings suggest an advance in style beyond the figures of Chartres and imply a stage between Chartres and Senlis. The tremendous influence and popularity of Chartres might well account for the addition of imitative decoration at St.-Denis.

But it is impossible to be dogmatic in defense of such a theory on the basis of the drawings because their accuracy is not to be trusted. It is included here because the problem of the relation between Chartres and St.-Denis has not yet been satisfactorily settled. Because of the established date for the construction of the façade of St.-Denis the theory of the precedence of the figures of St.-Denis is the better one, but the objections which the scanty internal evidence suggest ought not to be forgotten.

II. The "St.-Denis" Master of Chartres

How may one best designate the assisting Masters of Chartres? Any system must be arbitrary, but one which helps clarify the diverse elements in the façade and at the same time points out the relation of the work of the master to other monuments is preferable to one which records them as "First Assistant," "Second Assistant," and so on. Thus the style of the master whose work is closest to that of the headmaster, like his, suggests the drawings by Montfaucon of St.-Denis, and if it be understood that no claim is advanced for the sculptor's actual participation in the work at St.-Denis, he may be called the "St.-Denis master of Chartres" to point out the affinity of style between Chartres and St.-Denis.

The St.-Denis master did the three jamb figures at the right of the south portal, the portal of the Virgin. The likeness of his style to the headmaster's depends on its general effect; in execution and detail it is distinctly inferior. The headmaster's jamb figures are cut in a straight line from armpit to ankle, those of the St.-Denis master are clumsily shaped. One has only to glance from the awkwardly hipped queen at the right to the stately women of the central bay to realize the infinitely finer quality of the headmaster's work. The heads of the St.-Denis master are too high for their width. The features are badly articulated, the eyeballs prominent, the locks of hair long and spindly.

Did the St.-Denis master work anywhere else on the façade of Chartres? The little figure at the top of the pilaster which separates the central from the north bay is done in the style of the St.-Denis master, but the quality of the work is better than that of the jamb figures [fig. 48]. The pilaster figure is one of the most sensitive on the whole façade. The eyes are enormous, their prominence accentuated by the other features which are small and delicate. The body is frail, superbly animated. Yet the expression of the face is the expression of the king at the right of the south portal and the peering eyes are cut in exactly the same manner. It does not seem probable that a less important sculptor should have been selected for the jambs than for the pilasters. The jamb figure and the pilaster figure are probably the work of the same master, a master who could do small figures well but who was less successful in handling large figures.

A considerable mass of minor work belongs unmistakably to the master who did the pilaster. The pilaster which marks the junction of the central and south bays, the pilaster at the left of the south door, and the pilaster at the right of the north door are all his. He carved also many of the capitals in the half of the frieze which runs from the right of the central door across the portal of the Virgin. The head of the apostle at the right in the Supper at Emmaus[3] is a replica of the head of the pilaster figure. The same hand appears again in the Temptation,[4] in the Last Supper,[5] in the Presentation[6] and in the Three Maries[7] at the Tomb.

The discussion of the St.-Denis master involves one of the most

[3] Houvet Plate 95.
[4] Houvet Plate 88.
[5] Houvet Plate 90.
[6] Houvet Plate 86.
[7] Houvet Plate 93.

perplexing riddles on the façade, the purpose of the inscription at the top of the pilaster which separated the central from the right bay. The single word "Rogerus" is inscribed immediately above a headless figure carved by this assistant. This inscription has been accepted as a signature. Writers have even gone so far as to encourage the idea that it is the signature of the headmaster of Chartres. There is little defense for the first argument and less for the second. It is hardly reasonable to suppose that the headmaster would sign his name above the head of a small pilaster figure obviously done by another hand and entirely separated from his own work. The capital representing the Last Supper, which is the work of the St-Denis master, rests immediately above the inscription. Certainly if "Rogerus" is a signature it belongs not to the headmaster but to this assistant.[8]

But is there any good reason for considering the name a signature at all? Is it not far more likely that it is an explanatory inscription like the name "Jeremiah" which is cut on the scroll of the seated prophet on the pilaster at the left of the south door? The little figure [fig. 31][9] behind the head of which the name Rogerus was placed certainly has some deeper significance than a fanciful ornament. A man stands over an extraordinary animal which is bound to one of the framing colonnettes by a rope. This beast has the body of a horse. It has cloven front hoofs. It has the tail of a griffin. It has horns. Surely there is a direct reference to some story in this group.

Is there in early literature any legend which associates the name "Roger" with a supernaturally endowed horse? In the *Chansons de Geste* which have come down to us there is probably no definite mention of such a story[10] but there is sufficient evidence to make the existence of such a story as early as the Twelfth century extremely probable.[11]

The earliest story which connects a Roger with a horse is in the Orlando Furioso of Ariosto, the earliest edition of which was printed in Ferrara in 1516. One of the heroes of this epic is Rogero who is

[8] Herr Vöge maintained at the very beginning of modern criticism that this was the signature of one of the assistants. He did not try to find out which.

[9] I am happy to have Mr. Arthur Pope to thank for the sketch of this group. He has helped me more than anyone in the understanding of fine things of all periods and places.

[10] I have consulted Professor J. D. M. Ford and Professor G. L. Kittredge of Harvard on this point.

[11] I have in mind the case of the Fishmarket gate (c. 1106) of the cathedral of Modena, in the archivolts of which are scenes from some lost romances of the Arthurian cycle. [Note: See now R. S. Loomis and L. H. Loomis, *Arthurian Legends in Mediaeval Art*, London, 1938, *passim.*—Ed.]

possessed of a marvelous steed, the Hippogriff. In his notes on this animal Mr. Ford writes, "L'alato corridor, 'the winged courser' or Hippogriff of Ariosto brings to mind at once the Pegasus of classic antiquity. Fantastic aerial mounts figure in certain writings of the Greek Lucian. In the legendary lore of India—particularly in the *Pantachatantra* and in a tale in the *Thousand and One Nights*—we find mention made of wooden horses that fly through the air. These latter may have been present to the fancy of our Italian poet, for wooden mounts of the sort had already appeared in old French stories, as, for example, in the romance of Cleomades, of *Adénès li Rois*. Chaucer's *stede of bras* belongs to the category. In Pulci's *Morgante* (XXV, 247) we see Bojardo, a real horse, endowed with extraordinary powers of locomotion through the air, and in Boiardo's *Orlando Inn.* (I, xiii) we learn that the marvelous steed Rabicano, although in form but a horse, was created by the arts of enchantment. Ariosto insists that his Hippogriff is not a fictitious creature, but one actually born of a mare and a griffin, as of course, the name Ippogriffo (cf. Greek ἵππος, horse, and γρύψ, griffin, Latin gryps, gryphis) indicates. The idea of the strange parentage of Ariosto's hybrid may have come to him from Vergil's *Ecloques*, VIII, 27: *Jungentur jam gryphes equis*. Of the fabulous griffins we find an elaborate description in Albertus Magnus, *De Animalibus*, XXIII, where it is stated that they live on the Hyperborean Mountains. When saying that the Hippogriffs visit the Rhipaean Mountains, Ariosto is certainly thinking of this abode of the griffins."[12]

Perhaps there is another clue to the animal in a note by Panizzi on Alexander: "The story of the horse Bucephalus is well known and recorded by all the best writers of Alexander's life. In the narratives of the Middle Ages, however, this horse was graced with a horn, or if Boiardo's text be correct, with horns. But both in the Latin biography and in the English romance a single horn is mentioned."[13]

The animal at Chartres has horns, which would make it possible to argue that the Chartres group is a representation of the Alexander story. But the animal at Chartres is something more than a horned horse. It has a griffin's tail and cloven front hoofs. The ropes of course indicate a capture. It is interesting to note that Boiardo traces the descent of his Rogero on the maternal side back to Alexander.

The two notes quoted suffice to remind one of the popularity of

[12] J. D. M. Ford and Mary A. Ford, *Romances of Chivalry*, Canto IV, 16-3, p. 572. New York, Henry Holt and Co., 1916.
[13] *Orlando Innamorato* di Bojardo, vol. 4, p. 342 (note for St. 30), Antonio Panizzi, London, William Pickering, 1831.

equine monsters with poets and story tellers through the ages. Ariosto is given credit for the invention of the Hippogriff because the *Orlando Innamorato* from which he developed his poem has no hippogriff but only a magic horse, Rabicano, the steed of Orlando. But Ariosto is obviously harking back to earlier traditions when he mentions the Rhipaean Mountains, and after Pegasus and Vergil's griffins mated with horses there is nothing strikingly original in the creation of a Hippogriff. It is not necessary to maintain that the Chartres animal is actually a Hippogriff but only that an animal having some characteristics of horses and some of griffins certainly existed as early as the fourth decade of the Twelfth century.

Whether it is a mere coincidence that the Hippogriff of Ariosto is associated with Rogero, or whether Ariosto was acquainted with some now lost tradition which harks back to the Twelfth century is more difficult to say. Panizzi in his elaborate exposition of the legendary and historical origin of Boiardo's Rogero at least proves that the name was an old and famous one: "Ruggieri or Roger was a hero known in the old Romances. In the Excommunication of Ribaud, the extract of which was published by Le Grand, all those are excommunicated who do not welcome the minstrel singing of Roger Olivier and Roland."[14] Panizzi associates him also with the Ruggieri, and Riccieri, or Rizieri in the *Reali di Francia* and with the famous counts of Sicily. Boiardo apparently had no authority for making him the third paladin of Charlemagne.[15]

There were, then, in the tales of the Romanesque period heroes of the name of Roger and an animal of the horse and griffin family.

The group underneath that inscribed with the name Rogerus at Chartres is not a symbolic representation but is connected with some secular or chivalric story of the time. The three figures immediately below this group are of a secular character and might very well be other actors in the story. Immediately below Rogerus is a figure which is undoubtedly intended for a knight. A comparison of his costume with that of the twins of the sign of the zodiac for May which appears on the second [voussoir] of the first order of the archivolts at the left of the north portal proves this. The third figure carries a disc and is attended by an impish child or dwarf which carries a knife in his right hand and a gourd-shaped object in his left. Fourth is a man wearing a smock-like robe which falls to his ankles. He held something in his hands which has been broken. His left foot rests on a block of stone which suggests a forge tipped over to show the top.

[14] *Ibid.*, vol. II, p. lxxx.
[15] *Ibid.*, vol. II, p. cvi *et seq.*

The two bottom figures may or may not have any connection with the four just described. The upper one is reminiscent of the seated kings of the [voussoir] of the central portal. There is a suggestion of drapery falling about the neck (the head is missing) like those of the queen in the row of jamb figures at the right of the central door which leads one to believe it a female figure. Thus it might be either a religious figure or a secular queen connected with the other figures of the pilaster. Since she has no halo the latter is more likely. The sixth and last figure is seated and carries a scroll like the prophet Jeremiah. Is it another prophet or is it possibly a representation of the minstrel who recorded the story of which the other pilaster figures are the actors?

The suggestions about the lower five figures on the pilaster are not intended as a dogmatic explanation. They are included to call attention to the iconographical puzzle which they represent.

But the hypothesis that the name Rogerus refers to a lost story of a man named Roger and an animal, part horse, part griffin, is far more tenable than the theory that it is a signature.

III. The Master of the Angels

The work of the master who did the tympana of the north and south bays ranks next in beauty and importance to that of the head-master. Because he was supposed to have carved the Madonna in the Porte Sainte-Anne of Notre-Dame of Paris he was called "Der Meister der beiden Madonnen" by Herr Vöge, but the Madonna of Paris is at the best no more than a competent copy of the Virgin of Chartres and the old name has become a hindrance rather than a help to the understanding of Chartres. An analysis of this sculptor's part in the work at Chartres shows him to have been particularly happy in his carving of angels. His personality as it appears at Chartres is best distinguished by naming him after them.

In the work of the Master of the Angels an all pervasive sweetness is kept virile by restraint. It is a style less ecstatic, less abstracted than that of the headmaster. It has an earthly quality which is even better suited to the representation of the Virgin and the last incident in the earthly life of Christ.

The gentle wind which animates the draperies of the angels of Chartres blows from Burgundy. Burgundian influence is a fundamental component of the façade. Burgundian detail of drapery and attitude, especially in the work of the Master of Etampes, has always been noted. Lately Mr. Porter has pointed out that the compositions of all three tympana have Burgundian origins.[16] The *Maiestas Domini* of the central bay and the Ascension of the north bay come directly out of Burgundy. The composition of the tympanum of the south bay is a variation of the Burgundian Ascension in which a Virgin[17] has been substituted for the Christ. The lintels of the central and north bays have also Burgundian prototypes.

But the work of the Master of the Angels is Burgundian in more than composition and casual detail. The angels of the Ascension at Chartres are copied directly from the angels of the Ascension at Anzy-le-Duc.[18] Compare the angel at the left of Christ at Anzy-le-Duc [fig. 42] with the angel at the left of Christ at Chartres [fig. 26]: the same emotion sways their bodies, the same humility turns their faces from the Godhead, the same ecstasy lifts their wings. The angels of Chartres are more sophisticated in technique than those of Anzy-le-Duc. They may be considered the culmination of the Anzy-le-Duc tradition.

At Chartres the Master of the Angels did the tympana of the north and south portals, the upper register of the lintel of the north portal, the twelve angels of the first order of the archivolts in the central portal and the six angels of the first order of the archivolts in the south portal. This includes most of the angels of the façade. They are his great contribution to Chartres, a fact which seems to have been acknowledged by the headmaster himself when he executed his symbol for St. Matthew. The winged man of the central tympanum is certainly the work of the headmaster but it imitates the work of the Master of the Angels. The head of the man is copied from the head of the angel at the left of the Virgin, very different from the usual type carved by the headmaster.

The heads of the Master of the Angels are distinctly blocky. The foreheads are low, the cheeks broad and full, the chins heavily rounded. The eyes are small, but wide open. The hair is variously treated; sometimes parted in the middle, sometimes banged, sometimes falling over the forehead in rosettes. At the back of the head it

[16] A. Kingsley Porter, *Romanesque Sculpture of the Pilgrimage Roads,* Chapter VIII. Marshall Jones Co., Boston, 1923.

[17] In his chapter on St.-Gilles, Mr. Porter points out the Madonna of Marseilles as the direct prototype of the Madonna of Chartres. This is important in establishing Provençal influence on Chartres. *Ibid.,* ch. XIV.

[18] The master of the Angels did not copy the whole composition from Anzy-le-Duc; he was influenced also by Etampes. See below.

follows the rounded skull to the nape of the neck where it terminates in heavy curls.

One peculiar characteristic of the Master of the Angels is that he deliberately avoids defining the drapery edges at the feet whenever he can possibly do so. Usually he obscures them by conventional and, it must be confessed, rather stupid clouds. The figures of the tympanum of the Virgin are exceptions which help to explain the reason: the hem of the garment where the stone required deep undercutting apparently bothered him; in both the Virgin and the angel at her right it is laboriously dull. In the case of the Virgin the dullness might be explained as copying, but even so the quality is inconsistent with the rest of the work. This treatment of the bottom hem becomes more puzzling when it is compared with the extremely refined and graceful line which defines the fall of drapery from knee to ankle on the angel at the right of the Virgin. The apparent contradiction makes the problem of the archivolts difficult.

There are perhaps as many as four assistants beside the Master of the Angels at work in the archivolts. The most important of these worked on the four crowned elders [fig. 33 shows the left rows] which stand at the spring of the second and third orders of the archivolts in the central bay. The style of these figures combines elements of both the Master of the Angels and the St.-Denis master. The whole system of draperies is like that of the Master of the Angels but the boldness of posture and haughty smugness of expression are not his. The spindly locks of the beard have been copied from the St.-Denis master, the monotonously rhythmical drapery edge has a suggestion of both the St.-Denis master and the Master of the Angels. The assistant's individuality appears again in the thick mouths and broad noses.

The twenty elders who sit in the archivolts above the standing kings are probably the work of the same assistant. Here again the system of draperies is suggestive of the system of the Master of the Angels but the quality is not so fine, the drapery hems are facilely defined, and the heads are like those of the standing elders. It is not impossible that both master and assistant worked together on some of the [voussoirs].

The discussion of the assistant leads to the archivolts of the side bays. In the south portal the work of master and pupil is related in the same manner as in the central portal. All the angels of the first order of the archivolts are by the hand of the Master of the Angels. The sign of the zodiac for May (twins) is also his work. Most of the other [voussoirs] suggest the work of both master and assistant. To this group may be assigned the female figures symbolizing geometry, rhetoric, arithmetic, astronomy, and the historical personages associated with them, Euclid, Cicero, Boethius, Ptolemy. And in the left bay the same workmanship may be recognized in the sign of the zodiac for September (a virgin) and in the allegories which represent November and December.

To a second assistant, distinguished by over-large heads and consistent dullness of execution, belong the female figures in the [voussoirs] of the south portal symbolizing music, grammar, and dialectic. One figure in the lintel of the south portal, the female figure at the extreme right of the Presentation, is by the same hand.[19]

A third assistant did the historical personages which are associated with the symbolic female figures of the preceding sculptor. These are the Donatus,[20] Pythagoras[21] and Aristotle[22] of the portal of the Virgin. He did also the two-headed man representing January[23] in the [voussoirs] of the left bay and perhaps the allegory for February.[24] This sculptor, like the Master of the Angels, avoids drapery edges, but unlike the master his figures are squatty, the draperies blanket-like. The heads are done somewhat in the manner of the St.-Denis master, not unpleasant in appearance but superficial in execution.

The lower register of the lintel in the left bay is the work of this same assistant. The perky attitudes of the heads of the apostles are supposed to have been copied from the lintel at Moissac but Mr. Porter remarks that it is more likely that both the elders of Moissac and the apostles of Chartres have a common origin in Cluny.[25]

It is impossible to make a complete analysis of the [voussoirs]. The allegory for March and the signs of the zodiac for December and February (an archer and a water-carrier) are too badly damaged to ascribe and the other signs (a goat, a ram, a lion, a bull and a crab), are extremely problematical. Perhaps those of the [voussoirs] at the left of the north bay all belong to a fourth assistant who certainly did the allegories for April[26] and July[26] which stand at the springing of the archivolts, and probably the allegories for May,[27] June,[27] August[28] and September.[28]

---

[19] See below.
[20] Houvet, Plate 70.
[21] Houvet, Plate 72.
[22] Houvet, Plate 61.
[23] Houvet, Plate 33.
[24] Houvet, Plate 34.
[25] *Romanesque Sculpture of the Pilgrimage Roads*, ch. 8, pt. 1.
[26] Houvet, Plate 36.
[27] Houvet, Plate 37.
[28] Houvet, Plate 38.

IV. The Master of Etampes

Third in importance of the assisting masters of Chartres is he who did the three jamb figures at the left of the portal of the Ascension [fig. 36]. The bodies of these figures are crudely articulated, the draperies clumsily incoherent, and yet the bold furrows of the chisel have clothed the figures with effective magnificence. This master actually worked at Etampes. His appearance at Chartres makes necessary a careful consideration of the relation between the two monuments. Although Etampes is commonly supposed to be a derivative of Chartres, Buschbek is undoubtedly correct in dating it earlier.

At first glance the fourteen figures of the lintel at Etampes do suggest an imitation of the central lintel at Chartres where there are also fourteen figures [figs. 24, 41]. The lintel of Chartres represents the apostles but instead of the usual twelve figures there are fourteen. The two extra figures have been hitherto explained as space-fillers. The fourteen figures of Etampes have been considered a copy of the supposedly faulty iconography of Chartres. But there is a perfectly logical explanation for the fourteen figures of the lintel at Chartres and a different but equally logical explanation for the lintel at Etampes.

The subject of the central tympanum at Chartres [fig. 24] is the Christ of the Apocalyptic vision. The two little figures which stand one at each end of the row of apostles must be intended for the two witnesses of the Apocalypse.[29] Mediaeval symbolism definitely associated the two witnesses with the prophets Enoch and Elijah. At the beginning of the Twelfth century they became very popular especially in Lombardy.[30]

The subject of the tympanum at Etampes [fig. 41] is an Ascension. There is a very simple explanation for fourteen figures in this composition.

"And when he had spoken these things, while they beheld, he was taken up; and a cloud received him out of their sight.

"And while they looked stedfastly toward heaven as he went up, behold, two men stood by them in white apparel;

[29] This suggestion was made by Mr. C. M. S. Niver to whom I am indebted for its inclusion here.
[30] See A. Kingsley Porter, *Lombard Architecture*, vol. 1, pp. 408, 409. It is perhaps worth remark that Lombardy developed jamb sculptures at the beginning of the twelfth century. It is not impossible that Lombardy is the origin of the jamb sculptures of the Ile-de-France.

"Which also said, Ye men of Galilee, why stand ye gazing up into heaven? this same Jesus, which is taken up from you into heaven, shall so come in like manner as ye have seen him go into heaven" (Acts 1:9–11).

The two extra figures at Etampes must be intended for the two men which the Bible mentions. Mr. Porter has pointed out a lintel at Montceau-l'Etoile which proves this. At Montceau-l'Etoile where the subject is also an Ascension there are fourteen figures on the lintel, the Virgin and thirteen male figures. Although the Bible does not mention the appearance of the Virgin at the Ascension mediaeval iconography commonly represented her there. Two of the thirteen male figures have starred halos for the purpose of distinguishing them from the others. One of these stands directly below the ascending Christ and points upwards with a fine rhetorical gesture. The two figures with starred halos are indubitably the two men of the Bible. This leaves only eleven apostles while in the earlier representations as at Charlieu and Anzy-le-Duc there are twelve. But the Montceau-l'Etoile composition shows an advance by this omission because obviously Judas should have been left out.

The lintel at Etampes has been supposed to represent fourteen male figures, the central group of twelve being the twelve apostles. But an examination of the halos above the battered and headless figures show a differentiation much like that at Montceau-l'Etoile. At Etampes one halo at each end of the row is plain. These two belong to the men. Eleven of the halos are beaded—the apostles surely. The fourteenth halo which is almost in the middle of the lintel is starred. The presence of the single starred halo proves the presence of the Virgin on the Etampes lintel. If the Virgin appears at Etampes, the lintel can not have been copied from Chartres where she does not appear.

The discussion of the lintel at Etampes demands a consideration of the lintel of the north bay at Chartres. The subject of the tympanum at Chartres is an Ascension. The lintel has never been fully explained. The lintel has two registers, the lower representing ten apostles, the upper, four plummet-like angels. Bulteau, whose explanation is best, assumes that there was no room for the eleventh apostle and refers to the angels as the two "angels" who announced the Ascension to the apostles. Although neither the King James version of the Bible nor the Vulgate mention angels (they both use the word "men") their representation is generally accepted. The suggestion that there was not room for the eleventh apostle is not so satisfactory—there is obviously an abundance of room. The analogy of the seated figures of the lintel to Moissac and Cluny has been mentioned. Is it not possible that the subject was deliberately varied to avoid a repetition of standing figures such as were already planned for the central bay?

Nor does it seem likely that the tympanum at Etampes is a reflection of the Ascension of Chartres [fig. 26]. It is hard to believe that the Master of Etampes crowded two of the angels of the lintel of Chartres into his tympanum. It is much more likely that the Master of the Angels at Chartres copied the descending angels from Etampes, doubled them in number, and dropped them from tympanum to lintel to balance the two registers of the lintel of the south portal.[31]

The composition of the voussoirs at Etampes can hardly be an imitation of the harmoniously balanced archivolts of the central portal at Chartres. In the first and second order of the archivolts at Etampes are twenty-two seated elders. If the other two elders appear among the thirteen prophets of the third order of the archivolts they are not differentiated from them.

A comparison of the capitals of Chartres with those of Etampes show the former to be more coherent in the presentation of the lives of Christ and Mary, more complex in composition, and more elaborate in the development of the canopies. But fundamentally the frieze of Chartres depends on the frieze of Etampes. Even in detail there are many close analogies. The same thick-ribbed Burgundian draperies with the ends artificially hung out as if they were draped over pegs, appear in the Sacrifice of Joachim at Chartres[32] and in the same scene at Etampes. The Nativity[33] of the capitals at Chartres is almost a replica of the Nativity of Etampes. The canopies at Chartres are clearly an evolution from the canopies at Etampes. At Etampes the towers are all alike, single-storied with a decorated band at the top: in the Marriage of the Virgin at Chartres[34] a second band has been

---

[31] It is worth noting that the colonnette which separates the king from the queen at his right in the series of jamb figures done by the Master of Etampes at Chartres, is decorated with a vine interwoven with grotesques which are strongly suggestive of the style of the Master of Etampes, especially of the whirling draperies of the angels in the corners of the tympanum at Etampes.

Again: on the column which separates the king from the queen at his left are little nude figures climbing in a vine, a motive suggestive of the two scenes of the garden of Eden on the capital at the right of the door at Etampes. The Chartres nudes, which I believe to be by the same hand, are better in execution. This indicates an advance in style. Mr. Porter points out that the motive of nude figures climbing in a vine recurs on a capital of St-Etienne of Toulouse and in Apulia.

[32] Houvet, Plate 75.

[33] Houvet, Plate 80.

[34] Houvet, Plate 78.

added in the middle of the tower making two stories. This form at Etampes appears only in the more elaborate canopies of the jamb figures. At Chartres the canopy is developed with almost incredible variety.

There can be no doubt that the Master of Etampes worked on the Chartres capitals. His hand may be traced in the half of the frieze which runs from the right of the central door through the south portal. Not all the capitals are his work but his touch is evident from the Sacrifice of Joachim through all the scenes to the Magi before Herod at the left of the door in the south bay. The heads of the Magi suggest the St.-Denis master but the rest of the capitals can be ascribed neither to the St.-Denis master nor to the Master of Etampes. Some of the heads suggest the assistant who carved the figures of the lintel of the south portal, but the lively and precocious seated Herod is like nothing else on the façade.

The jamb figures at the left of the portal of the Ascension [fig. 36] have already been noted as the work of the same master who did the jamb figures at Etampes [fig. 35]. The two figures at the left are almost exactly like the corresponding figures at Etampes. The shape and attitude of the third figure are like the third figure at Etampes but the costume is different; from the girdle to the feet she is dressed like the headmaster's Bathsheba, third to the right of the central door. The beauty of the execution of the dress convinces one that the headmaster himself completed the figure.

The attribution of the heads of the three figures is an open question because many of the heads at Chartres have been broken off and one cannot be sure of their correct replacement. The heads of the king and queen at the left are in the style of the St.-Denis master and are probably by him. The much abused head of the queen at the right of the three may very well be the work of the headmaster himself. Criticism has noted the disagreeable personality of the woman; it has neglected the manifest excellence of execution.

The jamb figures of the Master of Etampes at Chartres, like as they are to his figures at Etampes itself, are infinitely superior in quality. For this the possible interference of the headmaster is not a satisfactory explanation. Surely the Master of Etampes came to Chartres with a hand matured and experienced by his work at Etampes. A mechanical reason supports the hypothesis. The figures of the headmaster are skillfully adossed and the columns heavily patterned to give the effect of support. At Etampes the jamb figures are clumsily stuck on with no hint of support, but this defect is remedied at Chartres by the addition of figures which hide the column below the adossed statues.

This aggregation of evidence for the precedence of Etampes is overwhelming. There is one more fact which would in itself vitiate any other verdict—there is not the slightest trace of the style of the headmaster of Chartres on the façade of Etampes. It is impossible that a sculptor who had worked under the direction of the headmaster of Chartres, or who had even seen his work, should have gone away uninfluenced by it.

Etampes is earlier than Chartres.

V. *The Little Master of St-Gilles*

Far more subtle is the problem of the lintel of the south portal [fig. 25]. It is plainly the work of an assistant to the headmaster, an assistant the origin of whose style is of great importance. In detail the style presents so many analogies to the style of one of the sculptors who worked on the early part of the frieze at St-Gilles that the assistant of Chartres may be called the Little Master of St.-Gilles.

The definition of his personality is a delicate undertaking. He is obviously working in careful imitation of the headmaster and it is only by the application of the Morellian method of connoisseurship that one may hope to catch him.

A comparison of the lintel with the frieze at Montmorillon reveals a significant fact.[35] Not only is the composition of the lintel a direct copy of Montmorillon but there is also extremely close copying of style. The central group of the Presentation at Chartres is the Presentation at Montmorillon reversed. The lower register of Chartres follows scene by scene the Montmorillon frieze; first an Annunciation; then a Visitation; a Nativity with the Virgin lying in a bed underneath an altar on which rests the infant Jesus and two animals (a scene symbolic of the sacrificial lamb of God); and finally the Angel announcing the Nativity to the Shepherds. More than the composition is copied. The cloak of the Joseph of Montmorillon appears again on the Joseph of Chartres. The attitudes and costumes of the shepherds are much the same at Chartres and at Montmorillon. The sculptor who executed the lintel of the portal of the Virgin is above all an expert copyist, a valuable assistant for any headmaster whom he may serve.

The headmaster of Chartres was able to stamp his own personality on that of his assistant very clearly. The fact that the figure at the extreme left of the Presentation is by another hand leads one to

[35] *Romanesque Sculpture of the Pilgrimage Roads*, ch. 8, pt. 1.

suspect that the headmaster experimented with another assistant before he chose the one who did the rest of the lintel. No doubt the headmaster directed his assistant very carefully, at times touching up the work himself but the individuality of the assistant is recognizable in numerous little tricks and mannerisms of style.

Curiously enough one of the assistants who worked on the frieze at St.-Gilles was the same kind of person. The frieze of St.-Gilles presents one of the most difficult problems of mediaeval archaeology. Mr. Porter has discussed the frieze carefully in his chapter on St.-Gilles. There can be no question that he is correct in dating the central part of the frieze earlier than the side parts. His explanation of the varying quality of the central part is equally logical. There are certainly two, perhaps more, hands at work on the central part of the frieze at St.-Gilles but the work done by each is anything but clearly defined. Very probably this is because they worked together over the same ground, one perhaps sketching the design and modeling part of the figure which was finished by the other. The present interest in the frieze is that one of the assistants exhibits all the characteristics of the assistant of the south lintel at Chartres. Just as the assistant at Chartres copied the composition of Montmorillon and aped the style of the headmaster, so the assistant at St.-Gilles copied scene by scene the composition of Beaucaire and aped the style of Brunus. And what is one to believe when one finds all the eccentricities of style identical?

The most striking analogy is the mode of representing the eye, the lids sharply undercut, the pupil indicated by a socket-like hollow. This is not common at Chartres; except on the south lintel it appears only twice; there only one figure, that by the other assistant, lacks it. This mannerism, so uncommon at Chartres, is the rule at St.-Gilles.

At both places the whole cast of the heads is too big, dwarfing the bodies. At Chartres this is less true of the lower register only because of the superior height of the figures. Look from the head of the man third behind Simeon [fig. 25][36] to the head of the Judas bargaining with the high priest at St.-Gilles [fig. 44]. Are they not very similar?

The difficulty of setting such heads on bodies too small for them has produced stiff woodeny necks. The heads of the first shepherd at Chartres [fig. 25] and the apostle second from the right in the Last Supper at St.-Gilles [fig. 45], of the Virgin in the Presentation at Chartres and of the Christ who drives the money changers from the temple at St.-Gilles all have a similar awkward tilt.

[36] Third from the left in this picture [Ed.].

Extremely popular at St.-Gilles is the use of pastry-like rosettes to represent hair as in the Peter in the Washing of Feet [fig. 45]. This same convention appears once on the upper register of the lintel at Chartres in the figure third from the left.[37]

Wattling of the sleeves of the upper arm is a motive by no means so common as wattling at the wrist and ankle, yet this convention is repeated again and again on the south lintel at Chartres and at St.-Gilles. Three of the figures in the Presentation, the Joseph of the Nativity, the recumbent Virgin, and all the shepherds at Chartres have wattling above the elbow; so have the high priest and Judas conferring, the high priest and two conspirators in the Payment of the Betrayal Money, the St. John of the Last Supper, and two of the soldiers in the Trial Before Pilate at St.-Gilles.

And where the lower part of the sleeve is not wattled it is often indicated by a series of close parallel lines as in the shepherds, the Virgin of the Nativity, the Gabriel of the Annunciation, and the figures about the altar in the Presentation at Chartres; and as in the priest and the soldiers in Judas Receiving the Betrayal Money and in the soldiers behind the cross at St.-Gilles.

The master of the frieze at St.-Gilles often indicates his stockings by a spiral groove; two of the fleeing money changers [fig. 44], a soldier in the Trial Before Pilate, and another in the Carrying of the Cross have stockings so defined. At Chartres the stockings of the Joseph of the Nativity [fig. 25] are done in exactly the same manner.[38]

The dress of the third figure from the left in the upper register of the lintel at Chartres has a perforated border, an ornament repeated on the bed of the Virgin. One of the floggers of Christ at St.-Gilles has a tunic so decorated. So too the collars of the money changers and the Christ in the same scene, and the collar of the Jew who seems to threaten Pilate in the Trial of Jesus.

Short tunics like those of the shepherds and the Joseph of Chartres are common at St.-Gilles where they were copied from Beaucaire. Except on the south lintel they do not appear at Chartres.

The likeness of the drapery edges of Chartres to those of St.-Gilles is very important because these lines are apt to be as revealing as a signature. At both places they have considerable variety; sometimes the line is simple, with or without a border, as in the right hand flogger at St.-Gilles and the attendant second from the right in the upper register of the lintel at Chartres; sometimes it progresses in heavy ribbon-like folds as in the flogger at the left of Christ at St.-

[37] The Master of the Angels uses a flattened variant of this.
[38] The stockings of one of the shepherds is a variation of this convention —they are spirally wattled.

Gilles and the second shepherd at Chartres; but most often it moves in slovenly disorder, exaggerated by time to raggedness, as in the drapery edges of the tunic of Christ and those of the soldiers in the Carrying of the Cross at St.-Gilles, and those of Simeon and the attendant at the right of the Presentation at Chartres.

The folds of the garments themselves are executed with a similar touch and in a similar system. The tubular character of the tunic of the soldiers behind Christ at the Pillar at St.-Gilles is repeated in the shepherds and in the St. Anna of the Visitation at Chartres.

A comparison of the lively animals of St.-Gilles with the armadillo-like sheep of Chartres shows that they are fundamentally far more alike than at first appears. The cutting of the eyes, the ears, the nostrils, and above all as Mr. Porter has pointed out, the peculiar curve of the horn around the ear are identical at both places. The awkward motionless bodies of the sheep at Chartres are probably literal copies of the missing sheep of the much admired Montmorillon.

Why should all these little mannerisms which one finds at St.-Gilles appear at Chartres? Can it be that the personality which they reveal worked at both places? The most serious objection is that St.-Gilles is violently animated, Chartres severely quiet. But may not the characters of the headmasters explain this? Brunus, robust and vigorous, the headmaster of Chartres, stately and tranquil, dominated everywhere the work on the respective monuments. Surely a minor assistant might be expected to work in the manner prescribed by whatever headmaster he happened to work under, and a sculptor as adept at copying as the man who copied Montmorillon at Chartres could certainly adjust himself to temperaments as diverse as those of Brunus and the headmaster of Chartres.

The analogies of the lintel of Chartres to the frieze of St.-Gilles are undeniable. If the same assistant did not go from one place to the other, one of the assistants must have seen the work of the other. These mannerisms occur in a very restricted area of the façade at Chartres but are common to the early part of the work (the central portal) at St.-Gilles. Moreover, distinctly Chartresque elements (other than those peculiar to the south lintel) do not appear in the early part of the work at St.-Gilles. It is only in the later part of the frieze of St.-Gilles that there is any suggestion of influence coming from Chartres. In that part of the frieze, which is either by one of the masters of the earlier part who has developed his style or by a new man who is carefully imitating the early part of the frieze, there is a certain rhythm and restraint suggestive of Chartres, and there are occasional details such as the little half-moon draperies over the elbows which are characteristic of the headmaster of Chartres. The direction of influence is certainly from the central part of the frieze at St.-Gilles to the lintel of the south portal of Chartres.

JACQUES VANUXEM

The Theories of Mabillon and Montfaucon on French Sculpture of the Twelfth Century—[1957]*

Vanuxem was the first to investigate the history of the often-repeated theory that the kings and queens on early Gothic portals represent the rulers of France. His essay is a milestone in the study of the meaning of the statue-column.

Towards the end of Louis XIV's reign, scholars turned their attention to the study of a number of sculptured church porches—including those of Chartres and Saint-Denis—which we now know to date from the twelfth century, and which became the cause of fierce controversies lasting throughout the first half of the eighteenth century. In the first volume of *Annales Bénédictines* (1703), D. Mabillon, the eminent author of the *Diplomatique*, announced that he had identified work dating from the Merovingian period in two of these doorways—those of Saint-Germain-des-Prés and of Nesle, in Champagne.

He was not the originator of the idea that the kings and queens represented in church porches were the ancient rulers of France; this was a popular belief, which the names often found painted on phylacteries only served to confirm. The actual age of these sculptures, however, was quite unknown. Now, in the *Annales Bénédictines*, Mabillon not only confirmed that they were indeed the figures of Merovingian rulers, but also stated that the statues were contemporary with the kings they represented.

Mabillon was most anxious to uphold the rights of the Benedictine abbeys, and to prove the authenticity and antiquity of the charters which had established them. Even during his lifetime he was accused of not always respecting the principles of sound judgment; in 1704, for example, the Jesuit Father Germon claimed that Mabillon should have examined certain ancient documents more closely, and with greater circumspection. After his death, criticism of his methods became more widespread. It was said that he had been too biased in favour of the Benedictine order, or that he had worked too hastily.

---

* This essay first appeared in the *Journal of the Warburg and Courtauld Institutes*, vol. 20, 1957, and is reproduced here by the kind permission of the author and the editor [Ed.].

All these criticisms are excellently summed up by de Rudder in *La vérité sur l'église de Saint-Omer* (1754):

> His very natural prejudice in favour of his own order was the endearing cause of some of these faults: but the greatest of them can only be attributed to the vast extent of his field of study. His attention was divided amongst a multiplicity of subjects; sometimes he forgot in one place what he had said in another; he judged by the objects he had in front of him, and those he lacked were the source of his errors. . . .[1]

Mabillon's writings on the church doorways confirm what his critics have said. He made no attempt to compare the various sculptures with one another; he hastily studied a few isolated examples, interpreting them in such a way as to favour "those of his own order." He believed that these sculptures could confirm, and even prove, the antiquity of certain documents and certain foundations.

He may have been misled by some works where historical events were represented; for example, the tomb of Ogier the Dane at St.-Faron-de-Meaux which he took to belong to the beginning of the ninth century, or the fine north doorway of St.-Benoît-sur-Loire, which actually dates from the end of the twelfth century. Mabillon believed it to be a ninth-century work; the lintel depicts an event of about 660—the translation of St. Benoît's body to the Abbey of Fleury. This discovery served to confirm the Benedictine scholar in the belief that the sculptures on church doorways should be interpreted as referring to events and persons directly connected with the history of the building concerned.[2]

Let us now consider the chief examples of the application of this method. At Villenoce, near Troyes, there formerly existed a doorway removed from the abbey of Nesle la Reposte (it is now destroyed) [fig. 50]. In the *Annales Bénédictines*, Mabillon attempted to identify the six figures on either side of the door. He recognized St. Peter without difficulty; the bishop is Saint Remi of Rheims or Saint Loup of Troyes. But the kings and the queen were a problem. Studying the image of the queen, a flash of inspiration came to him: it was Clotilde, the wife of Clovis, easily recognizable because she is the "Reine Pédauque" with the goose's foot, as she appears on other doorways of the same type. Why had Clotilde a goose's foot? Mabillon answered that this probably symbolized the queen's prudence; the goose was a symbol of prudence in antiquity. This argument satisfied him,

[1] *La vérité sur l'église de Saint-Omer*, 1754, p. 180.
[2] Martène and Durand, *Voyage littéraire de deux bénédictins*, 1717; first part, p. 65.

and having identified Clotilde it was obvious that the three kings were her three sons, or Clovis and two sons. This was all the evidence that was necessary for the discovery of Merovingians.[3] The proof is a very shaky one—all the more so because Mabillon had to admit that apart from these statues there was no known connection between the Merovingian kings and the abbey of Nesle. It is odd that so scholarly a person as Mabillon should have been unacquainted with the legends identifying the Queen of Sheba with the "Reine Pédauque"; to see Pédauque as Clotilde because the goose is the symbol of prudence is to display a knowledge of antiquity which had nothing to do with the matter. There stands revealed a man of the seventeenth century, familiar with the art of emblems and devices; the goose symbolized prudence because of the geese of the Capitol, and various legends to be found in the emblem books of Menestrier or Verrien.[4]

Mabillon was always ready to believe without hesitation in the authenticity and antiquity of any manuscripts or monuments with which he was concerned. In 1697, some tombs were discovered under the high altar of the abbey of Saint-Acheul, near Amiens. The Canons Regular who lived there immediately claimed to recognize one of these tombs—on the strength of a few indistinct carvings—as that of St. Firmin the Confessor, third Bishop of Amiens; a doubtful opinion, to say the least. Mabillon, in his letter on the unknown saints (1698), accepted it unhesitatingly. In 1711 the Canon de Lestocq, calling in question the claims of the community of Saint-Acheul, made use of Mabillon's own words in opposing him, pointing out that according to the principles laid down in the *Diplomatique* the carved inscription should be read with caution, and that it was by no means certain that it concerned St. Firmin.[5]

In connection with the St. Firmin affair, Mabillon had found an ardent supporter in the person of Thiers, the celebrated Curé of Vibraye, who was all in favour of the new ideas. But a few years later, in 1700, Thiers attacked Mabillon violently over the question of the "Sainte Larme de Vendôme."

In 1700, Mabillon had had an unusual task to perform; he was called on to defend the veneration of the so-called "Holy Tear," which the monks of Vendôme claimed to have been shed by Christ at the death of Lazarus. Thiers was attacking this old devotion; to uphold it against these attacks, and to confirm its antiquity, Mabillon made

---

[3] Mabillon, *Annales ordinis Sancti Benedicti*, Paris, 1703, vol. 1, pp. 50–51.
[4] Menestrier, *Sylloge Symbolorum*, Amsterdam, 1695, p. 757; Verrien, *Recueil d'Emblèmes, Devises, Médailles*, Paris, 1696, pl. 54.
[5] *Dissertation . . . sur Saint-Firmin le Confesseur*, by the Abbé de Lestocq, 1711, pp. 175–180.

appeal to the sculptures on the arcade in the abbey church of
Vendôme, where the relic was kept. Speaking of these sculptures,
he declared: "The authenticity of these figures is unquestionable . . .
they date from the foundation of this abbey" (i.e. the eleventh
century) [fig. 52].

Thiers vigorously denied the probability that the arcade dated from
the eleventh century; he even claimed that it could not be earlier than
the fifteenth, which was going too far to the opposite extreme. This
does not excuse Mabillon for not having examined the sculptures
more carefully, however, and for dating them as early as 1040.

In fact, their real date probably lies somewhere between those
allotted to them respectively by Mabillon and Thiers, though it is
difficult to make any definite statements about a composition only
known to us through a drawing.[6] However, one can safely rely on
the indications provided by certain details: the attitudes of the large
figures in the round, the folds of their garments, their style of dress,
especially of the female figures with head-dresses, and the architectural details of the upper part all go to prove that his monument
must belong to the second half of the thirteenth century. For the
sake of his thesis, Mabillon had added two centuries to its age; if he
had encountered a calmer and less impassioned opponent the weakness
of his case would have been made obvious.

The polemic carried on after Mabillon's death concerning the doorway of Saint-Germain-des-Prés was more acrimonious, and of greater
importance in connection with the subject under discussion.[7]

There is no uncertainty about the date of the main tower of the
abbey church of Saint-Germain-des-Prés. A document which had long
been well known attributed its construction—or at least that of the
lower part—to Abbot Morard, who died in 1014. In spite of this, even
such scholarly Benedictines as Mabillon and his disciple Ruinart, re-
suscitating a theory put forward in 1612 by Père Dubreuil, took the
tower to be much older, and to have been built in the sixth century
at the time of the foundation of the abbey. In spite of the documentary
evidence, therefore, the Benedictines claimed that it had not been
destroyed by fire under the Normans. In 1699 D. Ruinart, one of
Mabillon's collaborators, published the works of Gregory of Tours,

[6] *Bulletin de la Société Archéologique du Vendômois*, 1873, pp. 157–212.
The writings of Thiers and Mabillon on the Holy Tear of Vendôme are
published together in *Dissertation sur la Sainte Larme de Vendôme*, Amsterdam, 1751 (see especially pp. 353 and 417).

[7] See the *Mercure de France*: May, 1723, p. 895; January, 1724, p. 24;
March, 1724, p. 472; April, 1724, p. 613; May, 1724, p. 826; July, 1724,
p. 1472; also Dom Bouillart, *Histoire de l'abbaye de Saint-Germain des
Prés*, 1724, pp. 296 ff.

and reproduced in the appendix an illustration of the doorway under the tower [fig. 51]. This excellent engraving presented the statues as Merovingian, and as representing Merovingian kings—a weighty argument in favour of attributing the foundation of the abbey to Childebert, and some small consolation for the fact that the foundation charter was now known to be a forgery. As in the case of Nesle la Reposte or Vendôme, the very stones of the building were called upon to make up for the deficiencies of the documents. In short, from the time of Ruinart, the statues of Saint-Germain-des-Prés were accepted as sixth-century work representing Clovis, St. Rémi (who had baptized him), Clovis's four sons, and Ultrogothe, the wife of one of them —Childebert, the founder of Saint-Germain-des-Prés. In the *Annales Bénédictines*, 1703, Mabillon appeared to approve of Ruinart's opinion and confirm it.

An official Benedictine attitude on the subject of the doorway was established, and was all ready to be taken over by Dom Bouillart, when he published the *Histoire de l'Abbaye de Saint-Germain des Prés* in 1724. In fact, he was not satisfied with simply repeating the theory—he undertook to defend it. A Norman scholar, Claude du Moulinet, Abbé des Tuileries, saw the weakness in the Benedictine case. He was a man of outstanding intellect, independent and unprejudiced, who had gained much from his friendship with Richard Simon, the father of French biblical criticism. We cannot go into all the details of du Moulinet's observations on the theories of Mabillon and Ruinart in 1723 and 1724. He began by stating that among the figures of kings he thought he could identify not only Merovingians but also Charlemagne, Pépin and Bertrade; this immediately reduced the age of the doorway by two or three centuries. Not content with this, however, he went on to state that he suggested the period of Charlemagne as a date for the doorway only because he did not wish to oppose Mabillon too violently, since he had always had the greatest respect for the latter's authority; his own view was that the doorway dated from the eleventh century, since the tower belonged to the time of Abbot Morard. We are thus getting remarkably near the truth; in fact, the doorway was inserted in Morard's tower in about 1160.

The Abbé des Tuileries made a number of other very judicious statements; he affirmed, for example, that on the façade of Notre-Dame (which no one had ever claimed to include Merovingian material) there were statues on the Portal Ste.-Anne which were closely related in style to the figures on the doorway of Saint-Germain-des-Prés.

Our author was thus obliged to deprive the tower and doorway of Saint-Germain-des-Prés of its venerable antiquity. Nor was he prepared to give ground on this point; in his view, the identification of the statues was very doubtful, and he added ironically (speaking of Bouillart): "I must leave it to this skilful historian to enlighten me, since he, unlike myself, experiences no difficulty in the matter."

Du Moulinet attached no importance whatever to the story of Clotilde and the goose's foot at Nesle; and, returning once more to the statues of Saint-Germain-des-Pres, he goes into the question of the mitre worn by the figure of the bishop there. He rightly identified it as a style of mitre belonging to a later period than the Merovingian era, and appealed to Montfaucon on the subject. It was well known at that time (1724) that this Benedictine scholar was preparing his vast work on the *Monumens de la Monarchie française*, which had been announced in 1719 in the preface to the first volume of *L'Antiquité Expliquée*.

Referring to Bouillart, who was about to publish (in 1724) his history of the royal abbey of Saint-Germain-des-Prés, du Moulinet wrote: "This historian has the advantage of living with the learned Father de Montfaucon, who is collecting all that is known concerning secular and ecclesiastical monuments and preparing a vast work on them; he could find out whether Father Montfaucon has ever seen examples of similar mitres dating from the period in question, and produce his testimony in evidence. . . ."

The replies of Bouillart and Montfaucon, thus challenged, were awaited with interest. They were not very convincing. Bouillart discusses questions of detail in order to defend Mabillon's hypotheses on the antiquity of the porch of Saint-Germain-des-Prés. He does indeed try to follow the example of the Abbé des Tuileries and see the problem in a wider setting; but, for the most part, he shelters in craven fashion behind authority in countering his adversary's objections: "When I said that the big tower was as old as the abbey church, I was not speaking of my own accord; I was simply following the opinions of the most learned antiquarians . . . one can, of course, be mistaken in one's conclusions, but the risk of error is less when one is guided by such eminent scholars as M. du Tillet, Père du Breuil, Père Mabillon, Dom Thierry (Ruinart). . . ." Thus, Bouillart refused to examine du Moulinet's objections; and so did Montfaucon.

It is important to realize that these objections should have led anyone who studied the sculpture in question very near the truth; Montfaucon's attitude, in neglecting them or replying in such preemptory fashion, is therefore all the less excusable.

In 1729, in the first volume of *Monumens de la Monarchie française*, Montfaucon declared: "I know that a certain individual (du Moulinet, Abbé des Tuileries) has written that this doorway does not date from the original foundation . . . but I believe it can be shown," he added, "that the great tower was built at the same time as the first church." Naturally, we are curious to see how he will set about demonstrating this fact. He offers as "definite proof" the names of Merovingian kings inscribed on the scrolls of the statues. "Moreover," he adds, "the style can be recognized as belonging to that period; these figures are quite flat, and have nimbuses." Of course, this proves nothing; these characteristics are part of his own theory which we are about to expose. He claims to establish this theory by statements without any real foundation.

Further on, Montfaucon states that he will not refute du Moulinet, and in spite of the documentary evidence attributing the tower of Saint-Germain-des-Prés to Morard, he persists in maintaining that it is Merovingian. Although challenged personally, he refused to discuss the question of the style of the bishop's mitre. After remarking that mitres vary considerably and that one cannot draw definite conclusions from their shape, he adds: "The matter presented no difficulty whatever to Père Mabillon, who was familiar with a great many examples of early mitres" (p. 52).

Like Bouillard, therefore, Montfaucon withdraws behind Mabillon's authority, describing him as "one of the most scholarly and enlightened of authors," although disagreeing with him on points of detail. In order to keep in line with his master and his colleagues, he summarily dismisses du Moulinet's objections. The latter had brought forward as evidence the statues of the Porte Ste-Anne of Notre-Dame, which could not be Merovingian; Montfaucon retorted that they had been brought there from the earlier church. In a sense he was right —the statues were not made for the existing façade; but they are only about fifty years earlier in date, and therefore could not have come from the ancient cathedral church "which Gregory of Tours called *ecclesia senior*," as our good Benedictine has no hesitation in affirming.

In short, du Moulinet's attacks on the statements made by Mabillon and Bouillart leave Montfaucon's belief in his colleagues' theories quite unshaken; he even reaffirms his theory. It is therefore difficult to excuse this theory on the grounds that he was ignorant of the criticisms aroused by his ideas. The criticisms then levelled at him are the same as those we repeat to-day.

Montfaucon's theory is set out in detail in the first volume of *Monumens de la Monarchie française*, which was published in 1729, five years after the *Suppléments* to *L'Antiquité Expliquée*. In the preface to this work, Montfaucon states that pieces of sculpture survive from the time of the "deux premières races" (i.e. Merovingians and Carolingians), dating therefore from the end of the fifth century to the ninth century; ". . . Clumsy though they are, they provide information unobtainable elsewhere."

The system built up on these "grossières sculptures" is sketched out in the preliminary discourse on the inauguration of the first kings, and is confirmed in the course of the book. Montfaucon stated that the inauguration was full of reminiscences of antiquity; the Merovingian kings were inaugurated upon a shield, like the Roman Emperors or the Emperors of Constantinople. Like them, too, the Merovingians also received a divine character, since their images were graced with luminous haloes. This attribute of gods and emperors, Montfaucon explained, was transmitted through Christianity to Christ, the Virgin and the saints; it was also passed on to the kings, and our author adds:

> According to Gregory of Tours, when Clovis received the Codicils of the consulship from the Emperor Anastasius, he clothed himself in purple, took the chlamys, set the diadem on his head, distributed largesses of gold and silver, and was henceforth called "Consul" and "Augustus." It seems likely that he then also took over a number of other imperial trappings, and that since this inauguration the images of himself and his successors were provided with a nimbus. They are to be seen thus on the doorway of the church of St.-Germain des Prés, at the foot of the great tower.

Once more, Montfaucon asserts that this door dates from the foundation of the church. On the scrolls held by two of the kings one can still read the names of Clodomir and Clotaire. "This sculpture," he says, "is in the awkward style of the first dynasty, when statues were made completely flat, like all those with a nimbus—as can be seen on other churches. From the time of Pépin and Charlemagne, sculpture was more rounded, as we shall explain later." Around this doorway of Saint-Germain-des-Prés, Montfaucon went on to group a whole family of statues displaying, in his opinion, the same characteristics: statues which were flat, and which had a nimbus, therefore representing Merovingian kings assimilated to the gods and emperors of antiquity.

Among the statues which he took to be of the same period, he first showed those of the Porte Ste.-Anne of Notre-Dame (now lost). He rightly stated that they had transferred from an older church, but these two he claims to have been Merovingian. In spite of du Moulinet's objections, he identified St. Peter and St. Paul amongst them, and claimed that the four kings and two queens represented sovereigns of the first dynasty—Frédégonde, Arégonde, Chilpéric, Clo-

taire—although there were no inscriptions on their scrolls. The king
with a viol, who is nowadays recognized without difficulty as King
David, was believed by Montfaucon to be Chilpéric "who, according
to Gregory of Tours, composed hymns and canticles for the Church."

With Saint-Germain-des-Prés and Notre-Dame-de-Paris, Montfaucon groups the statues of the façade of Chartres. The west front is
earlier than the church itself; he does not believe it possible to identify
the kings and queens. "It seems certain, however," he says, "that they
belong to the first dynasty." According to him, the statues date from
that period; he illustrates them in engravings done after some very
poor drawings sent to him from Chartres [fig. 54]. Fortunately, these
statues are still in existence, so our knowledge of them does not have
to depend on the drawings. The latter, however, include a detail
which does not now exist, and which cannot be put down to a piece
of fantasy on the part of the draughtsman. All the crowns worn by
the kings and queens are "radial"—that is to say, surmounted with
points which have now disappeared—if, indeed, they ever existed.
Montfaucon seizes upon this detail and is thus enabled to establish
another line with antiquity: "Radial crowns," he says, "were much
used in the early days of the Roman Empire."

Finally, in the same group Montfaucon also includes "two statues
of kings with sculptured haloes, on two of the columns supporting
the cloister" in the abbey of Saint-Denis, in the oldest part of the
cloister. One of these figures is now in the Metropolitan Museum,
New York.

Montfaucon classes all these flat and haloed statues as Merovingian.
With the end of the first dynasty—in the reign of Pépin le Bref, to
be precise—he claims to discover new characteristics.

Montfaucon attributed to the end of the eighth century a most important monument: the façade of the abbey of Saint-Denis. He dated
it from the time of Fulrad (abbot from 750 to 784), pointing out
that the statues on the doorway have greater roundness than the earlier
ones and no longer have haloes. Pépin apparently discontinued the
custom of representing kings with haloes, out of respect for Our
Lord, the Angels and the Saints.

Montfaucon seems fortunate to have been able to find these two
features—roundness and nimbus—to assist him in determining a kind
of evolution in sculpture, or to show, in the words of his preface,
this "différent goût de sculpture . . . en divers siècles." Here, then,
is the basis of his theory. The engravings, made after excellent drawings, give an exact idea of the twenty statues of the doorway of
Saint-Denis, which Montfaucon believed to represent four queens

and sixteen kings who reigned in Paris after Clovis, and which he took to have been carved in the time of Pépin le Bref.

The first doorway on the left has six statues; five kings, and a queen whose head is missing. The second (middle) doorway has eight; five kings, and three queens (one headless). The third has six kings, of which the end one has fallen a victim to the ravages of time.

These engravings and the drawings they reproduce are of great value because the statues are now destroyed. They have made it possible to identify three sculptured heads (now in the Baltimore and Cambridge Museums in the United States) as fragments of the sculpture of Saint-Denis.

With the doorway of Saint-Denis Montfaucon also grouped another doorway, because the figures on it had no haloes: that of the abbey of Nesle, in Champagne, which as we have seen was discussed at some length by Mabillon.

Such, then, very briefly, is Montfaucon's theory.[8] Along with many of his predecessors and contemporaries, he was convinced that the figures on the church doorways represented kings and queens. He thought they were much older than was actually the case; he attempted to classify them and to find characteristics which would enable him to date them, and he unearthed two: first, the nimbus, proving a Merovingian origin, and a survival of the deified emperors of antiquity; and secondly, the degree of roundness which these statues presented.

Although Montfaucon's dating is entirely wrong, since the statues in question belong to the twelfth century and not to the sixth or eighth, it may be worth while considering the importance of the difference he claimed to observe between the "flat" statues and those which have, in his own words, "plus de rondeur." Those of Chartres, Saint-Germain-des-Prés, and Notre-Dame-de-Paris belong to the first category; those of Saint-Denis to the second.

All historians of mediaeval art now agree that although the statues of Saint-Denis and Chartres may have iconographic and stylistic connections, they show two very different tendencies. Those of Chartres are attenuated, static; those of Saint-Denis are more agitated and richer in spatial effects. Here we seem to be in the presence of Montfaucon's "flat" and "rounded" statues. Setting aside for the moment the chronological error, Montfaucon was therefore right in seeing these statues as two different groups. If, as has sometimes been

[8] This theory is spread throughout the first volume of *Monumens de la monarchie française* (introduction and text). Carolingian and Merovingian monuments are there interpreted according to the same principles.

supposed, Saint-Denis were later than Chartres, and the rounded statues therefore later than the flat ones, his theory would thus be confirmed on one small point. But the general belief is that his two groups were either produced in the reverse order of time or else were contemporary with one another, and simply revealed two different tendencies in twelfth-century French sculpture.

We have seen that Montfaucon's theory took no account of the criticisms directed at Mabillon by Thiers, or those levelled at Bouillart by du Moulinet. Yet, quite apart from these, a great many other objections should have occurred to him. Let us give some examples.

It will be remembered that Montfaucon attributed the main façade of Saint-Denis to the time of Fulrad and Pépin le Bref—that is, to the eighth century, thus accepting the opinion expressed by D. Michel Félibien in his history of the royal abbey of Saint-Denis (1706). But he disregarded the fact that in 1708, in a work opposing Mabillon's views on the antiquity of certain charters, the author pointed out that the abbey had often been sacked and burnt, and that "to-day there is no marble or bronze monument to be seen there which is any earlier than the time of the Abbot Suger."[9] This author was quite right, and it is difficult to understand why his wise observation was ignored by Montfaucon twenty years later. The attitude of the latter can only be explained by his desire to uphold the opinions of his *confrères* Mabillon and Félibien.

There were many further objections he could have found. He was perfectly familiar with the tombs of Childebert (the founder of the abbey) and of Childeric at Saint-Germain-des-Prés, and he dated them in the eleventh century.[10] Their style is very close to that of the statues on the doorways.

Even at Saint-Denis, Montfaucon was well acquainted with the north door of the church, which he took to be a twelfth-century work —as, indeed, it is. It is difficult to understand how he could have imagined an interval of five or six centuries between these sculptures and those on the doorways of the main front, when there was in fact only thirty or forty years between them. Faced with such problems, he calmly wrote: "Time will no doubt throw light on all these matters."[11] So it has; but its revelations are not what he anticipated they would be.

Convinced of the validity of his theory, he deliberately ignored any documents which contradicted it. When he was preparing the *Monu-*

[9] *Histoire des Contestations sur la diplomatique avec l'analyse de cet Ouvrage*, Paris, 1708, p. 93.
[10] *Monumens de la monarchie française*, vol. 1, Paris, 1729, pp. 58, 60.
[11] *Ibid.*, p. 194.

mens de la Monarchie française, and documents were being sent to him from all quarters, he received (in 1726) a very detailed description of the doorway of the abbey church of Ivry, part of which still survives. It was easy to see that this doorway was closely linked in style with those of Saint-Germain-des-Prés and Chartres. The abbey at Ivry, however, was not founded till the end of the eleventh century, and it was therefore impossible to claim that its sculpture was Merovingian; so Montfaucon carefully avoided making use of this document in the *Monuments*. It still exists among his papers in the Bibliothèque Nationale.[12]

As we have already said, Montfaucon's attachment to these manifestly erroneous theories arose from a desire to uphold the opinions of Mabillon and his colleagues. It was also an outcome of his particular attitude of mind, acquired during the course of his studies, which had been directed mainly towards antiquity and, more specifically, its religious mysteries. If one goes through the fifteen volumes of *L'Antiquité Expliquée*, one will find that he was fascinated by the mystery cults—those of Isis, Attis, and Mithra—and by anything to do with the gnostic sects; he dwelt at some length on the Abraxas, of which Saint-Germain-des-Prés possessed copies [fig. 53]. He found in them a curious mixture of Egyptian religion and Christianity.

Since he was so familiar with works of art which were the product of secret communities or gnostic religions, Montfaucon was ready to suspect a mystery everywhere. He was not alone in this; at that time it was quite usual to see esoteric meanings in mediaeval works of art. Leaving aside those who saw them as alchemical symbols, it should be pointed out that the Abbé Chatelain, a scholarly liturgist, believed that the monsters and fantastic figures on the arch of the twelfth-century doorway of the abbey of Chelles were Egyptian hieroglyphs.[13]

It was in such a spirit that Montfaucon had undertaken these studies. In *L'Antiquité Expliquée* he had had occasion to examine several mediaeval works, and had no difficulty in finding plenty of mysteries in them. He was always ready to find occult meanings and remote origins for any document sent to him; he would accept the most far-fetched legends if they partook of this character. He believed that the *octogone* of Montmorillon was a druidical monument, and in this

[12] MS fr. 15643, fol. 90; *cf.* A. Rostand, "La Documentation iconographique des Monuments de la Monarchie française de Bernard de Montfaucon," *Bulletin de la Société d'Histoire de l'art français*, 1932, pp. 104–149.

[13] Abbé Lebeuf, *Histoire de la ville et de tout le diocèse de Paris*, ed. Bournon, Paris, 1883, vol. 2, p. 487.

connection he built up a theory on the Druids and the octagonal shape of their buildings. He did not actually go as far as his colleague D. Jacques Martin, who tried to interpret the sculptures on this monument and looked for evidence of a moon-cult in them; but he did believe it to be contemporary with the Druids, whereas it was in fact twelfth-century work[14] [fig. 55].

When he discusses a mediaeval work of art in *L'Antiquité Expliquée*, he makes the most extraordinary comments on it. One of a series of ivory diptychs with which he deals is a ninth-century work in which sacred and profane subjects are represented together— Christ on the cross being depicted above Romulus and Remus. Montfaucon remarks: "A very strange feature, which I have never seen anywhere else, is a human eye clearly delineated on the abdomen of Christ. This extraordinary thing evidently refers to some story of marvel of which we are ignorant."[15] In fact, what Montfaucon took to be an eye was merely a somewhat clumsy representation of the navel of Christ [fig. 58]. But a reading of his text shows that he was ready to see such marvels everywhere, and to employ all his learning and subtlety of mind in defence of the most startling theories.

Everything at that time conspired to make him see Carolingian and Merovingian work in twelfth-century doorways. Seventeenth-century historians were familiar with these remote periods, which were then very much in the news. The discovery in 1653 of Childeric's tomb at Tournai created a tremendous stir. Chifflet's *Anastasis Childerici* (1655) described and illustrated this discovery; Menestrier, in his *Histoire de Louis le Grand* (1699), classes it among the most important events of Louis XIV's reign. Montfaucon could hardly do less; but, oddly enough, instead of going back to the actual treasure, which had been in the royal library in Paris since 1665, he simply reproduced Chifflet's plates.[16] Along with the medals and coins found in the tomb, he included Egyptian scarabs which his predecessor had introduced for purposes of comparison. Montfaucon thought that these, too, were Merovingian. Far from suspecting his mistake, he felt that some great mystery underlay the presence of these objects. He was always on the look-out for traces of antiquity; so he wrote: "I am surprised to find a stag-beetle here—an object of Egyptian superstition . . . could these beetles have reached France from Egypt at this early period? In another oval there is a frog, which is also to be found fairly frequently on Egyptian monuments."[17]

---

[14] *Supplément* to *L'Antiquité Expliquée*, 1724, vol. 6, pp. 220–224.
[15] *Ibid.*, vol. 3, p. 230.
[16] A. Rostand, *loc. cit.*, p. 117.
[17] *Monumens de la monarchie française*, vol. 1, p. 15.

Montfaucon was evidently delighted to find reminiscences of ancient Egypt (which he had discussed at some length in *L'Antiquité Expliquée*) amongst these Merovingian objects. Such a discovery was bound to redouble the enthusiasm with which he sought for similar mysterious *rapprochements*.

Additional finds also served to bring to mind these remote periods of history; for example, the altar stones discovered in Notre-Dame-de-Paris in 1711, where the deities of Gaul were represented side by side with Roman gods. Montfaucon had published a commentary on this find, pointing out its unusual features—the names of the Celtic gods, who with Esus and the bull with the three cranes represented all the mysteries of the religion of ancient Gaul, rediscovered beneath a medieval church. Once again, antique traditions were found linked with the monuments of Christianity.

For Montfaucon, Merovingian monuments followed on directly from those of Antiquity, and should be studied according to the same principles. He made this clear as early as 1719, when the first volume of *L'Antiquité Expliquée* was published. "This project . . ." he says, "can be continued for the succeeding periods. Although the fifth to the fifteenth century was an age of barbarism, a similar work devoted to that period is bound to be extremely useful." In the prospectus of 1725 announcing his *Monumens de la Monarchie française*, he is even more explicit: "This is, as it were, a continuation of *L'Antiquité Expliquée*, which I have just published. Both works are of a similar nature; one begins where the other leaves off."[18]

In fact, for Montfaucon there was no break in continuity between antique and Christian monuments. He was not surprised to find works of great antiquity in churches. While he was preparing the *Supplément* of *L'Antiquité Expliquée*, a Benedictine, D. Pierre Thivel, sent him drawings of Roman bas-reliefs on an arcade of the abbey church of Saint-Pierre-de-Flavigny. Montfaucon identified these as "most unusual victory marks, displaying a number of unique features."[19] Doubtless they were the remains of a monument to Augustus [fig. 56].

Thus, even in Christian monuments he found reminiscences of the Antiquity he knew and loved so well. "Knowledge of Antiquity," he wrote, in the preface to the *Supplément* of *L'Antiquité Expliquée*, 1724, "is the gateway to all the arts and all the sciences." He constantly brings the *Monumens de la Monarchie française* into relationship with antiquity. Since he had found many links with it in the

18 E. de Broglie, *Bernard de Montfaucon et les Bernardins*, Paris, 1891, vol. 2, p. 190.
19 *Supplément to L'Antiquité Expliquée*, 1724, vol. 6, p. 86.

statues on church doorways, it is not surprising that he tried to make these out to be even older than they were.

At the basis of his theory is the explanation of the nimbus on the King's head. Homer, Virgil and their commentators are called on for evidence in this connection; so are representations of Trajan and the Emperor Claudius. Montfaucon recalls the fact that Clovis was raised to the Consulate; it was therefore not surprising that he should be represented with a nimbus. For Montfaucon, these kings with a nimbus on church doorways were apotheoses *à l'antique*.[20]

It was the same story with the famous Sainte-Chapelle cameo, representing the apotheosis of Germanicus, to which Montfaucon devoted a good deal of attention. He was interested to observe that in the drawings sent to him the statues at Chartres had radial crowns;[21] in the cameo, one of the figures also wears a radial crown.[22]

According to Montfaucon, the *fleurs de lys* of the French kings are a legacy from antiquity; they are to be found on crowns in antique diptychs, and in mosaics at Ravenna. "Our kings," he concludes, "adopted the use of what we call the *fleur de lys* not as a symbol peculiar to themselves, but perhaps in imitation of the emperors of Constantinople."[23]

In antiquity, the sceptre was the symbol of command. On the doorway of Saint-Germain-des-Prés, the statue presumed to be Clovis held a sceptre surmounted by an eagle "like the consular baton of the Romans." Once more Montfaucon reminds us in this connection that Clovis had been appointed consul.

In the treasury of Saint-Denis, there was a sceptre, said to be that of Dagobert, which had at the upper end a representation of a man seated on a flying eagle. Montfaucon sees it as "an apotheosis in the style of Roman monuments . . ."; and he emphasizes the connection between the so-called throne of Dagobert, Roman curular chairs, and the consuls' chairs which he had reproduced in *L'Antiquité Expliquée*.

The kings and queens on the doorways wear the chlamys; even their footwear is reminiscent of the classical style of shoe.

Once he had found such connections between antiquity and the Merovingian kings, Montfaucon readily accepted that the statues

[20] *Monumens de la monarchie française*, 1729, vol. 1; Introduction, pp. xx ff.

[21] *Ibid.*, p. xxvii and p. 57.

[22] *L'Antiquité Expliquée*, 1719, vol. 5, Book II, Ch. X. See also Morand, *Histoire de la Sainte-Chapelle de Paris*, Paris, 1790, p. 63.

[23] *Monumens de la monarchie française*, 1729, vol. 1; Introduction, p. xxxiii.

which he presumed to represent the latter were close to antiquity in date, and contemporary with their subjects. This reasoning was, of course, completely false; but Montfaucon's authority and air of assurance succeeded in imposing it, and historians of French art were thus thrown off the right track for the best part of a century. His knowledge and love of antiquity guided him in the same direction at his desire to uphold the ideas of Mabillon; for both reasons, he greatly exaggerated the age of the monuments he examined.

It must not be imagined that his ideas were accepted without question. As early as 1739 Dom Plancher, a Benedictine, who was writing the *Histoire de Bourgogne*, came across some monuments similar to those studied by Montfaucon. He reproduced several of them, in good engravings. He undertook to question the theories of his colleague and predecessor; speaking of Montfaucon, he says: "He offers as proof a fact which has not been established," and goes on to add: "The representation of Clovis on a church doorway is no proof that the statue dates from the time of Clovis."[24] Plancher examines the nimbus theory and the dates given by Montfaucon; he criticizes the theory based on the flat and rounded figures. To him, that proved nothing; and he claimed that the doorways which Montfaucon took to be Merovingian were really twelfth-century work. All that Plancher says is full of good sense and moderation; the only point on which modern knowledge fails to agree with him is that he continues to accept the kings on the doorways as kings of France. We do not know how Montfaucon reacted to the criticism of his Burgundian colleague. In 1739, he was 85; he died two years later.

Ten years after his death, his theory was to receive the final blow. On April 30, 1751, the Abbé Lebeuf addressed a séance of the Académie des Inscriptions on the subject of "la Reine Pédauque." This scholar accepted Plancher's dating; and, what is more, he did not recognize "la reine Pédauque" on the doorway of Nesle as Queen Clotilde, as Mabillon and Montfaucon had done: he correctly identified her as the Queen of Sheba. He submitted that the statues on church doorways represented characters from the Bible, and not kings and queens of France.[25]

Thanks to Plancher and Lebeuf, Montfaucon's system was overthrown, the right lines were indicated, and investigators could confidently proceed with the study of these monuments. Unfortunately,

[24] Dom Plancher, *Histoire de Bourgogne*, 1739, vol. 1, pp. 503 ff.
[25] Lebeuf, *Mémoires de l'Académie des Inscriptions et Belles-Lettres*, 1756, vol. 23, meeting of April 30, 1751; *Histoire de la ville et de tout le diocèse de Paris*, ed. Bournon, Paris, 1883, vol. 1, p. 269.

Montfaucon's prestige was so enormous that there were still some people who appeared to disregard these refutations, and his theory continued to enjoy considerable esteem.

Half a century later, the attitude of the celebrated Alexandre Lenoir is of particular interest. True, he was not a scholar, even though he made himself out to be one—any more than he was the universal saviour of French monuments during the Revolution, a distinction which he also claimed.[26]

He published a number of writings on his museum, in which he not only revived Montfaucon's theory but also reinforced it in a manner which removed it still further from historical truth. In his vast eight-volume work, published in 1800, he enlarges on the subject of the nimbus "dont Montfaucon parle avec mystère." Far from criticizing the theory, he adds further to the mystery by interpreting as an image of the sun at its zenith. He writes: "This emblem of the sun was commonly placed on the heads of saints and of kings of the first dynasty . . . this nimbus simply expressed the apotheosis of the hero who was thus honoured."[27] This is a curious mixture of the theories of Montfaucon and of Dupuis—the author of *L'Origine de tous les cultes* (1793). In this work, he claimed to find sun-worship at the root of all religions, including Christianity; the Zodiac on the doorway of Notre-Dame-de-Paris and of Saint-Denis provided him with examples to illustrate his system. Lenoir was a great admirer of Dupuis, as he was of Montfaucon.

Unfortunately, Lenoir could not exhibit in his museum any of the haloed statues mentioned in the *Monumens de la Monarchie française*; all those of Paris or Saint-Denis had just been destroyed, or had disappeared.

A piece of good fortune enabled him to fill this gap. In 1803, he was able to obtain possession of two statues of a king and a queen from the church of Notre-Dame-de-Corbeil. These statues were of exactly the same type as those of Saint-Germain-des-Prés or Chartres. In 1806 Lenoir published a commentary; following Montfaucon's example, he held forth on the nimbus and the sceptre, and on flat and rounded statues, and added a sprinkling of reflections borrowed from Dupuis. It goes without saying that he took these statues to be sixth-century sculpture, representing Clovis and Clotilde.[28]

[26] J. Vanuxem, "La sculpture religieuse au musée des monuments français," in *Positions des thèses des élèves de l'Ecole du Louvre (1911–1944)*, Paris, 1956, pp. 200–203.

[27] Alexandre Lenoir, *Musée de Monuments français*, Paris, An. IX (1800), vol. 1, p. 156.

[28] *Ibid.*, vol. 5, pp. 218–222.

The admiration which Montfaucon had inspired revealed itself in other ways than the application of his method—in itself strange enough in 1806, so many years after it had been refuted by Plancher and Lebeuf. It was also displayed in the tomb erected to his memory by Lenoir in his *Jardin Elysée* [fig. 57]. This tomb, designed by Lenoir, is reproduced in an engraving; it is described as follows: "Tomb in an antique style, containing the body of Dom Bernard de Montfaucon, the learned antiquarian, who died at the age of 87 in 1741: hieroglyphs, Egyptian figures, Greek reliefs, figures from the late Empire and relics of the early days of the French monarchy have all gone into making up this monument to a man who was equally successful in all those fields."[29] In this strange monument, Lenoir was particularly insistent on Egypt, Antiquity, and "les mystères"; the tomb was to commemorate the "learned antiquarian" rather than the Benedictine who published the writings of the Fathers of the Church.

Yet Lenoir must have known very well that, contrary to his statement, Montfaucon had not met with equal success in all the subjects covered by his vast *oeuvre*. In 1800 and 1806 Lenoir accepted Montfaucon's theories without hesitation; in 1821, however, he gave them only qualified approval. Referring to the nimbus theory, he says: "This opinion is sound up to a point, but not entirely acceptable; while we are not in entire agreement with Montfaucon, whose judgment on works of art can be at fault, we will nevertheless refer to what he says on matters where he was most in a position to have a thorough knowledge."[30]

The appeal to authority is still there; but the authority is no longer accepted without a certain degree of mistrust. At long last, Lenoir must have been put on his guard.

With the defection of Lenoir in 1821, darkness finally envelops Montfaucon's theory. It had enjoyed a long twilight, since as early as 1738 it was known that this theory had no solid foundation.

[29] *Ibid.*, vol. 5, p. 202.
[30] *Ibid.*, vol. 7, p. 53.

[Note: A sequel to this article, entitled "L'abbé Lebeuf et l'étude méthodique des monuments du moyen âge," appeared in the *Société des fouilles archéologiques et des monuments historiques de l'Yonne*, no. 3, 1963.—Ed.]

5

THE SCULPTURE OF THE TRANSEPTS

The sculpture of the transepts of Chartres forms a separate body of work in the Cathedral, one that merits independent study. In the following selections, Henri Focillon discusses the general position of the transept sculpture in the history of Gothic art; Peter Kidson gives a clear account of the building history and describes the central portals; and Vöge, in an epoch-making essay, isolates the work of one Master. Each author has a different approach to style and each helps us to grasp the beauty and the meaning of the works under consideration.

HENRI FOCILLON
[Architectural Sculpture and Gothic Humanism—1938][1]

The combination of the ribbed vault with Romanesque masses, by its inherent conflict, helps us to realize that Romanesque art and Gothic art were not successive forms, following naturally one from the other, but that the former opposed the advance of the latter and, over and above this, that whereas Romanesque art was the scion of an ancient lineage, with links that led far back into the past, the researches which allowed the architects of the Ile-de-France to develop a style out of the vault rib, and to pursue its consequences down to the structural paradoxes of *Rayonnant* architecture, were essentially modern. This view receives remarkable confirmation from the study of the sculpture. The image of human life, as displayed in the cathedrals, shows nothing that is foreign to us, or which we cannot recognize as familiar. Whereas Romanesque sculpture led us into

---

[1] From Focillon, *The Art of the West in the Middle Ages*, edited and introduced by Jean Bony, published by Phaidon Press, London and Phaidon Publishers Inc., New York, vol. 2, pp. 71–78 [Ed.].

an unknown realm, into a labyrinth of transformations, and into the most secret regions of spiritual life, Gothic sculpture brings us back again to ourselves and the things we know in nature. We do not feel that it is centuries away from us. It seems of yesterday, like a collection of family traditions, which are tinged but not weakened by the passage to time. In these great expanses of stone, despite the size and majestic character of the figures, we feel that intimacy of emotion produced only by works which, their age notwithstanding, remain the eternal contemporaries of man. If one were called upon to give a psychological characterization of the various phases of medieval sculpture, one might perhaps convey something of the difference, even irreconcilability of their qualities by saying that Romanesque sculpture was the expression of faith, that Gothic sculpture was the expression of piety, and that the sculpture of the decline was the expression of devotion. Romanesque faith, shot through with visions and prodigies, accepted and cherished the mysterious; it moved among superhuman things; it trembled in anticipation of rewards and punishments; the miracle was its law, and the unknowable its nourishment. From these epic heights, round which resounded the thunders of Sinai, the piety of the thirteenth century bring us back to the paths of the Gospel; in God-made-man, it cherished humanity; it loved and respected God's creatures as He loved them; it accepted the benefit which He brought to men of good will—peace on earth—and extended it to include even death, which was no more than a sleep in the Lord. Finally, the devotion of the decline, more demanding and perhaps more sensitive in its emotions, replaced this serenity with its own unease, passionately devoted itself to the terrible scenes of Calvary, fixed them, contemplated them, made them live again, suffered them anew, with a dramatic pageantry and mystic power of re-creation which conferred holiness even on the accessory and the indifferent object. Iconography, style and technique were all equally expressive of these profound differences.

It is true, of course, that the iconography of the twelfth century had foreshadowed to some extent the Gothic iconography, in its general interpretation of the Old and the New Testaments, in its recognition of symbolic correspondences between the two—an idea revived by Suger—and in the attention which it devoted to the cult of the saints. But it was dominated by the Apocalypse, from which it derived its fearful visions and its image of Christ the Judge, enthroned in glory, with His inhuman *entourage*. From the Apocalypse it drew, if not all its resources, at least its predominant tonality, which was that of the epic poem. It transformed the *Psychomachia* into a *chanson de geste*. It gave an oriental tinge to Christian poetry, and exaggerated proportions to its heroes. Into its world it welcomed monsters conceived out of chaos, and obeying laws foreign to those of actual life. Thirteenth-century iconography made simultaneous renunciation of the visions, the epic, the East and the monsters. It was evangelic, human, Western and natural. It brought Christ down almost to the same level as His people; He stands, with His bare feet on the asp and the basilisk, between the Apostles, who seem to move aside to make way for Him, so that we may see Him the better, as He raises His hand, a grave and gentle Teacher, a young and loving Father. True, He is still enthroned on high in the tympanum, presiding over the resurrection of the dead and the eternal doom, but even there He is the Christ of the Gospels and retains His gentle humanity. This latter quality completely irradiates the scene of the Coronation, wherein Mother and Son are tenderly united. The thirteenth century surrounded the youthful image of the Virgin with an affectionate fervour which, while glorifying woman, respected her femininity, just as, in the beauty of the angels, it preserved, as a fadeless flower, the fleeting charm of adolescence among the children of men. From Annunciation to Coronation she retains her birthright of grace, derived from her human clay; she is no longer the stone idol of earlier ages, but the celestial sister of human mothers. This perfect moment, when art takes hold of life between the uncertainties of the juvenile form and the fatiques of maturity, this moment of poise and of the first blossoming, like the ἀκμὴ of the Greeks, was present in all its poetry in thirteenth-century iconography, which extended it even to the features of the dead, rejuvenated and at peace, and even the prophets, Martyrs and Confessors, burdened with years, even the diocesan saints, grown old in their apostolic labours, still draw from it a tranquil majesty which illumines their decrepitude.

This iconographical period and tone, however, were not the expression of a false idealism. The accent of life is not effaced in the great peace of the cathedrals. They are not dedicated to the beatitudes alone. The whole of creation, full and frank, takes its place within them. Built and decorated, as they were, in the days of the great encyclopaedias, when the middle age sought for the first time to assess itself, its intellectual resources and its stock of knowledge, and, in short, tested its possession of the world and of man, they too are encyclopaedic. In adopting the plan of the *Speculum majus* of Vincent of Beauvais in order to render an account of their treasures, Emile Mâle[2] was not forcing them into an alien mould, but revealing the

[2] *L'art religieux du XIIIe siècle en France,* 7th ed., Paris, 1931, intro., pt. II, "Méthode à suivre dans l'étude de l'iconographie: Les miroirs de Vincent de Beauvais," p. 23. [Note: In paperback see, *The Gothic Image,*

harmony of the system of the images and the system of the ideas, developing the basic thirteenth-century conception of the hierarchy of the created world, and respecting the imposing structure, not of an expositional framework, but of the "realms" of spiritual life. In each of these divisions the latter moves in accordance with a rhythm of concealed relationships, to which art gives a musical quality, and whose symbolic significance it translates but does not reveal. The forms obey the law of numbers and the law of symbols. The world is in God, the world is an idea in the mind of God, art is the writing down of that idea, and the liturgy is perhaps its dramatization. Each "mirror" reflects, not a group of inanimate images, but the perpetual rising up in God of beings and forms. When we say that the iconography of the thirteenth century is encyclopaedic, we mean, not only that it is universal and all-embracing, but also that, within its immense orb, of which God is the centre, a secret force binds together, and draws into its gravitational field, all the aspects of life.

This conception was at its most ardent and poetical in this period. It seems to be inventing and evolving its whole universe simultaneously. But the profound harmony which existed between religious thought and contemporary iconography must not mislead us into thinking that the latter was a by-product of theology. It was theological, and the theologians had a considerable share in it, but this art goes far beyond any definition which might seek to confine it to the interpretation of scholastic, liturgical or symbolic themes. It is still too close to the discovery of the world, too much absorbed in its wondering contemplation. The supernatural is the underlying principle of the natural, but nature exists none the less. It was the error of the Romantic school, and, no doubt, of Huysmans, to confer on thirteenth-century iconography a hieroglyphic character. The cathedral interpreted according to Guillaume Durand and Vincent of Beauvais is certainly a valid conception, but it also possesses a poetic strength which lies outside the scope of the systems. "Man walks there through forests of symbols," but they are symbols which wear the youthful features of living things. This is the point which is so well brought out by M. Mâle. "The sculptors of the Middle Ages . . .

---

tr. D. Nussey, New York, 1958, intro., pt. II, "Method used in this study of Mediaeval Iconography."—Ed.] The *Speculum majus* probably dates from the middle of the thirteenth century. The Jesuits produced a four-volume edition, Douai, 1624. It includes only three parts—The Mirror of Nature, The Mirror of Science, and The Mirror of History. The Mirror of Morals dates from the beginning of the fourteenth century, but was probably envisaged in the original scheme. Mâle, *op. cit., loc cit.,* p. 24. n. 2. See *ibid.,* Livre I, "Le Miroir de la Nature," pt. III, pp. 46–62.

do not seek to read into the tender flowers of April the mystery of the Fall and the Redemption. On the first spring days, they go off into the woodlands of the Ile-de-France, where humble plants are just breaking through the crust. The ferns, curled up like strong springs, are still covered with their downy wool, but already, along the streams, the arum is about to flower. They gather the buds, and the leaves which are ready to open, and contemplate them with that loving, passionate curiosity, which we others feel only in earliest childhood but which true artists retain all their lives." Thus youthful humanity is surrounded by youthful vegetation. The stone of the churches is radiant with perpetual spring.

The Mirror of Nature shows us the wood outside the little town, and the small suburban garden close at hand where hazel nuts grow, and strawberries, and a few stems of vine. It is as if some infant hand had gathered these altar decorations and hung them in the church, fresh-plucked, for an unending holy day. There too are the beasts of the earth and the creatures of fable; but even more than the wonders from the bestiaries, the sculptors loved the old familiar companions of human life, studied them endlessly, and prodigally multiplied their images, now with the zest of a ribald tale, now with a kind of affectionate respect. Sixteen draught-oxen, hoisted to the tops of the towers of Laon, high above the field, celebrate in stone the patient beasts which dragged up the hill the stones of which the cathedral is composed. On all this creation, sprung from His thoughts, the Eternal Father meditates, and rests His cheek on His hand, like a good gardener, his day's work done. And man also, as he appears in the Mirror of Science,[3] gives himself up to labour as to a work of redemption; no distinction is made between the skill and labour of the hands and the skill and labour of the mind. On the plinths of the churches, the calendar of Works and Days, carved in rectangle or quatrefoil, warned the passer-by of tasks to be performed, and the figures of the Seven Liberal Arts promised him the delights of Knowledge.[4]

Just as Nature is the thought of God, and just as hand and mind work according to His ways, so also the history of the world.[5] is the history of the Lord extended through the lengthy annals of human

[3] See E. Mâle, *L'art religieux du XIIIe siècle en France*, Livre II, "Le Miroir de la Science," p. 63.

* [4] See J. C. Webster, *The Labors of the Months in Antique and Medieval Art*, Chicago, 1938; W. Déonna, *Die Darstellung der freien Künste in der Kathedrale Saint-Pierre in Genf*, Pro Arte, pt. VI, 1947.

[5] See E. Mâle, *L'art religieux du XIIIe siècle en France*, Livre IV, "Le miroir historique," p. 133.

life. It begins with the Creation, and its main episodes are the Fall of Man and his Redemption, between which lie the long series of prophetic centuries, when the elders of Israel, the heralds of Christ, prefigured His word and proclaimed His mission. The cathedrals were first and foremost the genealogical tree of the Saviour, and the tall regal and priestly figures which adorn them outline not only His fleshly descent but also His spiritual lineage. The notion of the concordance of the two Testaments here achieves its fullest meaning, so that one might almost say that the thirteenth-century cathedrals composed, in monumental terms, a kind of third Testament, formed from the intimate union of the Jewish and the Christian Bibles. The ranks of the kings of Judah are deployed on the façades—at Paris, Amiens, and Chartres. The procession of the Prophets advances out of the depths of ages. At last, the promise is fulfilled, and Christ is born in the stable. Under the influence of the liturgy, the thirteenth century retained of His life only those cycles which correspond with the major festivals of the year, the Christmas cycle and Easter cycle, the Nativity and the Passion. These are also the most moving pages of the whole moving story; above all, they are perhaps the most human. The Parables have their place—the Wise Virgins, the Good Samaritan, the Prodigal Son, Dives and Lazarus—as the direct expression of the Word of God. The apocryphal gospels are not excluded: they serve especially to enrich the story of the Virgin, her glorious and anguished life, her Dormition, her Entombment, her Coronation, and her miracles. The thirteenth century did not set her apart from the Son, but associated her intimately with His earthly career and seated her beside Him in the regions of eternity. Here, certainly, is the most sublime aspect of this iconography. The cult of the Virgin was not only a phase in the history of piety, but was at the very heart of the life of the Middle Ages, and implied no diminution of its energetic character and virile grandeur. In the Child who rests in her strong arms, the Virgin bears the whole weight of the crucified Christ. On these images and examples the Saints fix their gaze. As the lives of the Prophets were a prefiguration, so their lives are an imitation, by virtue of their renunciations, labours, miracles and sufferings. The history of the world is the history of the saints, and the geography of the world is that of their hermitages, their miraculous springs, their tombs and their pilgrimages. The church militant stands in the doorways alongside the church prophetic and the church apostolic. Each diocese finds room for its local saints, and the guilds have theirs also; these patrons of the Christian life strengthen by their example the lessons of the Mirror of Morals. The Virtues no longer fight; the age-old duel which was carved in the Romanesque churches of Poitou and Saintonge is now concluded; calm and erect, the victors trample on the prostrate vices.

The vast panorama of life, extending through the untrammelled realms of faith, included also a few of such remnants of the antique world as could be put to didactic uses, by showing, for instance, the frailties of the flesh among the great (Aristotle and Virgil deceived by the wiles of woman and by their own weaknesses), or perhaps the herald of the Last Days, the Erythraean Sibyl.[6] Of profane history, it recalled and celebrated the Christian heroes, such as Charlemagne and St. Louis. On St. Theodore at Chartres it bestowed the pride and charm of the young knight of the time. But there is nothing to compare with the memory of the epic deeds of knightly prowess which was revived in the portal of Modena, except the windows at Chartres dedicated to Charlemagne and those at Saint-Denis which commemorate the Crusades: but these latter were earlier by half a century, and still belonged to the age of the epics.[7] The great epic of the new period was the Last Judgment. It no longer possesses the tumultuous violence of Apocalyptic art, though this did, in fact, survive in certain representations of the Four Horsemen—for instance, at Amiens and Paris. A terrible silence reigns over the various episodes of the Judgement, ranged in the several registers of the tympana. At Laon, no disorder attends the separation of the good from the evil. So it is also at Chartres, where blessed and damned follow one after another in neat files [fig. 65]. So, too, at Reims, where demons, dragging on a chain, drag off to their torments the resigned sinners, clerks and laymen, with a king and a bishop among their number. In the Portail des Libraires at Rouen, and at Bourges, the damned break out in frenzy. But St. Michael weighing souls is full of the grace of youth, and the scene of the general Resurrection, in the lintel of Rampillon, has nothing tragic or funereal about it. These delicately formed nudes, this slim adolescence of the flesh, holds the promise of beatitude in its beauty of form, no longer subject to decay.

The history of art can show nothing comparable with this sculptured exegesis of a great system of religious thought. In spite of the abundance of its myths, the Greek genius did not multiply the representations of them on its buildings. Those which it selected are

* [6] See J. Adhémar, *influences antiques dans l'art du Moyen-Age français*, London, 1939.
* [7] The Crusade window did not belong to Suger's first scheme. E. Panofsky, *Abbot Suger on the Abbey Church of Saint-Denis and its Art Treasures*, Princeton, 1946, p. 195, places this addition in the third quarter of the thirteenth century, but L. Grodecki is of the opinion that it was made by Suger himself, probably c. 1150.

admirable, but the very principle of the selection precluded variety and was still more inimical to profusion. The distinction, in fact, goes still deeper, for it involves two opposing conceptions of life and nature. Medieval art set man in the centre, but the rich diversity of the world was indispensable to it, as was also the arrangement of episodes and prodigies according to a higher order, conceived by God. But antique art, in its best period, saw man surrounded only by light, and the order which it imposed on its figures was a harmony born of reason. Thus these two classic states of the human spirit are fundamentally distinct, though they drank from the same fountains of eternal youth and often show striking similarities in the treatment of forms. If some parallel to the Western iconography of the thirteenth century is required, it is perhaps in Buddhist iconography that its elements may best be found. That, too, evolves, not around an inaccessible deity or a perfect athlete, but around a god who assumed human form, whose life was a model of holy living, and a commentary and symbol of a philosophy. The numerous scenes are arranged in fixed cycles: the cycle of the innumerable *jatakas*, or previous existences; the cycle of the Nativity, notable for the episode of the seven steps taken by the Predestined One immediately after his birth into the world; the cycle of the vocation, with the scenes of the four meetings by which he was persuaded; the ascetic cycle, with his temptation; the cycle of teaching, and finally the cycle of Nirvâna. Admittedly, there is nothing resembling the scenes of the Gospels, but there are a great number of edifying stories, and exalted mission, and a life whose every chapter has a meaning and whose representation is a lesson. The Buddha is surrounded by his apostles and the saints of his church. His and their teaching breathes the purest charity and counsels renunciation. The life about them is illusory, but the forms which it assumes are inhabited by the spirit, and worthy of respect, compassion and love. The plants which sheltered the reverie of the Sage, or bore his body, are sacred. All creation mourns the Nirvâna, and all the beasts of the earth come running to the death-bed of the Buddha. A strong spirit of naturalism animates the iconography of this religion, despite the fact that it holds nature to be but a dream. It expresses, moreover, a conception of man and life, based on detachment and charity, which is not different in essence from the moral teaching of the Gospels. Finally, it had, like early Christian art, a Hellenistic period prior to its assumption of true Asiatic forms. In this aspect, the narrative length, and the symbolic and didactic character of the temple-sculptures make them comparable with the art of the Western cathedrals. But Indian iconography, by its very nature, turned early to formulae, and life ebbed away from the Sage, so that his meditation tended towards a complete vacuity, which enfolded a vacant soul and an immobile body, the shrine of his sacred absence. Though human and evangelical in his origins, the God of Asia drifted into sleep, and grew rigid, as an idol of gold. Furthermore, the buildings which bear his image and his story are quite unrelated to those of Christian architecture, and it would be difficult to explain or even to imagine Gothic iconography apart from the profoundly original architecture in which it is embodied and located.

PETER KIDSON
[The Transept Programs—1958]¹
North and South transept portals

The fire of 1194 spared not only the western block which contained the Portail Royal, but also the XI century crypt of the previous church. Both were incorporated into the new building, and in effect, they were the limits which determined its length. The decision to retain the Portail Royal as the western entrance for the new church was particularly important, as it meant that any new sculptured portals would have to be set in the transept façades. Several problems have their origins in these circumstances.

It can be shown that the present magnificent ensembles which are spread in depth across the full width of the north and south walls of the transepts, came into being piecemeal [text illus. 3, 4]. First of all, it is apparent that both sets of porches were built on after the façades, or at any rate the lower parts of them, were finished. Then, an examination of the masonry of the north transept façade allows us to deduce that the original provision was for no more than a single portal in the central bay. But when we compare this with the terminal wall of the south transept, it becomes clear that the latter was intended to have three portals from the moment it was begun. It is unlikely that the two façades were planned like this from the outset, and we are entitled to infer from the difference between them that the north transept was started first, and that there was a change in the design before the south transept was put in hand. What form the south transept façade was to have taken before the change, we cannot say for certain. Perhaps it was intended to match the north transept in having just one portal. But it is conceivable that an asymmetrical arrangement, like that finally achieved at Reims, was

¹ From Peter Kidson, *Sculpture at Chartres*, London, Alec Tiranti, 1958, *passim*, reproduced by permission [Ed.].

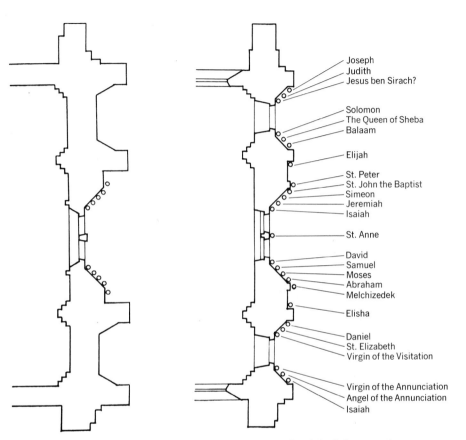

Text illus. 3. North transept, reconstruction of original form and reconstruction of final form before addition of porches, after Grodecki (Kidson)

envisaged, i.e. with a north transept portal, but none on the south transept. Later, the north transept at Chartres was brought into line with the actual south transept, when two new side portals were pierced. This probably coincided with the construction of the porches on the north side. Then, finally, porches were added to the south transept as well to complete the symmetry. The entire operation must have been carried out in a very short space of time, especially by

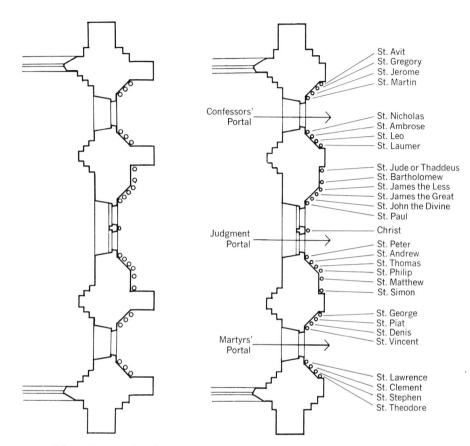

Text illus. 4. South transept, reconstruction of original form after Grodecki, and present form (Kidson)

medieval standards. The only evidence we have for exact dates are a reference to a flight of stone steps on one side of the cathedral in 1210 when King Philip Augustus visited Chartres; donations for the windows of the south transept façade between 1217 and 1220; and the removal of a temporary wooden porch against the south transept façade in 1224. It is generally agreed that the latter was done to allow the south porches to be built. If this was the final stage of the work, the total time taken can have been little more than thirty years. The

steps which were there in 1210 presumably led up to the north transept, which ought by then to have been partly built; and the donations
seem to imply that the portals of the south transept were already
well advanced by 1217. The changes and additions to the north
transept façade should therefore be placed somewhere between say
1220 and 1224. The sequence was so rapid that the work must have
been not only continuous but much of it even simultaneous.[2] In spite
of this, however, it is clear that there were two major changes, each
of which entailed a dramatic increase in the amount of sculpture
envisaged for the transept façades. The first, which probably occurred
between 1210 and 1215, expanded the number of portals from two to
six. The second, in the early 1220's provided each of the six portals
with a corresponding porch * * *.

North transept centre bay: Virgin portal

The first portal to be considered * * * is the Virgin Portal of
the north transept. But as in the case of the Portail Royal, we must
guard against the propensity of names to limit the significance of
what we see. It is true that the Virgin figures very prominently in
this portal, both in the tympanum and lintel, and also on the trumeau,
which functions as a sort of focal point for the lower part. But the
meaning of the portal is by no means centered exclusively in the
Virgin. There is a definite division between the upper and lower
parts. The voussoirs, tympanum and lintel are devoted to the precursors of Christ 'after the flesh,' and it is with these that the Virgin
properly belongs. The statues in the jambs of the portal, however,
might be called the spiritual precursors of Christ; and the whole portal has its unity in the notions of anticipation and foreshadowing
which, as we have already seen, inspired the interest of the Middle
Ages in the Old Testament.

Let us start with the voussoirs [fig. 62]. Among the rows of voussoirs, two stand out in having their several figures intertwined as it
were in the branches of a tree. This is a version of the Tree of Jesse,
one of the most celebrated of all medieval allegories, which had its

[2] The most recent discussion of the chronology of the portals and porches
of the transepts is by L. Grodecki, "The Transept Portals of Chartres
Cathedral," *Art Bulletin*, vol. 33, 1951. Some of the general presuppositions
of Grodecki's article have been criticized by P. Frankl in another article
in the *Art Bulletin*, vol. 39, 1957, "The Chronology of Chartres Cathedral,"
but this does not affect Grodecki's case about the portals. [Note: Most
recently, see J. van der Meulen, "Recent Literature on the Chronology of
Chartres Cathedral," *Art Bulletin*, vol. 49, 1967, pp. 152–172.—Ed.]

origins in the prophetic passage of Isaiah, chapter 11: "And there shall come forth a rod out of the stem of Jesse, and a Branch shall grow out of his roots. . . ." The idea came to have a special association with the Virgin through the fortuitous similarity between the Latin words for "rod" (*virga*), and "Virgin" (*virgo*). The Tree of Jesse had already been used at Chartres in the XII century, to decorate one of the windows over the Portail Royal. Here, in the north transept there are twenty-six figures altogether. Presumably they represent the twenty-six generations in St. Matthew's catalogue of the ancestors of Christ from David to the Virgin. If David is the first, the generation of Joseph and Mary would be the twenty-seventh, but the Virgin is accorded special honour on the lintel and tympanum.

The three scenes on the lintel and tympanum are closely related and form a single narrative [fig. 61]. On the eastern half of the lintel is shown the death of the Virgin. Her body is surrounded by the apostles, and among them appears the figure of Christ himself, indicated by the cross and halo, who has come in person to receive the soul of his mother, and to administer the last blessing. The other half shows the resurrection of the Virgin; her body being lifted out of the tomb by a company of angels. Finally, the tympanum presents her apotheosis. She has been received into the heavenly city and sits on the right hand of Christ, who is on the point of crowning her Queen of Heaven. They are surrounded by a great company of angels: four on the tympanum itself, and the rest in the innermost row of voussoirs. The scene of the coronation has undeniable connections with the cult of the Virgin, which assumed impressive dimensions in the course of the XII century. There is an element of delicacy and tenderness beautifully expressed in the tympanum, where Christ, in admitting the Virgin to the seat of majesty alongside his own, allows her special access to his compassion—an idea that was taken up in the Judgment portal of the South transept. But in this context, the coronation is also a recognition of the Virgin's special place in history. She is the last and most favoured of all the ancestors of Christ, the one in whom the Old and the New Testaments meet, and through whom all the portents and prophesies of the Old Testament receive their fulfilment.

A similar idea—of signs and portents in the Old Testament gradually becoming more and more precise until they are made explicit in the Church of Christ—links together the statues in the jambs of the portal. It can be seen that the portal itself makes provision for eight statues, four on each side. The conventional form of Virgin portal, which we find at Senlis, Laon, and Mantes at the end of the XII century, required precisely this number; and it is possible that the sculptors at Chartres started with the idea of simply reproducing an arrangement with which they were familiar. But when the statues were made, two more were added, presumably with the intention of removing any lingering doubt as to the meaning of the cycle. These were placed at the beginning and the end, and they represent Melchizedek and St. Peter. As there was no room for them in the portal itself, they were set against the wall between the portal and the buttresses on either side.

Melchizedek, the priest and king of Salem who came to be regarded as the archetype of all priests, and, as St. Paul argued in Hebrews, chapter 7, of the priesthood of Christ in particular, could also serve as the Old Testament counterpart of St. Peter, the first priest of the Church of Christ [figs. 63, 70]. The antithesis between these two figures is not far removed from that which was more usually expressed by allegorical representations of the Synagogue and the Church. But the meaning here is more precise. Melchizedek has a chalice in his hand and carries a censer, and he stands over the sacrificial lamb. Like St. Peter, his attire includes the tiara of a medieval pope, and this, in conjunction with his kingship, contains an unmistakable allusion to the claim of the medieval papacy to exercise supreme authority over all secular rulers. "The order of Melchizedek" was invoked continuously by Pope Innocent III in his assertion of this claim, at the very moment the north portal at Chartres was being built, and the inclusion of these two statues reveals a great deal as to the mood in which the whole programme of Gothic sculpture at Chartres was conceived. Next to Melchizedek and turned toward him, or rather looking over his head, is Abraham on the point of sacrificing Isaac. The distraction above Melchizedek is in fact the angel who intervened to save Isaac. The ram that took his place on the altar is beneath their feet. Then comes Moses, holding the Tables of the Law, and the column with the brazen serpent which was to become in St. John's Gospel a symbol of the crucifixion. He is trampling underfoot the golden calf which the children of Israel worshipped during his absence on Mount Sinai. After Moses comes Samuel with another sacrificial lamb. At his feet is the figure of Saul. Finally on the western side is David—a somewhat unusual representation of him—crowned, and holding the instruments of Christ's passion, the lance in one hand and the nails and crown of thorns in the other. This is David in his role as prophet as well as king, the allusion being to his remarkable premonition about the crucifixion in Psalm 22.

On the western side the chronological sequence is continued with Isaiah, the special prophet of the Incarnation and the author of the allegory of the Tree of Jesse [fig. 64]. At his feet is the recumbent

figure of Jesse, and in his hand is the rod which bursts into flower
at the top end. Isaiah points to the flower to emphasize the point.
After Isaiah comes Jeremiah, the prophet of suffering and lamentation.
He carries a halo on which is superimposed the cross, signifying the
manner of Christ's death and glorification. At his feet is one of the
Jews who attempted to stone him. The last of the precursors are
Simeon and St. John the Baptist, each of whom bore witness to Christ
in his lifetime. Finally, there is St. Peter. In him, the whole cycle
seems to find its appropriate consummation. The link between these
figures is that they all acknowledge Christ. But they do so in differing degrees of explicitness. From Melchizedek to Samuel, they anticipate Christ symbolically through their actions, and especially in their
reiteration of the idea of sacrifice. With David, Isaiah and Jeremiah,
the anticipation takes the form of prophesies. Simeon and St. John
go further and recognize the living Christ as the Messiah. But it
remains for St. Peter to acknowledge him as the Son of God. And
for this reason, St. Peter stands not only over against Melchizedek,
but over against them all. He is the first representative of the new
dispensation.

In the midst of the sequence of the spiritual precursors of Christ,
on the trumeau of the doorway, is a statue of St. Anne, the mother
of the Virgin, with the Virgin herself as a small child in her arms
[fig. 72]. It would be difficult to explain the presence of this statue
without a piece of definite information that sheds light upon it. We
know that some time after the sack of Constantinople by the Fourth
Crusaders in 1204, an infinitely precious relic of St. Anne, namely
her head, was presented to the cathedral. There can be little doubt
that the statue on the trumeau is connected with the arrival of this
relic, and its location follows from the kinship between St. Anne
and the Virgin. But it is later than the other statues in the portal,
and it is slightly extraneous to their meaning.[3]

One cannot help being struck by the apparent overlapping with
parts of the Portail Royal in the iconography of this portal if we
are right in regarding its theme as the ancestors and precursors of
Christ, then it performs the same kind of function as the lower parts
of the Portail Royal. The contents are not the same, it is true. But
the solution reached in the Portail Royal was not final; and when,
towards the end of the XII century, a new formula was devised, bringing together in a single portal the Tree of Jesse, the Coronation of
the Virgin, and the prophets and patriarchs who foreshadowed Christ,

[3] The role of the St. Anne in this portal is analogous to that of the
Joachim and Anna capitals of the Portail Royal.

it was clearly felt that this was a more satisfactory way of doing what the Portail Royal had done with its representative figures of the Old Testament. In particular, the association of the Virgin with all the other antecedents of Christ was a logical improvement. But the necessary inference to be drawn from this is the new portal made part of the Portail Royal superfluous, at least so far as its iconographical function was concerned. As we shall see, the south transept portals entail a similar consequence for the rest.

Although there is a basic similarity to be seen in the execution of these figures, they vary considerably in quality, and there seem to have been several hands engaged upon them. The Isaiah, Jeremiah, and Simeon seem to go together, and perhaps the Melchizedek ought to be placed with them. The David stands apart in respect of the proportions of his body: his head is small in comparison with his height. The same reasons applied in the opposite way allow us to attribute the Abraham and the Samuel to the same man. When we compare them with the statues of the Portail Royal, we are no doubt impressed by the way the figures have loosened and matured as human likenesses in the course of half a century. The sculptors have begun to take notice of the forms of the body beneath the draperies, and the draperies themselves have begun to do the sort of things we expect of them when they are stretched over limbs in movement. Although as yet the movements are not very strenuous, at least the rigidity of the Portail Royal figures has been broken, and some of them, notably the Abraham, are turning to one side. Both movements and draperies are more flexible and interesting in the smaller figures of the voussoirs. But these are general characteristics which denote a change of style, not an improvement of quality. Few would contend that as works of art any of these statues can compare with the best of the Portail Royal. The David has an expression of noble, contemplative sadness; the power and vigour of the Abraham, though crude, is striking enough to anticipate the unrestricted movements of later Gothic statues elsewhere. By far the best of them, however, is the St. John, whose emaciated and rather pathetic features stand out from a row of otherwise expressionless faces. Not only is it outstanding in its context; but it is an unusual and singularly penetrating characterization of St. John, as unforgettable in its way as that by Botticelli nearly three hundred years later. As for the rest, they have an even, average degree of competence which suggests an harmonious workshop rather than a collection of individual geniuses. The origins of this style, like the iconographical formula of the portal and, one might add, the architectural antecedents such as they are, can be

sought in the Laon-Braisne-Soissons area. But it is necessary to remember that the increase of scale, and the impetus of such a vast
undertaking invited many developments which had no warrant in
tradition.

The Virgin portal leads us through the Old Testament to the
point where its promises are fulfilled in the persons of Christ and
St. Peter; or, to put it another way, Christ and his Church. These
two themes, the decisive elements in the second half of historical
time, are taken up and amplified in the portals of the south transept.
Although from an architectural point of view these are separate
entities, their iconography only makes sense when it is read as a
single programme.

South transept centre bay: Last Judgment portal

Like the Virgin portal on the north transept, the central bay falls
into two distinct halves. In the upper parts, there is the Last Judgment;
and below, the Apocalyptic vision [fig. 65]. Or perhaps it would be
better to say that this portal brought together for the first time two
closely related episodes from Christian eschatology which had hitherto
been treated separately, and in so doing presented a truly compre-
hensive picture of the Last Things. Inevitably, the component parts
underwent a radical transformation. Not only did they become the
nucleus for a greatly enriched iconography; but the entire mood
changed. The new themes were drawn from the history and teaching
of the Church; and in effect, the eschatology merges into the triumph
of the Church of Christ.

The combination of the Last Judgment and the Vision of St. John
allowed and even demanded considerable changes in the traditional
forms. Thus the apostles usually appeared in both scenes, so it became possible for one set of these figures to be eliminated. They are
in fact consigned to the jambs of the portal where they are able to
assume much larger dimensions than in the lintel or tympanum. The
exclusion of the apostles from the scene of the Last Judgment left
the whole of the tympanum free for the major protagonists: Christ
and the two intercessors who are the Virgin and St. John. In at-
tendance are angels holding the instruments of Christ's passion. The
clarification achieved is very striking when this tympanum at Chartres
is compared with older versions of the Last Judgment at St. Denis
and Laon, although these comparisons would have more point if we
still had the two examples which came between Laon and Chartres,

those at Corbeil and Sens. The really unusual feature of this tympanum, however, is the prominence given to the two intercessors. They are made as large as Christ himself, and introduce into these awe-inspiring proceedings a note of mercy which would not be lost upon those who passed beneath. The cult of the Virgin was particularly directed to the end of obtaining mercy, and it is perhaps no accident that she sits here on the right of Christ in a very similar posture to that which she adopts in the north transept portal when she receives the crown of Heaven; as though the recollection of her eminence inspired confidence in the power of her intercessions.

On the lintel below Christ is the archangel Michael who divides the saved on the left (west) from the damned on the right; and each group is shepherded toward its eternal destiny by angels emerging from the shadows beneath the tympanum. The scenes on the lintel actually spill over into the lower voussoirs [fig. 66]. It is there on the left that we see Abraham with the souls of the blessed in his bosom; while on the right five rather disconsolate little souls are being returned to the jaws of hell which they seem to have escaped, and into which their companions in despair are being tumbled. The devils presiding over these operations are conceived in the most lurid and melodramatic forms. There is no doubt that medieval imaginations were stirred much more readily by the task of representing the powers of evil than those of good. At any rate, they found it easier, for in every case of a Last Judgment portal the scenes of damnation are depicted with a fervour and power born of conviction, whereas the scenes of beatitude are presented in a perfunctory and conventional way.

Above the scenes of the blessed and the damned on the voussoirs we see the bodies of the dead rising from their graves, their hands clasped, summoned by angelic trumpeters. All the rest of the voussoirs are given up to the nine choirs of angels which constitute the hierarchy of the heavenly host. These are placed in successive rows of voussoirs: Seraphim and Cherubim in the innermost row; Thrones and Dominations in the second; Powers and Principalities in the third; Powers again and Virtues in the fourth; and finally Angels and Archangels. Thus the whole company of Heaven is represented at the court of Christ.

As we have said, the apostles who formerly figured in scenes of the Last Judgment were transferred to the jambs where they have their place in an expanded version of the Vision of St. John. No less than the Last Judgment, the traditional presentation of the Vision was irrevocably altered in its new setting. The four Beasts, which were perhaps the most characteristic of the Apocalyptic images, have gone; and so, at least for a time, have the twenty-four Elders. (They were to re-appear later on the piers of the adjacent porch.) To compensate for these losses, the significance of Christ and the apostles becomes at once clearer and more profound.

Unlike the St. Anne in the corresponding portal of the north transept, which was an afterthought, the Christ on the trumeau here is a true focal point for the whole design [fig. 73]. This benign figure was one of the most inspired inventions of the Chartres iconography. It was in effect a new conception of Christ—Christ as the *Beau Dieu*, the source of man's beatitude, who tramples underfoot all the manifold forms of evil. In line of descent, the Beau Dieu derives from the triumphant figure of the Vision of St. John; but emotionally he is as far removed from the Christ of the Portail Royal as the latter was from the Christ of Moissac. Here, he has stepped down from the tympanum, as it were, into the midst of the congregation passing into the cathedral. The change is important, for it places him between the faithful and the Last Judgment on the tympanum, so that he seems to assume the role of Christ the Mediator. The tone is no longer that of the traditional Apocalypse. Rather, it is that of Psalm 91, to which an explicit allusion is made in the lion and the dragon under the feet of Christ. It is as though he were saying to those on whom he bestows his benediction: "A thousand shall fall beside thee, and ten thousand at thy right hand; but it shall not come nigh thee. Yea, with thine eyes shalt thou behold and see the reward of the ungodly." It is perhaps no accident that the benefactor whose donations financed the windows of the south transept, should have had himself depicted in the performance of his act of piety "under the shadow of the Almighty."[4]

This new conception of Christ was appropriately expressed in a new form. It was the first statue of Christ in cathedral sculpture to be carved in the round. The type was to prove extremely popular. Paris, Amiens, Reims and Bourges each acquired its own Beau Dieu, in some cases even without the apostles which are strictly complementary.

The apostles at Chartres are arrayed along the jambs of the portal, six on either side [figs. 67, 68]. As in the corresponding portal of the north transept, the jambs made provision for only eight statues. There was never any question of restricting the number of the apostles, however. The two outer statues on each side were placed, like

---

[4] Peter of Dreux, Duke of Brittany.

Melchizedek and St. Peter, against the wall between the portal and the buttresses that divide the portals from one another. They were re-arranged slightly when the porches were built.

When we compare these statues with those of the Virgin portal, the monotonous regularity of their postures, the uniformity of their draperies, and the absence of any strong individuality or emotion in their faces, are apt to seem even more striking. Considered one after the other at close hand, they are undeniably uninspired. But equally there is no doubt that they were never primarily intended to be considered in this way. It is as a group, as the apostles altogether, that they make their effect; and the best place from which to see them is some little distance back; where their serried ranks can be seen converging on the Christ of the trumeau. Their shortcomings then seem irrelevant, or even transformed into virtues.

Nevertheless, they also reward closer attention, especially their attributes and the little figures under their feet. First on the west side is St. Peter. Unlike the other statue of St. Peter on the north transept, there is no allusion to his special place at the head of the papacy. He is attired in exactly the same way as the other apostles; and carries the keys, the symbol of the mission entrusted to him by Christ, and the cross on which he was martyred. Next to St. Peter is St. Andrew, his brother, who also carries a martyr's cross. The figure beneath his feet has been identified as Egias, the proconsul of Achaia, who ordered his execution. Then come St. Thomas and St. Philip, both carrying swords which are again symbols of their martydom, and both standing on the pagan kings who were responsible for the deeds: the king of Hieropolis in the case of St. Philip, and the king of India in the case of St. Thomas. Likewise, St. Matthew is coupled with the king of Ethiopia who was supposed to have had him put to death. Finally, St. Simon, standing between the central and western portals, is shown once more with a sword and yet another malignant pagan at his feet.

On the eastern side, the series proceeds in precisely the same way. St. Paul, slightly bald and carrying a sword, stands over the emperor Nero. St. John the Divine, the only one to be shown without a beard and with slight variations in his dress, holds a book containing his writings in one hand, and what is thought to have been a palm branch in the other. Under his feet crouches Aristodemus, the priest of Diana at Ephesus. Next come the two SS. James: first St. James the Great, with a sword and a pilgrim's pouch slung over one shoulder which is embroidered with scallop shells—the badge worn by pilgrims who travelled to his shrine at Compostela; and St. James the Less, holding the fuller's club by which he was beaten to death. The former is coupled with his persecutor Herod Agrippa; and the latter with one of the Jews who began to stone him. Next to these comes St. Bartholomew who at one time held the knife by which he was flayed alive at the order of a prince of Armenia. The latter duly appears under the apostle's feet. And last of all St. Jude or Thaddeus, the inseparable colleague of St. Simon whom he faces across the portal: he carries a book representing his epistle, and tramples on one of the sixty priests of Sannyr who, according to the legend, procured his death.

There is clearly one over-riding idea running through these images. The apostles are shown in triumph over their earthly adversaries. With the exceptions of St. Peter and St. John these adversaries were the agents of their several martyrdoms, which in Christian eyes were deeds of wickedness and folly matched only by their futility. For all the suffering that was inflicted upon the apostles failed utterly to impede their divine mission. Their victory over death at once ensured and foreshadowed the ultimate victory of the church. By endowing them with the attributes of martyrs the sculptors of Chartres turned the apostles of the Apocalypse into archetypes of all the martyrs and confessors who were to become the heroes of the church, an idea which they amplified in the two supporting portals. In this way they transformed the Vision of St. John into a vision of the Church Triumphant. One calls to mind the words of St. Paul in the Epistle to the Hebrews: "But ye are come unto mount Sion, and unto the heavenly Jerusalem, and to an innumerable company of angels, to the general assembly and church of the firstborn, which are written in heaven, and to God the Judge of all, and to the spirits of just men made perfect, and to Jesus the mediator of the new covenant . . ." (Hebrews 12, 22 *seq.*). The change is very characteristic. Here, again, they started from an idea that had been used in the Portail Royal, and gave it a new and wider interpretation. We may regret the passing of the Beasts, and we can hardly deny that by the end of the XII century they belonged to an out-moded imagery. They stemmed from the exotic and bizarre language of Revelation as literal, reverent and naive transcriptions. The new version is perhaps less colourful, but it reflects a more profound, or at least more rational understanding of the Biblical text. And as with content, so also with form. The transcendence of earlier times has yielded to a spirit of Christian humanism which infects the sculpture to an extent far beyond the discreet manifestations of the Portail Royal.

WILHELM VÖGE

Pioneers of the Study of Nature around 1200—[1910][1]

I

French sculpture of the thirteenth century is a field of study as yet barely touched by stylistic criticism. In Germany, those concerned with matters of attribution have shunned it. This is partly due to the erroneous view that artistic individuality is rarely found in the full flower of Gothic art. France, on the other hand, has never shown much interest in stylistic criticism or questions of style (these overlap in medieval research). There, interest in iconography is dominant. The most important French work about developed Gothic, that of Mâle's,* is an iconographic study. André Michel's interests and talents also lie essentially in this direction. How well he interprets the iconography of the transept statues of Chartres and recreates the subtleties of medieval character portraiture! But he tells us little about the flourishing of style, or the participation of the leading workshops, or the individual masters; and he does not mention what others have said.[2]

The French have certainly been willing to make attributions in the field of medieval *architecture*.[3] The figures of individual architects appear in light silhouette: Jean d'Orbais, Pierre de Montereau, Jean Langlois. While one might therefore be more inclined to view the history of thirteenth-century architecture from the standpoint of its artists, the facts are scarce. It is remarkable how much knowledge can sometimes be drawn from so few words (for instance about Pierre de Montereau).[4]

---

[1] This essay is based on an inaugural lecture delivered at the University of Freiburg i. Br. in 1910, at which time Part 1 was more elaborate and documented with source material. The latter will be cited elsewhere. [Note: This essay originally appeared in the *Zeitschrift für bildende Kunst*, N. F., vol. 25, 1914, pp. 193–216; the translation, by Mrs. Barbara Chabrowe, does not attempt to reproduce the style of the original.—Ed.]

* E. Mâle, *L'Art religieux du XIIIᵉ siècle en France*, Paris, 1898 [Ed.].

[2] André Michel, *Histoire de l'art*, vol. 2, pt. 1, pp. 125 ff.

[3] P. Bénard, Anthyme Saint-Paul, Eugène Lefèvre-Pontalis, Louis Demaison, and Marcel Aubert are among the serious, cautious scholars who have made attributions to individual medieval architects.

[4] Only since we learned from Henri Stein that Pierre de Montereau was the rebuilder of the nave and transept of the abbey church of St.-Denis, have we been able to see that the St.-Chapelle in Paris was wrongly

Unfortunately, hardly a line of importance survives about the great *sculptors* of the thirteenth century.[5]

Was Jean de Chelles, who is attested by an inscription on the south transept of Paris Cathedral, the sculptor of the portal as well? Sculptor and architect were not infrequently, I believe, one and the same person in the early and mature stages of the Gothic style.[6] But perhaps we will never dare attach the names of the architects to particular statues and reliefs of portals, façades, and so forth—that is to say, the great sculptors will remain nameless,[7] and hence more obscure than the great medieval Italian artists such as Niccolò and Giovanni Pisano and Arnolfo di Cambio. And without signatures and documents, the *oeuvre* of the French masters must also remain hazy and marginal for us. Only rarely will we be able to separate related works, for example the *oeuvre* of the teacher from that of the pupil.[8] We would not even be able to separate the Pisani from one another if we did not have documents, charters, and signatures, which sometimes provide absolute authentication.

Thus, the matter of inadequate documentation is far from unimportant when the personalities of the individual artists are so unclear. But we are also to blame. So far, we have dealt too superficially with

---

attributed to him and that, more likely, the lovely court chapel of St.-Germain-en-Laye was his creation. See Anthyme Saint-Paul, *Bulletin monumental*, 1906, p. 302, n. 1, and 1901, p. 91.

[5] Although we have diverse information concerning the sculpture of this period, it hardly adds anything to the question of stylistic criticism.

[6] Without the assumption of a union between architecture and sculpture at decisive moments of the development, the character and development of sculptural style in France would simply be incomprehensible. Franck-Oberaspach's opinion (*Repertorium für Kunstwissenschaft*, 1900), according to which one would have to accept a systematic separation between sculptors and architects (as the carriers of structural knowledge), is not tenable, although some new literature seems to be in favor of it (*Bulletin monumental*, 1902, pp. 219 ff).

[7] We will be concerned with the many sculptors, some highly important and even gifted, who worked on the transept façades of Chartres Cathedral. Maître Berthaud is the only one whose name we know. But he made only a few small repairs on a pier of the north porch, which was restored in 1316. The two small reliefs with David and Goliath may perhaps be attributed to him. See Eugene Lefèvre-Pontalis, "Les architectes et la construction de la cathédrale de Chartres," *Mémoires de la Société nationale des Antiquaires de France*, ser. 7, vol. 4, 1905.

[8] The problems of the west façade of Notre-Dame in Paris (left and central portals) are unusually great for stylistic criticism [See now W. Sauerländer, "Die kunstgeschichtliche Stellung der Westportale von Notre-Dame in Paris," *Marburger Jahrbuch für Kunstwissenschaft*, vol. 17, 1959—Ed.].

these medieval men; we do not know them. We must not reproach
them with being nonpersonalities or personalities of too vague a
nature without, as it were, having seen them.

"Nothing," we are told, "differentiates Italian art of the Middle
Ages from the High Gothic of the north as profoundly as the appearance of artistic personalities and the individual transformation of the
basic style of the time in their works."[9] In France, as well, where the
"basic style" changes significantly, the decisive steps taken by the
leading personalities are still perceptible today, both in architecture
and in sculpture. Painting played no role in this, as it did in Italy.

At the turning points, at the highs of the development, extraordinary
works emerge, original works, which express the new in the clearest
way and, at the same time, reflect those which precede and tower
over them, striking the finest spiritual note. Usually, such leading
works, in sculpture and architecture, are surrounded by minor ones,
"shopworks," that depend on them for models.[10] In the places where
significant stylistic trends originate, the traces of important masters
are recognizable. We may assume that it was *they* who gave the
period its character.[11] There can be no possibility of the omnipotence
of the "school." The relationship between school and master was a
mutual one, just as in later periods. Using the school as a footing, the
pioneering master prepared new, untrodden paths.

Yet the medieval outlook[12] and the French psyche prevented a
onesided domination by the individual. The community of large
workshops together with the sociability that was peculiar to the
French character produced a balancing and leveling effect. But one
must not confuse a tendency toward individualism with individual
talent.[13] The tendency toward individualism was far weaker in France
than in Italy, despite the fact that expressions and symptoms of artists'
self-consciousness were not wholly lacking.[14]

[9] *Repertorium für Kunstwissenschaft*, vol. 27, p. 89.
[10] The master who created the upper parts of the Virgin Portal on the
west façade of Paris, and who was perhaps the first to make Paris famous
as an artistic center, seems to have been surrounded by pupils, imitators,
and successors, both in and around Paris.
[11] E.g., the so-called "Head Master" of the west portals of Chartres, who
was mentioned in the previous note (see Vöge, *Anfänge des monumentalen
Stiles im Mittelalter*, Strasbourg, 1894). About the Rémois Master of the
Peter and Paul, see below.
[12] Alfred v. Martin, *Mittelalterliche Weltanschauung*, Munich and Berlin,
1913.
[13] See Bernhard Schmeidler, *Italienische Geschichtsschreiber des 12. und
13. Jahrhunderts*, Leipzig, 1909, pp. 69 ff.
[14] See my remarks in the *Zeitschrift für christliche Kunst*, 1903, p. 368,
about the most delightful expression of this kind (Belgium).

The leveling influence of collaboration is certainly perceptible in the large workshops along with a certain coarseness that accompanies mass production, especially in long, drawn-out programs, in sculpture meant to be seen from afar, and in similar instances. On the other hand, in the large workshops, one sees masters with different approaches competing with one another. Indeed, one perceives profound contrasts of temperament and talent in artists who have worked side by side for years, in the shadow of the self-same wall! In sculpture, one discovers distinctive talents in the orbit of a single workshop. On one side there are deeply serious men, discoverers and rediscoverers of the individual, men who strive for form; and on the other side are the great masters of style, the monumental-decorative, the linear. They stand side by side, just as Donatello stood next to Ghiberti in the early Quattrocento.

I can identify one of these realistic minds on the transept façade of Chartres Cathedral and can isolate one of his larger works: the "Master of the Kings' Heads." A second one, similar to him, worked at Reims. Both belong to the very early thirteenth century. Both stand out sharply from their workshop companions. Both are, so to speak, born sculptors. Both stand outside their time in that only a later period (one of free-standing sculpture) could have allowed their genius to mature fully. And both seem to have had a similar fate: we do not find them in the front rank; they did not work on main portals, but only on side entrances.[15] Other masters, the virtuosi of line, shine on the main portals. It was to them that the age gave the laurels. Furthermore, a few leading builders may be concealed among them—namely, the architect-sculptors.[16]

The fact that the sculpturally gifted masters were employed on side portals is partly to blame for their remaining unstudied up to the present. How many statues of Chartres Cathedral were cast for the Trocadéro Museum without so much as a single piece by the Master of the Kings' Heads among them! The gifted Rémois, the pioneer of a realistically oriented school, has hitherto been equally ignored. Michel does not mention him.[17] Thus, may I be permitted to say, regarding these two men, that *the most distinct artistic personalities which medieval France produced have not yet been discovered!*

[15] Also the Rémois; see below.
[16] For comparative purposes, one might also think of the architect, Arnolfo di Cambio, and the more severe, linear character of his sculpture.
[17] See *Histoire de l'art*, vol. 2, pt. 1, p. 165.

II

When the Cathedral of Chartres went up in flames in 1194, the west façade, with the old Portal of the Kings, remained standing. The idea may have come up to demolish the façade for the sake of unity in the majestic new structure.[18] But this plan was soon abandoned. Evidently, the hope for a new west façade had already disappeared by the time the plans for the transept façades were worked out. Otherwise the latter would not have been loaded with sculpture, a procedure contrary to tradition, nor would the themes normally reserved for the west façade have been displayed here. Moreover, the "program" of the transept portals was inspired by another west façade— that of Laon Cathedral—whose sculptural cycle of around 1200 was the most recent solution.[19]

Eagerness for the newest and latest was never so great as it was in France at that time. In all creative centers, reports of the new and the most recent must have spread like wildfire.[20]

What stood side by side on the west façade of Laon could be expanded and further developed on the north and south transept façades of Chartres. Both of the latter façades were given three portals each and all six had statues. Never before in Christian times had a school of sculpture been confronted with a task of such scope! The Marian themes (with the statues of the Prophets) were placed on the north side—the female side—and the Christ-Judge with the Apostles on the south. The clarity with which everything is organized and the impressive architectural unity (even in the portal bases, jambs, and

[18] According to Hans Kunze, *Das Fassadenproblem der französischen Früh und Hochgotik*, Leipzig, 1912, p. 31, n. 1: "That the first master counted on the destruction of the old towers is beyond all doubt."

[19] Laon also provided essential stimuli for the architectural organization of the Chartres transept portals; see my remarks in *Repertorium für Kunstwissenschaft*, vol. 27, 1904, pp. 8 ff. and Franck-Oberaspach, *Der Meister der Ekklesia und Synagoge*, Düsseldorf, 1913, pp. 108 ff. In essence, the thesis is that Laon and the north transept of Chartres are closely connected, as was indicated by Bulteau, *Monographie de la cathédrale de Chartres*, vol. 2, pt. 1, pp. 125 ff. A detailed explanation of the relationship, including the church at Braine, is urgently needed.

[20] That is the reason, for example, why influences from the west façade of Paris (which had been completed in the meantime) appear soon afterwards in the south porch of Chartres. See below.

profiles of the cornices)[21] testify that everything grew out of one plan.[22]

We do not have a fixed date for the portals. Only the outside steps are mentioned, and not before 1210;[23] but the work on the portals probably goes back further.[24] Even at that early time, the influence of its sculpture can already be perceived (in Reims, in the reconstruction of the Cathedral from 1211 on).[25] The statue of St. Anne, however, which has the place of honor on the north façade of Chartres (on the trumeau of the central portal), could hardly have been given this place before 1204. Only then did the Saint's head come into the possession of the Cathedral.[26] but its relations with the west façade of Paris[27] and its influence in Germany (upon Magdeburg and Strasbourg) also oblige us to push forward the date of the *oeuvre* of this

[21] The profiles of the portal moldings on the north as well as on the south sides and the articulation of the posts on the main and side portals are *graduated in the same way!* It is equally strange that the columns on the outermost flanks (on the outer jambs of the side portals, far left and far right) are strikingly related to each other on the north as well as on the south sides, while differing from all the other columns. There, the fluting shows a slighter groove and a flatter bulge. The foliage, in which the fluting terminates, is always very simple and consists (in part) only of scales receiving the flutes. This can be seen on the right portal on the south side (outer jamb) and on the left one on the north (also the outer jamb).

[22] The tendency toward a unified treatment of the entire structure is very strong at Chartres. H. Kunze made several appropriate remarks on the subject. This tendency increases in the course of the thirteenth century. It is somewhat characteristic of High Gothic (according to my division of periods, High Gothic begins only about 1225–1230, and is the glass-house type; the history of sculpture definitely demands a period division around the thirties!); that is, the desire of the "leader" to realize his ideas also becomes stronger in incidental details of the decoration and of the miniature motifs (very beautiful ones are to be observed at Reims on the canopies of the transept statues).

[23] See Lefèvre-Pontalis, *op. cit.*, pp. 11 ff.

[24] In my opinion, H. Kunze wrongly assumes the date of 1210 as *terminus post quem* ("but the portals were started soon after 1210").

[25] To mention one: the representation of Job on the Dung Hill (Chartres, Solomon Portal, see below) is repeated in a somewhat watered-down version at Reims on the central portal of the north transept. The Reims is certainly the later one because the scene is transposed into a completely foreign legendlike context. In its overflowing tendril ornamentation, the Reims portal shows almost all the characteristic leaf formations of the large capitals of the choir piers, so that the portal must also be dated in the earlier phase of construction.

[26] *Cartulaire de Notre-Dame de Chartres*, E. de Lépinois and L. Merlet, eds., Chartres, 1863, vol. 1, p. 60, n. 4, 6.

[27] See below, where I will explain them further on the basis of more recent photographs.

younger Chartres School as much as possible. The Master of Magdeburg already knew the sculpture of the marvelous porches, which were placed in front of the transept portals at a later date [figs. 59, 60]. He copied the motif of the so-called Mahaut (of the northern porch),[28] not as early as 1215 but certainly before 1234.[29] The creations of the Strasbourg Master (from the second quarter of the thirteenth century, the date of 1230 having recently been suggested)[30] presuppose that the most beautiful pieces were already in existence on the porches at Chartres.[31] Some of the "celestial beatitudes" from the upper part of the north porch are very closely related to the Strasbourg Ecclesia and Synagoga, a point I will discuss elsewhere.

The project for the porches was therefore not conceived as late as about 1240, as is usually assumed, but rather about twenty years earlier. The date of 1240 has no substance. One can even "feel" the connection between the sculpture of the porches and that of the portals—in the folds [of the garments] (especially in the ruffles of the hems); in the type of heads. The head-ideal of the two leading portal masters lives on in the sculpture of the porches.

III

And now I come to the central portals. The one on the north side, with the Coronation of the Virgin [fig. 61] and especially its tympanum and archivolt statuettes, is a classical example of that stylization which delights in curved lines and seems to have its most important sources in Laon and Sens.[32] At Chartres, one can observe

[28] As A. Goldschmidt has said ("Französische Einflüsse in der frühgotischen Skulptur Sachsens," *Jahrbuch der Königlichen preussischen Kunstsammlungen*, 1899, vol. 4). Yet, on the whole, the work of the Magdeburg Master is more closely related to the sculpture of the Chartres portals than that of the porches and one is almost tempted to trace it back to the portals alone. In my opinion, one must note, above all, the upper parts of the left portal on the north side, especially the Wise and Foolish Virgins and their drapery motifs (particularly the hems). Yet, the motif of the Mahaut is nowhere to be encountered on the portals. See also a capital of the Chartres porch copied in Magdeburg, as R. Hamann has pointed out. (R. Hamann and Felix Rosenfeld, *Der Magdeburger Dom*, Berlin, 1910, fig. p. 91).

[29] For the dates, see the thorough investigation by Hamann and Rosenfeld, *op. cit.*, pp. 140 ff.

[30] *Zeitschrift für christliche Kunst*, vol. 25, pp. 97 ff.

[31] Already recognized by Franck-Oberaspach, *op. cit.*, who discovered the relationships.

[32] Something that can be investigated in the larger context of the history of style.

in some Prophets' heads in the central portal how the masters of this
tendency wove their beautifully fluid lines into head types. These
heads were not all made by the Master of the Coronation tympanum
and the archivolt statuettes. Only the four statues of the right jamb
are his.³³ Figure 64 shows [some] of these heads with their semicircular, gently bulging foreheads, their curvilinear brows, lids, and
cheek folds, the flowing lines of their beards, the arched contour of
Isaiah's face [on the left], and so on.³⁴

The principal Master of the south façade, who created the central
portal with the Last Judgment [fig. 65], was not averse to beautiful
lines either. But his line is less fluid and flows more calmly. He is
more reserved, more austere, sometimes tightening the vertical folds
of the long garments of his Apostles (on the jambs; see especially
James the Elder, right) in a way which cannot be found anywhere
in the north portal. The Last Judgment Master [fig. 93] is not as
flexible in his language of *form*. To see this, one need only contrast
the slender, supple Virgin of the Coronation [fig. 94] with the more
heavily built Virgin of the Last Judgment [fig. 93] and compare their
faces—the peculiar, motionless oval face of the south Virgin with the
more animated, slimmer one of the Coronation. Notice also the
former's large, somewhat fixed eyes (with straight lower lids) and
its somewhat square though touchingly demure mouth, and the
latter's more alert eyes and sharp, talkative corners of the mouth.³⁵

³³ There is even more feeling for rhythm and flow of line in the right-
hand statues (Isaiah, Jeremiah, Simeon, John the Baptist). Note the beards
and hair in the left-hand statues, and the type of heads in general. The
wrinkles on the foreheads of the left statues (David, Samuel, Moses) are
very finely chiselled; that is, they do not quite have their full effect as
lines. On some of the left statues, the hairline is strangely pointed (Moses,
Abraham), something that cannot be found on the right side or in the
tympanum or archivolts. This contrast, which I found only after repeated
comparisons, could be followed up further. It is uncertain whether a pair
of the archivolt statues on the left side (Jesse, Moses) are by the Master
of the Abraham and David statues.
³⁴ It is unfortunate that in these older centers (Sens, Laon) it should
be the heads that are destroyed. A pertinent example of the stylization of
the beautifully fluid line of a head is offered by a bearded head in Sens
(formerly in the Archiepiscopal Museum). This head could well come from
one of the Apostles from the west façade of Sens Cathedral (central
portal). This is further suggested by the calm gaze and the lowering of
the eyes, external characteristics of the stylistic phase of Laon-Sens, which
brought about the dissolution of archaic tenseness both in the wrinkles
and in the expression of the heads. [This may be the head reproduced by
W. Sauerländer, *Von Sens bis Strassburg*, Berlin, 1966, fig. 35.—Ed.]
³⁵ In addition to the Virgin's head [fig. 94], the capital should also be
noted.

The Master of the Judgment is more ceremonial, more rigid in his overall composition (consider the sharply raised arms of the Christ-Judge in contrast to the calmer, more relaxed figure giving the blessing in the Coronation).[36] The gravity of the composition demands a strong accentuation of the central axis.[37] This emphasis is complemented by vertical lines on the sides, and even by the fluting on the seats of the throne. The Master of the Coronation, on the other hand, relates the seats vigorously to one another by means of horizontal moldings (he is less heavy in his profiling).

The rigid arrangement of attributes is striking in the Apostles of the Judgment Portal, which, as I have said, are by the same Master who did the tympanum, or by his shop. The spirit of Chartrain archaism is still alive in the principal Master of the south side, or comes to life again like sap from a root. The archaic straight stance, with the feet pointed uniformly downward, is also symptomatic. This does not occur in the Prophets of the north side. Though they, too, are archaic enough, they stand in a more relaxed way with a trace or reminiscence of heaviness. As was mentioned before, the style of the Coronation was inspired by Laon. Its program also stemmed from there. With the Master of the Last Judgment, one might almost think of connections with Paris (west façade of the Cathedral). At the beginning of the thirteenth century, a new austere style in sculpture emanated from Paris. But the Paris influences—which had already come to Chartres from the *central* portal of Notre Dame—are first clearly evident in the sculptures of the south *porch*.

It is very strange that the imaginative, spirited architects of the porches [figs. 59 and 60] should have adopted for their architecture the keynote of the central portals of the north and south sides. The north porch has the more supple rhythm of the Coronation built into it; the south porch has the more ceremonial verticality of the Judgment. The system of arches on the north porch is more complex, as is the articulation of the supports, but its vertical lines were not supposed to appear too rigid. The ingenious artist edged them with the large statues and with the irregularly-stepped candelabralike pedestals underneath. The effect is now spoiled because most of the statues are missing. The severe architectonic line was also muted above; a triple row of reliefs and fine-leaf filigree borders the front edge of the barrel vault. In the south porch, the entire sculptural decor is more severe architecturally; it was not supposed to be exuberant. The edge of the barrel vault is marked off and the surfaces,

[36] The subject matter does not explain anything. Rather, the Last Judgment is done violence by the rigid alignment of the Saved and the Damned.
[37] It emphasizes the figure of St. Michael below.

not covered by agitated tracery, emerge plainly. Statues decorating the piers of the porch were renounced. The straight lines of the verticals were meant to prevail. And they are carried upward by steep pilasters which then continue in the columns of the crowning canopies—indeed in a columniation of the whole façade [fig. 60]! On the north front, this is not employed.

Thus, the vertical rigidity of the Last Judgment resounds throughout the whole south façade. Just as the west portal sculptures took up the severity of the architectonic line at the very start of the work, so too something of the severity of the sculpture flows back into the building here. It is a circle that shows us how sculpture and architecture were merely parts of one and the same body in the Middle Ages.

As has been indicated, the more static, rigid character of the Judgment Master is also to be found in his character types. Figure 67 shows several of his Apostle heads. There are no semicircular foreheads bulging out as on the Prophets [fig. 64]. The Apostles' foreheads are carved in straighter lines; the cheeks are sometimes framed by the beard in a peculiarly square way; and the brows really slant in tense lines. The lower lid of the eyes is often almost straight—something that is even more noticeable in the softer Parisian style of the early thirteenth century, where the drapery is also straighter.

In Paris, this straight line of the lower lid helps bring about a particular sweetness, a French one. This lid, together with the smile, first appears in Paris.

The head-ideal of the Apostle statues can also be seen very well in Abraham with the Souls, on the portal archivolts. It can be found again in other archivolt statuettes which, in addition, reveal the spirit of the Master in the garments and monumental pose. He places the "statuettes" on the arches in rigid frontality. Not infrequently, the Coronation Master turns them toward the center (toward the tympanum) or even shows them in contrapposto.

Thus, despite the poor preservation of the upper parts, one may, with some assurance, attribute the whole sculptural decoration to the Master of the Judgment and his workship.[38]

Where the decorative-monumental forms are concerned, one can-

[38] It seems that in the Middle Ages the larger sculptural cycles were not infrequently divided up by portal, although that was not a fixed rule (see below about Reims). This separation of the collaborating masters contributed to their feeling of independence. It was in the medieval tradition to leave the executor on his own up to a point. Still, as has been said, the tendency to preserve the unity of the whole appears to have been strong at Chartres.

not do justice to his talent when one stands close to the works. One has to step back, stand in front of the porch, and look at the sculpture with half-closed eyes, in order to feel the effect of the whole.[39]

IV

How monotonous these Apostle heads are [figs. 67, 68]! They are minor variations on one type. Of course, the artist had a certain range even in his simplicity; this is proven by the heads of the holy people, such as Christ (also the one on the trumeau) and the Virgin. Here, the type is intensified and transfigured, softer in line and full of other-worldliness, full of soul [fig. 93].[40]

But the form is never thoroughly realized. This is also generally true of the Coronation Master and, very noticeably, of the leading Parisian, the Master of the Virgin portal at Notre-Dame. The impulse toward nature was a timid one in these "leaders" of 1200. In their mastery of form, they did not go beyond, or much beyond, the late twelfth century; among the later works on the old west façade of Chartres, for example, are some that could overshadow them.[41] They certainly brought life to their works, especially the heads; but they are general, typically French, as the Parisian heads show quite clearly, and the undercurrent of tradition can always be felt. "It is the hour

[39] The artist who created the left portal of the north façade is close to the Judgment Master. Note especially the heads of the statues to the left of the doorway and the three statues on the right jamb. We meet identical types in the archivolts of this left portal (compare to the head with the hood on the extreme left side of the archivolts in the lowest row). It appears that here, too, just *one* master (and his shop) worked on the portal. Realistic elements can be seen, particularly on the door frame and in some of the archivolt statuettes. But this realism is more a matter of large mouths and noses than of anything profound. A distant but kindred spirit of the Judgment Master is the artist who worked on the left portal on the north side; see below. The statues of the porches, especially "St.-Ferdinand" (Bulteau, *op. cit.*, p. 252), clearly show the survival of the head-ideal of the Apostles on the Judgment Portal. Only eight of these stand on the actual portal jambs. Were the remaining four, on the colonnettes at the left and right of the portal, added only when the porches were built, or did the sculptural decoration originally extend to the colonnettes between the portals? The four Apostles on the colonnettes are strangely close in style to those on the portal jambs. Perhaps the construction of the porches was started with the completion of the statue cycles of the two main portals.

[40] I admit to having underestimated the expressiveness of these Chartres figures (*Repertorium für Kunstwissenschaft*, 1901, pp. 3 ff.).

[41] Some sages' heads, in the cycle of the Arts in the archivolts of the right side portal, have strikingly realistic wrinkles.

of enchantment when, approaching nature and life with a care that is still apprehensive and with a virginal shyness, art gently takes hold," says André Michel.[42]

But the whole generation of 1200 in France was not that timid, not that lacking in vigor. In addition to the lofty-minded masters of line, there were bolder sculptors, as was mentioned above, more serious searchers after *form*. And one of them, the Master of the Kings' Heads, can still be traced in Chartres itself.[43]

France was a leader not only in the articulation of monumental line but also in the discovery of realism. It is not surprising that the first men to seek form were masters of statuary—sculptors. Sculpture creates form and molds bodies.[44] The great sculptors often arrived at an understanding and a detailed realization of form earlier than contemporary painters, even before Donatello. Alberti seems to have suspected that this was already the case in the Middle Ages.[45] Just as the whole central portal of the south side of Chartres can now be attributed to the Master of the Judgment and his workship, so can the whole Solomon portal (north side)[46] be attributed to the Master of the Kings' Heads.

The Solomon portal, dedicated to Old Testament images, ancestors, prefigurations of Christ and the Virgin, is the counterpart of the portal with the Birth of Christ (north side, left).

Rather high up, at the foot of the archivolts, are those large heads of Kings after which I have named the artist [figs. 78, 80, 81, 83]. These are his masterpieces, the strongest revelation of this ebullient man. They cannot be appreciated from below.[47]

In the six large statues on the jambs, which are certainly by this

---

[42] *Ibid.*, p. 146; mentioned in reference to the Virgin Portal at Paris.

[43] It is strange that Franck-Oberaspach (who rediscovered the connection with Strasbourg) failed to notice the existence of such different spirits side by side at Chartres. Franck was so sure that the extensive shopwork on the Chartres transept was done "according to one and the same rule," that were it not for the large amount of work, one would be tempted to attribute everything to one hand! Chartres appeared to him the citadel of conservative tendencies, even continuing the "idealistic" style of the twelfth century into the thirteenth. He had a one-sided view of certain characteristics of the drapery, i.e., the thinly folded kind which remained in favor at Chartres for a long time.

[44] Although the essence of sculpture (or painting) exists in the final analysis only for the gifted (for the most sensitive natures).

[45] "Et s'o non erre, la sculptura più sta certa che la pictura" ["and if I am not mistaken, sculpture is surer than painting"], says Alberti. He thought that there existed a few passable sculptors even in the artistically incompetent Middle Ages, although the painters were completely laughable.

[46] I call it that for the sake of brevity.

[47] I myself became aware of their magnificence from a scaffold about six

Master and were presumably done before the upper part of the portal, the impulse toward lifelike treatment is still unclear. But the wonderful head of Solomon [fig. 76], immediately to the left of the entrance, is equal in quality to the heads above.

The sculptural ambitions of this Master could not be realized in the small scale of the upper archivolt figures, and so he himself may have had the idea, out of the born sculptor's urge toward the life-sized, of placing large heads there. But these heads are not decorative masks; they belong to the "program" of the portal. Even Bulteau correctly interpreted them as oppressors of the Jews.[48] Whenever they appear, passion and vice are implied. That is manifest.

[Figure 78] shows the first head on the left, a stunning reflection in spirit and form of reality, where suspicion, fear, a tyrant's dull and brutal egoism without grandeur are convincingly expressed. The close-set slit eyes, embedded between forehead and cheekbones and slanting upward and out, are slightly tense, tightened at the lower lid, and accompanied by little wrinkles. They obviously go back to a definite model, like all the rest. It is striking how free the Master is of all schematism in the eyes! We must remember how hesitant even realistic portrait sculptors of the fourteenth century, such as André Beauneveu, are in the representation of the difficult parts around the eyes; they gladly relied on formulas even in portraits from life.

The wrinkles of this immobile, dead forehead [fig. 78] seem to be engraved by life itself. Other sculptors, too, attempted heads which expressed character. The Elizabeth, an old woman's face, on the left portal of the north side [fig. 79][49] may have been admired as a

years ago. The illustrations are from my own photographs made then. I am indebted to M. Mouton, Architect of the Cathedral, who kindly allowed me access to the scaffolding. [Note: some of Vöge's photographs have been replaced by more recent ones.—Ed.]

[48] Though the identification of each one remains uncertain, especially of heads 1 and 4 (counting from left to right). These two heads are at the foot of the outermost archivolt, with the story of Tobias, and are probably Manasseh and Sennacherib. On the left of the adjoining archivolt (second from the outside) is the story of Esther, which gives us the reason for why head 2 [fig. 80] probably has to be identified as Ahasuerus. On the right side of this row (with the story of Judith) should be Nebuchadnezzar [head 3, fig. 81].

[49] By a master close to the Judgment Master, but not identical with him. See note 39, and compare especially certain female types, for example the head of the Virgin from the Visitation group (with the strangely hard mouth, the large eyes with a straight lower lid) and the head of the Virgin from the Last Judgment (fig. 65).

masterpiece of "realistic" treatment by connoisseurs of the time.[50] Yet it is nothing but a play of lines.

Hair and beard meant no more than a play of lines to other artists. But our "realist" sought here and there to free himself from the linear by trying to represent the curls as a sculptural mass. In [figure 78], the small, tight tufts of the beard appear as if dropped on the face, accompanying an apathy of the soul. Look also at the hair of the Moorish king to the right [fig. 83] and at some heads in the tympanum.[51] This Master knew that some of man's character is expressed in his hair and he therefore made use of a striking wealth of nuances, from the fiery to the smoothly combed.

In the second king's head [fig. 80], one can also see the minute observation of nature in the lines around the eyes. Compare the eyes of the first and second heads. There are no tautologies; the contours of the eye are completely different, individual: the line of the lid in the second rises in indignation while the eye itself is less protruding and slightly cushioned—more lifelike.

The beard, in slight disarray, is kept short. Grace of line is not of interest; the treatment is more massive. The mouth is open as if calling—a heroic trait in the cut of the profile. But the front view shows a touch of cowardice.

The momentaneity is significant. As soon as Gothic moves toward realism, it immediately tends also toward the grimace. It seeks form and attains form in movement. This is a prognosis not only for further developments in France (for the realism of the school of Reims), but also for Italy (Giovanni Pisano, Donatello, the busts of the Early Renaissance).

The third head [fig. 81] on the right side of the portal is an antithesis as well as an intensification of the second. It is of a different character. The energetic element now emerges powerfully. The forehead protrudes, as if it were pushed out from the inside, and the bridge of the nose is raised in a similar way. The eyes are wide open and full of anger. The figure represented here is capable of terrible hate and of heroic passions. One feels that there is a new understanding of the structure of form, of the inner coherence of the parts.

And the fourth head [fig. 83] is a marvelous contrast to the third. Here, the mouth, with full lips, is pushed forward; the nose, irregu-

---

[50] That is, first of all, by the artists themselves, as in medieval Italy, where the artists were the best connoisseurs. However, there were enough aesthetically-minded people in France during the Middle Ages, though the indications of this would have to be brought together.
[51] The warrior at the extreme left on the doorframe with the Judgment of Solomon, and so on.

larly fleshy, is depressed; and the forehead is flat as if a band lay about it. Flat, unimaginative brows shade the deep-set eyes, the expression of which is cowardly yet piercing.

The wonderful head of Solomon [fig. 76][52] on the jamb of the portal should be mentioned next. The broad mouth with the strongly protruding lower lip recalls the first king's head [fig. 78]. But in comparing them, differences emerge showing the wealth of lively observation and the rich psychological outlook of which the sculptor is a master. There, the mouth is sullen and stubborn; here, noble and steadfast. Underneath the broad, "bushy" brows, in the portrayal of which the Master is especially inventive, lie almond-shaped eyes which do not rise but slant slightly outward and are pensive (although they will thunder in judgment). The forehead is not deeply lined, only lightly wrinkled, and projects over the brows. It is strangely powerful in its breadth and height, giving a spiritual expression to the broad, energetic, even vigorous face with its strikingly broadened nose. Solomon is meant to be a ruler and a prophet at the same time. Energy flickers in the capricious array of his curls. And his head seems even prouder from below, where one can see how majestically it is carried. The worldliness of these features becomes even more apparent when looked at in relation to those of Sirach. Sirach's features are purely spiritual.

The master depicts Joseph, the interpreter of dreams,[53] as a clever, well-preserved man of rank and limited horizons.[54]

Even though one cannot see it as clearly in the statues of Sirach and Joseph or in the figures of the two women [fig. 76], there is a richness of perception in this Master's work which makes the work of the "leaders" seem pale and empty.

There are also some lifelike heads among the small sculptures above,[55] [figures 82 and 90] show this. In particular, compare [figure 82] with the third king's head ([fig. 81]; note the opening of the

[52] On the left side of the door, to the left of Solomon, is the Queen of Sheba, and to the left of her, Balaam. The three statues of the right jamb are Jesus, son of Sirach (next to the door and opposite Solomon), Judith (in the center), and a young ruler. Bulteau calls the last one Joseph, the Dream-Interpreter (the type of Christ). The representation on the base, a woman to whom a dragon whispers something, might belong to the story of Samson, which is told on the archivolts, though one is hard-put to accept this.

[53] The statue on the extreme right; see the note.

[54] Tiny eyes beneath raised brows, superior but phlegmatic.

[55] Unfortunately, the upper parts (the peak of the tympanum, the upper archivolt figures) are badly weathered, as are the remaining portals. The Cathedral of Chartres is situated on the highest point of the Beauce, thus the wonderful porches could not protect the portals.

mouth!), in order to be convinced of the identity of the sculptor. Types which are harsh and masculine in character predominate. The powerful noses, especially of the tympanum heads, come close to caricature. Like certain realists of the Quattrocento, the sculptor took pleasure in the uncouth and had a preference for the heavy-set. The heads are often too heavy for the body [fig. 86]. Women have hard features and coarse spirits. Masculine seriousness is the basic theme of this work, reaching from the heights of joy to the depths of gloom. This was the keynote of the Master's personality. We are as little surprised by his harshness as we are by those of the conquering artists of the Quattrocento. To conquer has always been a masculine task.

The large heads have already shown us that this fiery artist knew how to depict passion. Passion permeates his interpretation of narrative. The beginnings of a deeper characterization are noticeable. In the representation of Solomon's Judgment on the lintel [fig. 77], one sees the dead child's mother storming against her opponent in violent rebuke. This portrayal, worthy of a poet, is woven into her character. The text says only "But the other said: 'Let it be neither mine nor thine, but divide it.'" The clothing—the sloppiness of the wide, hanging sleeves—is also made to serve the characterization here.

Passion, too, fills the scene of Job's Suffering (on the tympanum). Maliciousness and coldness of heart are showered on Job simultaneously. And in contrast to the liveliness of his gesticulation, the serenity of God the Father at the very top is impressive. But gentle as well as tender traits—and forms—are not entirely lacking in this work either. The loveliness and shyness of young Esther, the gentle circumspection of old age, and the patient waiting of the blind Tobias are expressed in the scenes of the archivolts, which become more sketchy toward the top.[56] The Master possessed a wider psychological range, had greater resonance, saw more sharply and deeply than others.

But if the heads were so much more important than the bodies to this Christian sculptor,[57] and the psychological insight was as important as the form, and the form was primarily a vessel of the soul, must he not have been occupied with specific sculptural problems, such as balance (to the degree this question can arise with statue-

[56] Apart from the innermost row of angels, the second row of archivolts (counting from the inside) depicts the stories of Samson (left half of the archivolt) and Gideon. On the third row are the stories of Esther (left half) and Judith; on the fourth, that of Tobias. See Bulteau, *Monographie*, vol. 2, 1888, pp. 243 ff. The reclining lion (innermost row, left) refers perhaps to Num. 24:9.

[57] The nude body of Job is disappointing and, comparing it with its counterpart at Reims by the Master of the central portal, one might at first glance be inclined to prefer the latter.

columns)? He really did think about this problem. This is proved by
the statue of Solomon, which goes beyond all contemporary work in
the stability and freedom of the stance [fig. 76]. The distance between the feet is as great as the limited space allows. The problem
of contrapposto is touched upon perhaps for the first time in a
Christian statue since Early Christian times. There is an attempt to
project the hip over the more heavily weighted left foot, although
more is suggested by the drapery folds than is actually carried out.
Something else is also noticeable in the drapery. The Master tries to
make the body appear beneath the garment. He intentionally pulls the
thin material of the two tunics in between the legs in single, deep,
channellike folds. The bare space between ankles and knees is made
perceptible to the viewer, who is thus led to feel the shape of the
leg and the volume of the body. The Apostles of the Judgment Master
[figs. 67, 68] and the Prophets on the central portal of the north side
are boardlike in comparison. Solomon's arms are more fully rounded
and his elbows are clearly detached from the body, while those of the
Apostles remain attached. And it becomes evident that his arms have
joints. The left arm is turned upward and the right arm, with the
scepter, downward.

A whole series of the Master's most personal and most beautiful
motifs depends upon this feeling for the function of the wrists. I
speak of the statue of Judith, from the right jamb, where a long scroll
rests on the fingers of her left hand which reaches upward in beautiful
movement, and that of Job [fig. 77], who, scraping the wounds on his
left arm, automatically turns his left hand downward. The hands of
God the Father are calmly bent downward side by side. Both angels
with the sun and the moon, on the innermost archivolt, clasp the
rims of the disks with a beautiful bending of the wrists.[58] The young
Tobias (left archivolt), sitting at the foot of the old man, is resting
his chin on the back of his hand.[59] The "Judith in prayer" [fig. 89,
much reduced] may explain these ingenious, though groping, attempts
to represent arms endowed with joints.[60] Contrast this sculpturally
significant motif of the arm strongly bent back—with a light accentuation of the wrists—with the praying attitude of the Virgin in the
Last Judgment [fig. 93], which is absolutely meaningless sculpturally.

[58] They are the two bottom ones, left and right.
[59] The outermost row of the archivolts, left, sixth scene from the bottom.
[60] From the right side of the archivolts. It is remarkable and, as one
might expect, a testimony to the *Master*'s seriousness, that *this* scene, and
not the bestowal of the jewelry, was chosen. The left arm is broken off;
the motif of the right arm has to do with Judith 9:1 ("and sprinkled ashes
on her head"). Bulteau already said this.

Notice also Joseph's hand holding the scepter, with its emphasis on the knuckles and the stretching of the finger [fig. 87] in contrast to the stiff hands of the Apostles [figs. 67, 68].

Now, consider the following scene: Judith, leaving the town with her attendant, is shown turning her head over her shoulder in a way that is sculpturally highly effective. Here are motifs of which Giovanni Pisano made brilliant use eighty years later with a born sculptor's talent—a feeling for the organic coherence of the body that was rare in Gothic and was stimulated by Antiquity.[61]

Although the Chartres Master was able, in these large heads, to express his sculptural genius successfully and—even for *our* eyes— effectively, he was incapable of indicating sufficiently the stance, movement, and development of the body. The limits set for the Gothic monumental statue were still rigid; the whole species was a parasite. And thus, the figure of Solomon, in which the struggle to make a *statue* is so clear and so moving, is a sculptural failure. The jamb[62] did not provide enough space. The loosening up as well as the more extensive rounding out of the arms could take place only at the expense of the body volume. That is why the figure has such a strangely tied-in waist.

The jamb, with its rigid angle, was more restrictive for this artist, who longed for lifelike qualities, than it was for others. On the right side of the portal, he conceived of the idea of expanding the space by turning the central figure inward, which would, at the same time, introduce a gentle rhythm into the row of statues.[63]

His work is lively and always as rewarding to find as that of later masters. Indeed, we even become interested in the man himself. But with regard to the more serious questions that arise, his aims seem noteworthy even where they are unfulfilled. Therefore, a few more remarks should be added about the treatment of drapery. The linear system of Gothic folds was a snare in which all artists were caught. Donatello's freshness was needed to tear this asunder; Donatello tore up the line out of his urge for form.[64] Yet, with these sculpturally

[61] This is given too little attention. Only because Giovanni knew how to represent movement as a function of the body can he be called a great sculptor and be said to have inspired the sculptors of the Renaissance.

[62] Or the block.

[63] The Joseph statue is now by itself.

[64] The flying cloak, in the scene of Tobias burying the Jew (archivolts, left side), is not only devised as an ornamental animation of an empty spot but also indicates the blowing of the night wind of which the text speaks. The contours are peculiarly melancholy. In the scene where Tobias is leaning over to catch the fish, a flying cloak is again represented, though it is a rare motif in Gothic art.

inclined artists in medieval France, there were already beginnings in this direction—attempts to make the drapery more plastic. It was not the Master of the Kings' Heads, but the slightly later, similarly inclined Master at Reims, the creator of the Peter and Paul statues (now on the north transept of Reims Cathedral), who seriously began to work out this more sculptural view of drapery [figs. 100, 101]. He blurred the linear arrangement of the ridges of the folds, crumpled it, folded the material in and out, entangled it, sought to knead it more than to delineate it. Indeed, certain of his sculpturally conceived drapery motifs—especially the cluster motif—found imitators at Reims.

In the case of the Master of the Kings' Heads, on the other hand, one must look more closely to detect similar things. Line dominates, but nowhere does it run to nought. Ornamental swirling folds are not found on the borders, although these were still favored by the masters of the porches. With his richer psyche, this Master was bound to express more in drapery than the others. He sought to give the curve gravity and weight. There emerged certain heavy, inflated, flamboyant motifs [see also fig. 86], characteristic of this Master but not of others.[65] Sometimes he was capable of the most tender effusions although he was generally much more vigorous than the others [fig. 88]. He was also capable of infusing line with his fire. His rhythms are more interesting; they have pulse.[66] Compare the hem lines on the left side of the Affliction of Job [fig. 91] with similar motifs of other sculptors. [Figure 92] gives a detail of the *left* tympanum on the north; how much duller its rhythms are. Compare the edges of the clouds. Those of the Solomon portal [fig. 88 above] are more animated than those of the Last Judgment [fig. 65]; they lack the latter's monotonous repetition and tedious embroidery. In addition, the surface of clouds by the Master of the Kings' Heads is carved more deeply and is gouged out and is not activated by lines—through engraving—as in [figure 65].

The lines of this Master's folds are also less abstract, because the drapery, particularly of his large statues, is more expressive. Notice the folds blousing above the belt of the Queen of Sheba [fig. 76] and contrast them with the schematic motifs of the "leaders." The wavy movement of the hem does not appear at the bottom of Judith's trailing dress [fig. 84], but the curves are created by a zig-zag movement of the material, which is seen plastically and has clothlike quality. Compare this to the ornamental, snakelike line of the Virgin's

---

[65] See the two lowest Tobias stories (outermost archivolt, left).

[66] Just as Dürer's line has a stronger character than the Late Gothic one from which it is derived.

hem in the Last Judgment [fig. 65] or to the harder, emptier, swirling folds of figures in the Visitation group.

In [figure 84], the animal is also noteworthy, as are the lions in the Samson relief [fig. 85], which can more properly be called the Lions of Atlas (according to H. David).

Unfortunately, I cannot attribute to this Master any works at Chartres except the Solomon portal.* But his influence can be felt in the tympanum and archivolts of the right portal on the south side,[67] which seem to be by the hand of a younger artist.

V

I will only refer briefly to the related Rémois Master. He also combines realistic tendencies with sculptural ones. A sculptural spirit was in Reims, in the air. The Cathedral of Reims, even its architecture, was conceived sculpturally. The accent lies definitely on the exterior,[68] a point which also has to be made about the Cathedrals of Chartres and Laon, the ones most closely related to Reims. (Laon is really the first great manifestation of Gothic "exterior architecture.")

---

* See now W. Sauerländer, "Tombeaux chartrains," *L'Information d'histoire de l'art,* vol. 9, 1964, pp. 47–59 [Ed.].

[67] The manner alone recalls the Solomon Portal, as in the tympanum above, where the half-figure appears over the clouds and between two approaching angels. It also recalls the rich, somewhat rigid types of the young Levites (innermost archivolt). On the archivolts at the left, we encounter a few truly hard king's heads which, in their powerful conception, recall those of the Master of the Kings' Heads. The head of St. Giles, with pensive, deeply embedded eyes, also reflects his spirit. Note, in addition, the manner in which the heavy fold of cloth next to the foot is spread out on the ground, similar to the draperies of Job's wife [fig. 88]. Yet, one still cannot accept him as the artist. The miniature architectural motifs on the canopies and bases of the archivolts do not show any specific relation to those of the Solomon portal. The bases of the canopies by the Master of the Kings' Heads, which serve as plinths to the figural representation of the archivolts, are formed in a strangely heavy and rich manner, probably as a result of the Master's feeling for the unmoving. In this respect, his portal is different from the five others, as are also his socle designs for the large jamb statues. The small, stocky columns, which frame the large heads [figs. 78 and 80] with their heavy bases and their heavy, bulbous capitals, can be seen again further up on the archivolts. It is a characteristically favorite motif of this energetic artist. Characteristic as well of the Solomon portal is the economic use of halos (only God the Father and Jesus, son of Sirach, have them), while on the right portal of the south side, halos are frequent.

[68] See Vöge, "Die Kathedrale von Amiens," *Münchner Allgemeine Zeitung,* July 30, 1902.

But, as I have emphasized once before, Reims also has a broad, calm quality, less tense, less commanding, less Gothic.[69] Therefore, the sculpture on its walls dared to follow its instincts more freely than usual—in two ways. First of all, it resulted generally in an affirmation of plasticity of form as well as in freedom of manner; an Antique fullness and weight. Secondly, it resulted in a realistic treatment of form; a sharpness and fineness of observation, especially in the heads, which, all things considered, is unique in the Middle Ages. But even at Reims, medieval linearism prevailed, except for the Peter and Paul Master; like all other Gothic schools of sculpture, the one at Reims ended in the linear manner.

At the peak of the Reims development, around the middle of the thirteenth century, the most beautiful combinations of linear and portraitlike treatments appeared.[70] Note the head of the youthful Prophet [fig. 98].[71] Although linear, it is based on an understanding of the structure of form. The profile is both expressive and elegant.[72] Even more sensitively felt is the head of the old French woman [fig. 99]. The sympathetic line of the profile and of the lower part of the face have an almost Early Renaissance intimacy, even though it was not meant to be a bust. The head is that of a statue of St. Anne, which stands, among many other statues of saints, rather high up in the niches on the inside of the west wall of Reims. They can hardly be seen from below and are never appreciated. Furthermore, the head of St. Anne does justice to its monumental and decorative function in the way in which it is set off and framed by the sharp lines of the folds [of the head covering]. Voll said,[73] "Medieval art shapes one saint just like any other. . . ." How unfair he is toward these Rémois masters of 1250! In their urge toward realism, in their realistic mood, they occasionally forget all iconographic etiquette: there are heads of Prophets of an earthy ugliness (the Prophet cycle on the south rose of the Cathedral).

It is true, however, that the realistic attitude then reigning in

[69] *Repertorium für Kunstwissenschaft*, 1904, pp. 1 ff. and *Münchner Allgemeine Zeitung*.

[70] Among other things, the head of Joseph on the central portal of the west façade belongs here.

[71] According to a cast in the possession of the sculptor, Coutin, of Reims, who kindly gave permission for the photograph. The original is in the interior on the west wall of the Cathedral.

[72] The medieval artists were generally masters of profile because of their gift for line. Among the Early Gothic sculpture at Reims is a whole series of heads which have a personal quality in their profile, but which are of a type and lack true form when seen frontally, as, for example, the angels between the windows of the choir chapels.

[73] *Die altniederlaendische Malerei*, Leipzig, 1906, p. 23.

several Rémois workshops was shared by only a few forceful artists during the early period of construction. It is the Master of Peter and Paul (on the north side of the Cathedral) who must be considered the true pioneer. His concern for form, like that of the Master of the Kings' Heads, originated in a truly sculptural spirit. Soon after the start of construction (1211), we find this sculptural genius[74] in opposition to a group of masters of line who are far behind him in the mastery of form. The large "formless" heads on the statues of the central portal—in the place of honor on the north side![75]—best show this [figs. 102, 103]. "How monotonous these heads are" is a phrase that can also be used here. It is as if the same head were repeated.

We know dozens of heads by this Master of the central portal. He, it seems, together with his shop, made almost the whole, vast sculptural decoration of this wide double portal.[76] Endlessly, he returns to his slit eyes with their hard, slightly curved lids. He is certainly one of those rare medieval artists that might be called "otognostic"

[74] Apparently, his two Apostles were originally made for the right portal of the west façade (first project). So were the four others (the bases on the left side have been reworked!), as well as the equally archaic Prophets now standing on the far right of the right portal of the west façade, which go back to the figures on the north transept at Chartres, and which belonged on the central portal (west façade). We may imagine the oldest sculptural cycle for the Reims west portals by referring to the cycle at Laon, at least to the extent that the original plan called for the Reims Last Judgment (with six Apostles) on the right portal and the Virgin theme (Coronation of the Virgin) with the Prophets in the central portal.

[75] Recently, Hans Kunze (*op. cit.*) claimed that this central portal was the main portal for the old west façade. This clever thesis can hardly be maintained as it stands because the central portal and the Apostles and Prophets cannot be considered parts of a unified façade project (the oldest one). Nor could the Prophets and Apostles have been opposite each other on the two *side* portals of the west façade, because the Prophets are considerably larger than the Apostles. The Prophets were originally planned for the central portal, a point to which I will have to return later.

[76] Perhaps single pieces are to be excepted. The archivolt figures strikingly show the stamp of the same style just as the large jamb statues do. The peculiar, flat depressions on the forehead (as if formed with the finger), parallel to the arch of the brow (on the statues of the Pope and of Eutropia), also occur on the statues in the archivolts as well as those on the large tympanum. The latter is to be attributed entirely to this Master. The Master's head-ideal is echoed in some of the giant statues of the upper story (head of the statue of Eve next to the north rose window; see below). This Master is much more successful in the small heads in the tympanum and in the archivolts of the portal than in the heads of the large portal statues. He does not know how to execute large forms. It is touching how he tries to compensate for his weakness by a wealth of ornament!

[figs. 96 and 97]; the ears [of his sculpture] are made of an undulating line[77] which also plays a part in the folds of the drapery, especially in the often archaic, stiff hems of the tunics [fig. 95]. Unfortunately, at this moment we have nothing from the Peter and Paul Master except for the Apostles, including the statuette on the base of Peter [figs. 100, 101]. But there can be no question of the repetition of a type in these. There is a remarkable wealth of forms in this tiny *oeuvre*. The head of Paul [fig. 101] can hold its own with important Renaissance works, not least of all because of the nobility of its spirit.

The form, too, shows great genius. The eyes, the manner in which they are set and slightly pouched, are absolutely free of beautiful but vacuous linearism. The inner corners are carefully marked; the pouches are somewhat puffy and are set off from both cheek and lower lid (in Peter, they are a little lighter). This motif of the pouches, along with the deep position of the eye, recurs frequently in Rémois sculpture from this time on. Like the sculptural clusters of folds which have already been discussed, it is one of the characteristics of this pioneer's decisive influence. The ear, always a test of sculptural ambition, is surprising for this period. Peter's is more slender and not quite so good, but Paul's shows a beautiful wide curve of the auricle—a thing Michelangelo loved. Only the front view of the head permits one to see that the auricle also projects outward. There are a number of Renaissance busts which are inferior in this respect. Also sculpturally effective is the way the hair lies in tight clusters and the way the bulk of the moustache protrudes more than the beard. The slight lift of the upper lip gives the mouth its resigned look. The Master of the Kings' Heads never created a character of such dignity; the Rémois Master was certainly of a wiser nature!

The Peter [fig. 100] shows definite study of nature: he is more temperamental, with fuller lips; he is a human being more oriented toward life, with a more abrupt forehead, a peculiar, egotistically pointed and protruding nose, and a fleshy cranium. In both heads, the transition from the bridge of the nose to the curve of the brows is particularly good, as is the way in which the peculiarly soft curves of the eyes are surrounded by wrinkles in the Peter.

The hair, voluminous and heavy, lies in small, thick, spiraling curls. A deeply incised groove, not visible in the pictures, divides the beard. The sheer volume of the head is frightening and the vigorous jutting

---

[77] The rim of the conch, drawn into the lobe, forms a loop shaped something like a keyhole.

forward of the chin from the neck contributes to this impression. In the Andrew on the next column, executed by a master of line, the chin is pulled back; the head and the whole figure are flattened, in a plane, as are the hands. The statue of Andrew is one of the finest works of line in this period; one which at first makes one overlook its lack of form because of the delicacy and linearity of its head. The snakelike lines of Andrew's curls seem to be pressed flat almost as in Late Gothic mannerism. The folds of Andrew's garments are similarly pressed one on top of the other; they are limply supple, in low relief, and in round patterns. Both statues, as well as the Paul with its neighbor, should be compared in all their parts down to the unimportant details. The handle of Paul's sword, carved free of the body, was never meant to have a fine, flat coating of fishscales as does that of its neighbor, but was conceived sculpturally and was thus ribbed. The same is true of the scalloped halo. Now, I have already mentioned how the sculptural attitude was vehemently opposed to the linear one, as is particularly noticeable in the treatment of drapery on the two chief Apostles [figs. 100, 101]. The vigorous plasticity of the folds alone, contrary to normal medieval usage, would assure the attribution of both statues to *one* master in this early period. The illustrations do not show everything. The most ruffled parts on the Peter are on the left side of the right sleeve where the cloak seems to be crammed up against the column. But from the extreme right side one can see the agitation in the loops.

One thing more should be said: the Master attempted to "detach" the figure from the shaft of the column. In the case of the Peter, he made a big opening into the stone between the shaft and the figure as if the sculpture were meant to be in the round. Perhaps this very advanced Master thought it was time to break the fetters binding the statues to the walls of the Church.[78] There is a heathen, anti-Christian attitude and a worldliness in all sculpture in the round. This is the reason why the spirit of the Early Renaissance was nowhere more threatening than in the full-round statue.

It is a bit discouraging that we can hardly attribute anything to this noble Master except these two statues. But an unfortunate event took place. The portal, with the six apostles (among them Peter and Paul), was not completed according to the original plan, most likely because the construction of the west façade, for which it was intended, was postponed. The tympanum, archivolts, and Beau Dieu were added only after a lengthy interval, and according to another plan devised

---

[78] In this, he had successors at Reims: the cutting-back of the statue-column is found later in the Visitation Master of Reims (central portal of the west façade).

by a master of different training.[79] Whatever else is extant of the sculpture from the earliest period of Reims, it is not by the Peter and Paul Master.[80]

One must, therefore, look at the somewhat newer, stylistically more advanced[81] sculpture in the upper story of the choir and transept, among the large statues of angels and kings on the buttresses, and among the large heads and masks on the consoles.

The most beautiful of the large statues of kings high up on the transept point, in the final analysis, to the manner of our Master: the so-called Pepin the Short on the south transept [fig. 104],[82] the closely related king with the cluster of folds on his arm,[83] and the most impressive figure, the archetype of the Bamberg Rider.[84] These are, most likely, by younger Masters whose art is rooted in his, rather than his own works.

In the head of Pepin [fig. 104], there is a similar realism and one should compare it with the Peter [fig. 100]. The large, fiery eyes with light shadows beneath, the strange way they lie directly under the brows; the bold arches of the brows and the manner in which they are connected to the bridge of the nose; the full, vigorous lower lip, and even the way the mouth is framed by the beard; everything recalls the Peter.[85] Everything is similar, and, yet, everything is different.

[79] The work of the Beau-Dieu Master, rather voluminous and artistically significant, is equally interesting in that it allows an insight into the development of the artist.

[80] A number of angels standing between the windows of the choir chapels are connected to the art of another very great Rémois, the Visitation Master.

[81] For the most part, at least. I should add a few comments to my remarks about the position these things take in the development of style at Reims (*Repertorium für Kunstwissenschaft*, 1901), but on the whole they are accurate.

[82] It is on the west side of the south transept and is the first one, counting from the south façade.

[83] It is immediately to the right of Pepin the Short, the first one on the south façade; A. Weese, *Die Bamberger Domskulpturen*, fig. 24.

[84] See *Repertorium für Kunstwissenschaft*, 1901, fig. on p. 18.

[85] That the workshops are interconnected cannot be doubted by anyone who views the work of the Reims School in its entirety. Furthermore, there are connections between these large statues of the upper walls at Reims and various other Early Gothic groups of Rémois sculpture. The head-ideal and the schematic treatment of the Master of the central portal survive in the head of Eve (next to the north rose window). Compare this head with those in [figs. 78 and 79] and notice its slit eyes with pointed and slightly curved corners, the bandlike upper lid, the cut of the mouth, and so on. Even clearer, is the relation of the statue of the king on the right of the south rose window (with its rose-curls) to those of several angels of the choir chapels and also to the figures of the Visitation.

Everything is intensified in the King's head and made outwardly effective. It is less robust, but it is intended to appear livelier (High Gothic).[86] The forms are less powerful, but more agitated. The brows and the contours of the cheeks shoot down abruptly. The hair is like a cape in flight. Everything is concentrated on the pathos of the line. Form is sacrificed to line; form is flatter.[87] But the eyes are more deeply set and a stronger shadow is produced. The whole is more agitated and at the same time more rigid. The sculptural spirit has vanished; the decorative-monumental has won out. And effects of distance have been taken into consideration.[88]

Attributing such a change to the Master of Peter and Paul would be permissible only on the basis of a document. But here we remain in the dark.

The problem of the masks is even more elusive. I cite only one [fig. 105],[89] which may be from the Master's hand. It is a piece of astonishing quality despite its decorative treatment. It is badly damaged, like the Pepin. How can one let these exquisite testimonies to the history of French art go to ruin in wind and rain!

[86] See my remark in *Repertorium für Kunstwissenschaft*, pp. 24, 26 ff.

[87] The planar spreading-out of the hair and flattening-out of the beard.

[88] Just as Donatello gave his heads a stronger shadow to make up for greater height, or deepened the eyes, among other things.

[89] From the north transept façade, if I am not mistaken.

6

THE STAINED GLASS

The stained glass of Chartres is almost as varied as the sculpture, but
it has never been studied in the same detail because close-up photographs of all the windows have never been taken. The glass continues
to fascinate people, however, exercising an almost irresistible attraction
on such different personalities as Maurice Denis and Henry Adams.
Denis was a painter and his approach to the glass of Chartres is that
of the intelligent, informed artist. Adams, whose chapters on the glass
are perhaps the most brilliant ever written, approached the windows
as a literary artist.

MAURICE DENIS
[The Splendor of the Windows—1927][1]

What seduces us above all in that art (the art of the thirteenth
century) is its freshness, its candor, its freedom, and its sensitivity,
its love of life. (Color Plate IV)

I would not hesitate to say that what strikes us most in a monument like Chartres is less the perfection than the youthfulness of art.
Elsewhere, Greco-Roman antiquity has left us no models of impec-
cable beauty. Here, we clearly see that the artist must seek that beauty
in life. And it is not a useless lesson, in a complex era such as our
own, to remind artists that one of the essential characteristics of art
is naturalness and spontaneity. * * *

Feeling, even religious feeling, does not make the search for
beauty less necessary. Art is the play of materials, colors, and forms,
with a view to delectation. It was Poussin who said so. It is also the

---

[1] Translated by Robert Branner from a 1927 lecture by Maurice Denis
printed in R. Gobillot, *Hauts lieux de la chrétienté. Chartres*, Tournai,
Casterman, 1947, pp. 162–164.

opinion of Maritain and the scholastic thinkers. And the stained-glass makers of Chartres give us the most beautiful example of it ever known.

In these windows, surely, it is neither the subject—which one sees only after a long look—nor the resemblance of the figures or objects represented that are deeply moving. It is the splendor of the windows that at first charms us like divine music: it is the play of colors, of light, in admirable proportions, that first incites us to prostrate ourselves. Whatever the dogmatic or iconographic meaning of these mosaics in glass, they emit an irresistible charm at first sight, because they are beautiful. Neither do we understand the precise meaning of all the psalms of the religious service, which, all the same, are ravishing, and even ravish us in God because lyricism and poetry, like color, have a magnificent power over the spirit.

Their free sensitivity enchants us, but their art also edifies us; it has frankness, a smiling gravity, a serious conviction of Christianity. From the history of the *Miracles of the Virgin*, we can gain some idea of its sort of faith—neither more nor less than a good Christian of our own time. But it knows that it is the spokesman of Christianity, and the whole world, ancient and modern history, and all visible creations are, for it, disposed according to revealed truth. * * *

HENRY ADAMS
[The Twelfth-Century Glass: The Legendary Windows—1904][1]

The Twelfth-Century Glass

At last we are face to face with the crowning glory of Chartres. Other churches have glass,—quantities of it, and very fine,—but we have been trying to catch a glimpse of the glory which stands behind the glass of Chartres, and gives it quality and feeling of its own. For once the architect is useless and his explanations are pitiable; the painter helps still less; and the decorator, unless he works in glass, is the poorest guide of all, while, if he works in glass, he is sure to lead wrong; and all of them may toil until Pierre Mauclerc's stone Christ comes to life, and condemns them among the unpardonable

[1] From Henry Adams, *Mont-Saint-Michel and Chartres*, Houghton, Mifflin and Co., Boston and New York, 1936, chaps. VIII, IX, by permission of the publishers [Ed.].

sinners on the southern portal, but neither they nor any other artist will ever create another Chartres. You had better stop here, once for all, unless you are willing to feel that Chartres was made what it is, not by the artist, but by the Virgin.

If this imperial presence is stamped on the architecture and the sculpture with an energy not to be mistaken, it radiates through the glass with a light and colour that actually blind the true servant of Mary. One becomes, sometimes, a little incoherent in talking about it; one is ashamed to be as extravagant as one wants to be; one has no business to labour painfully to explain and prove to one's self what is as clear as the sun in the sky; one loses temper in reasoning about what can only be felt, and what ought to be felt instantly, as it was in the twelfth century, even by the *truie qui file* and the *ane qui vielle.* Any one should feel it that wishes; any one who does not wish to feel it can let it alone. Still, it may be that not one tourist in a hundred—perhaps not one in a thousand of the English-speaking race—does feel it, or can feel it even when explained to him, for we have lost many senses.

Therefore, let us plod on, laboriously proving God, although, even to Saint Bernard and Pascal, God was incapable of proof; and using such material as the books furnish for help. It is not much. The French have been shockingly negligent of their greatest artistic glory. One knows not even where to seek. One must go to the National Library and beg as a special favour permission to look at the monumental work of M. Lasteyrie, if one wishes to make even a beginning of the study of French glass. Fortunately there exists a fragment of a great work which the Government began, but never completed, upon Chartres; and another, quite indispensable, but not official, upon Bourges; while Viollet-le-Duc's article "Vitrail" serves as guide to the whole. Ottin's book *Le Vitrail* is convenient. Mâle's volume *L'Art Religieux* is essential. In English, Westlake's "History of Design" is helpful. Perhaps, after reading all that is readable, the best hope will be to provide the best glasses with the largest possible field; and, choosing an hour when the church is empty, take seat about halfway up the nave, facing toward the western entrance with a morning light, so that the glass of the western windows shall not stand in direct sun. (Color Plate I)

The glass of the three lancets is the oldest in the cathedral. If the portal beneath it, with the sculpture, was built in the twenty or thirty years before 1150, the glass could not be much later. It goes with the Abbé Suger's glass at Saint-Denis, which was surely made as early as 1140–50, since the Abbé was a long time at work on it, before he died in 1152. Their perfection proves, what his biographer asserted, that the Abbé Suger spent many years as well as much money on his windows at Saint-Denis, and the specialists affirm that the three lancets at Chartres are quite as good as what remains of Suger's work. Viollet-le-Duc and M. Paul Durand, the Government expert, are positive that this glass is the finest ever made, as far as record exists; and that the northern lancet representing the Tree of Jesse stands at the head of all glasswork whatever. The windows claim, therefore, to be the most splendid colour decoration the world ever saw, since no other material, neither silk nor gold, and no opaque colour laid on with a brush, can compare with translucent glass, and even the Ravenna mosaics or Chinese porcelains are darkness beside them.

The claim may not be modest, but it is none of ours. Viollet-le-Duc must answer for his own sins, and he chose the lancet window of the Tree of Jesse for the subject of his lecture on glass in general, as the most complete and perfect example of this greatest decorative art. Once more, in following him, one is dragged, in spite of one's self, into technique, and, what is worse, into a colour world whose technique was forgotten five hundred years ago. Viollet-le-Duc tried to recover it. "After studying our best French windows," he cautiously suggests that "one might maintain," as their secret of harmony, that "the first condition for an artist in glass is to know how to manage blue. The blue is the light in windows, and light has value only by opposition." The radiating power of blue is, therefore, the starting-point, and on this matter Viollet-le-Duc has much to say which a student would need to master; but a tourist never should study, or he ceases to be a tourist; and it is enough for us if we know that, to get the value they wanted, the artists hatched their blues with lines, covered their surface with figures as though with screens, and tied their blue within its own field with narrow circlets of white or yellow, which, in their turn, were beaded to fasten the blue still more firmly in its place. We have chiefly to remember the law that blue is light:—

But also it is that luminous colour which gives value to all others. If you compose a window in which there shall be no blue, you will get a dirty or dull (*blafard*) or crude surface which the eye will instantly avoid; but if you put a few touches of blue among all these tones, you will immediately get striking effects if not skilfully conceived harmony. So the composition of blue glass singularly preoccupied the glassworkers of the twelfth and thirteenth centuries. If there is only one red, two yellows, two or three purples, and two or three greens at the most, there are infinite shades of blue, . . . and these blues are placed with a very delicate observation of the effects they should produce on other tones, and other tones on them.

Viollet-le-Duc took the window of the Tree of Jesse as his first illustration of the rule, for the reason that its blue ground is one continuous strip from top to bottom, with the subordinate red on either side, and a border uniting the whole so plainly that no one can fail to see its object or its method.

The blue tone of the principal subject [that is to say, the ground of the Tree of Jesse] has commanded the tonality of all the rest. This medium was necessary to enable the luminous splendour to display its energy. This primary condition had dictated the red ground for the prophets, and the return to the blue on reaching the outside semicircular band. To give full value both to the vigour of the red, and to the radiating transparency of the blue, the ground of the corners is put in emerald green; but then, in the corners themselves, the blue is recalled and is given an additional solidity of value by the delicate ornamentation of the squares.

This translation is very free, but one who wants to know these windows must read the whole article, and read it here in the church, the Dictionary in one hand, and binocle in the other, for the binocle is more important than the Dictionary when it reaches the complicated border which repeats in detail the colour-scheme of the centre:—

The border repeats all the tones allotted to the principal subjects, but by small fragments, so that this border, with an effect both solid and powerful, shall not enter into rivalry with the large arrangements of the central parts.

One would think this simple enough; easily tested on any illuminated manuscript, Arab, Persian, or Byzantine; verified by any Oriental rug, old or new; freely illustrated by any Chinese pattern on a Ming jar, or cloisonné vase; and offering a kind of alphabet for the shop-window of a Paris modiste. A strong red; a strong and a weak yellow; a strong and a weak purple; a strong and a weak green, are all to be tied together, given their values, and held in their places by blue. The thing seems simpler still when it appears that perspective is forbidden, and that these glass windows of the twelfth and thirteenth centuries, like Oriental rugs, imply a flat surface, a wall which must not be treated as open. The twelfth-century glassworker would sooner have worn a landscape on his back than have costumed his church with it; he would as soon have decorated his floors with painted holes as his

walls. He wanted to keep the coloured window flat, like a rug hung
on the wall.

The radiation of translucent colours in windows cannot be modi-
fied by the artist; all his talent consists in profiting by it, according
to a given harmonic scheme on a single plane, like a rug, but not
according to an effect of aerial perspective. Do what you like, a
glass window never does and never can represent anything but a
plane surface; its real virtues even exist only on that condition.
Every attempt to present several planes to the eye is fatal to the
harmony of colour, without producing any illusion in the spectator. . . . Translucid painting can propose as its object only a design
supporting as energetically as possible a harmony of colours.

Whether this law is absolute you can tell best by looking at modern
glass which is mostly perspective; but, whether you like it or not, the
matter of perspective does not enter into a twelfth-century window
more than into a Japanese picture, and may be ignored. The decoration of the twelfth century, as far as concerns us, was intended only
for one plane, and a window was another form of rug or embroidery
or mosaic, hung on the wall for colour,—simple decoration to be seen
as a whole. If the Tree of Jesse teaches anything at all, it is that the
artist thought first of controlling his light, but he wanted to do it not
in order to dim the colours; on the contrary, he toiled, like a jeweller
setting diamonds and rubies, to increase their splendour. If his use
of blue teaches this lesson, his use of green proves it. The outside border of the Tree of Jesse is a sort of sample which our schoolmaster
Viollet-le-Duc sets, from which he requires us to study out the
scheme, beginning with the treatment of light, and ending with the
value of the emerald green ground in the corners.

Complicated as the border of the Tree of Jesse is, it has its mates
in the borders of the two other twelfth-century windows [cf. figs.
110–112], and a few of the thirteenth-century in the side aisles; but
the southern of the three lancets shows how the artists dealt with a
difficulty that upset their rule. The border of the southern window
does not count as it should; something is wrong with it and a little
study shows that the builder, and not the glassworker, was to blame.
Owing to his miscalculation—if it was really a miscalculation—in the
width of the southern tower, the builder economized six or eight
inches in the southern door and lancet, which was enough to destroy
the balance between the colour-values, as masses, of the south and
north windows. The artist was obliged to choose whether he would
sacrifice the centre or the border of his southern window, and decided that the windows could not be made to balance if he narrowed

the centre, but that he must balance them by enriching the centre, and sacrificing the border. He has filled the centre with medallions as rich as he could make them, and these he has surrounded with borders, which are also enriched to the utmost; but these medallions with their borders spread across the whole window, and when you search with the binocle for the outside border, you see its pattern clearly only at the top and bottom. On the sides, at intervals of about two feet, the medallions cover and interrupt it; but this is partly corrected by making the border, where it is seen, so rich as to surpass any other in the cathedral, even that of the Tree of Jesse. Whether the artist has succeeded or not is a question for other artists—or for you, if you please—to decide; but apparently he did succeed, since no one has ever noticed the difficulty or the device.

The southern lancet represents the Passion of Christ. Granting to Viollet-le-Duc that the unbroken vertical colour-scheme of the Tree of Jesse made the more effective window, one might still ask whether the medallion-scheme is not the more interesting. Once past the work-shop, there can be no question about it; the Tree of Jesse has the least interest of all the three windows. A genealogical tree has little value, artistic or other, except to those who belong in its branches, and the Tree of Jesse was put there, not to please us, but to please the Virgin. The Passion window was also put there to please her, but it tells a story, and does it in a way that has more novelty than the subject. The draughtsman who chalked out the design on the whitened table that served for his sketch-board was either a Greek, or had before him a Byzantine missal, or enamel or ivory. The first medallion on these legendary windows is the lower left-hand one, which begins the story or legend; here it represents Christ after the manner of the Greek Church. In the next medallion is the Last Supper; the fish on the dish is Greek. In the middle of the window, with the help of the binocle, you will see a Crucifixion, or even two, for on the left is Christ on the Cross, and on the right a Descent from the Cross; in this is the figure of a man pulling out with pincers the nails which fasten Christ's feet; a figure unknown to Western religious art. The Noli Me Tangere, on the right, near the top, has a sort of Greek character. All the critics, especially M. Paul Durand, have noticed this Byzantine look, which is even more marked in the Suger window at Saint-Denis, so as to suggest that both are by the same hand, and that the hand of a Greek. If the artist was really a Greek, he has done work more beautiful than any left at Byzantium, and very far finer than anything in the beautiful work at Cairo, but although the figures and subjects are more or less Greek, like the sculptures on the portal, the art seems to be French.

Look at the central window! Naturally, there sits the Virgin, with her genealogical tree on her left, and her Son's testimony on her right, to prove her double divinity. She is seated in the long halo; as, on the western portal, directly beneath her, her Son is represented in stone. Her crown and head, as well as that of the Child, are fourteenth-century restorations more or less like the original; but her cushioned throne and her robes of imperial state, as well as the flowered sceptre in either hand, are as old as the sculpture of the portal, and redolent of the first crusade. On either side of her, the Sun and the Moon offer praise; her two Archangels, Michael and Gabriel, with resplendent wings, offer not incense as in later times, but the two sceptres of spiritual and temporal power; while the Child in her lap repeats His Mother's action and even her features and expression. At first sight, one would take for granted that all this was pure Byzantium, and perhaps it is; but it has rather the look of Byzantium gallicized, and carried up to a poetic French ideal. At Saint-Denis the little figure of the Abbé Suger at the feet of the Virgin has a very Oriental look, and in the twin medallion the Virgin resembles greatly the Virgin of Chartres, yet, for us, until some specialist shows us the Byzantine original, the work is as thoroughly French as the flèches of the churches.

Byzantine art is altogether another chapter, and, if we could but take a season to study it in Byzantium, we might get great amusement; but the art of Chartres, even in 1100, was French and perfectly French, as the architecture shows, and the glass is even more French than the architecture, as you can detect in many other ways. Perhaps the surest evidence is the glass itself. The men who made it were not professionals but amateurs, who may have had some knowledge of enamelling, but who worked like jewellers, unused to glass, and with the refinement that a reliquary or a crozier required. The cost of these windows must have been extravagant; one is almost surprised that they are not set in gold rather than in lead. The Abbé Suger shirked neither trouble nor expense, and the only serious piece of evidence that this artist was a Greek is given by his biographer who unconsciously shows that the artist cheated him: "He sought carefully for makers of windows and workmen in glass of exquisite quality, especially in that made of sapphires in great abundance that were pulverized and melted up in the glass to give it the blue colour which he delighted to admire." The "materia saphirorum" was evidently something precious,—as precious as crude sapphires would have been,—and the words imply beyond question that the artist asked for sapphires and that Suger paid for them; yet all specialists agree that the stone known as sapphire, if ground, could not produce translucent colour at all. The blue which Suger loved, and which is probably the same as that of these

Chartres windows, cannot be made out of sapphires. Probably the "materia saphirorum" means cobalt only, but whatever it was, the glassmakers seem to agree that this glass of 1140–50 is the best ever made. M. Paul Durand in his official report of 1881 said that these windows, both artistically and mechanically, were of the highest class: "I will also call attention to the fact that the glass and the execution of the painting are, materially speaking, of a quality much superior to windows of the thirteenth and fourteenth centuries. Having passed several months in contact with these precious works when I copied them, I was able to convince myself of their superiority in every particular, especially in the upper parts of the three windows." He said that they were perfect and irreproachable. The true enthusiast in glass would in the depths of his heart like to say outright that these three windows are worth more than all that the French have since done in colour, from that day to this; but the matter concerns us chiefly because it shows how French the experiment was, and how Suger's taste and wealth made it possible.

Certain it is, too, that the southern window—the Passion—was made on the spot, or near by, and fitted for the particular space with care proportionate to its cost. All are marked by the hand of the Chartres Virgin. They are executed not merely for her, but by her. At Saint-Denis the Abbé Suger appeared,—it is true that he was prostrate at her feet, but still he appeared. At Chartres no one—no suggestion of a human agency—was allowed to appear; the Virgin permitted no one to approach her, even to adore. She is enthroned above, as Queen and Empress and Mother, with the symbols of exclusive and universal power. Below her, she permitted the world to see the glories of her earthly life;—the Annunciation, Visitation, and Nativity; the Magi; King Herod; the Journey to Egypt; and the single medallion, which shows the gods of Egypt falling from their pedestals at her coming, is more entertaining than a whole picture-gallery of oil paintings.

In all France there exist barely a dozen good specimens of twelfth-century glass. Besides these windows at Chartres and the fragments at Saint-Denis, there are windows at Le Mans and Angers and bits at Vendôme, Chalons, Poitiers, Rheims, and Bourges; here and there one happens on other pieces, but the earliest is the best, because the glassmakers were new at the work and spent on it an infinite amount of trouble and money which they found to be unnecessary as they gained experience. Even in 1200 the value of these windows was so well understood, relatively to new ones, that they were preserved with the greatest care. The effort to make such windows was never repeated. Their jewelled perfection did not suit the scale of the vast churches of

the thirteenth century. By turning your head toward the windows of
the side aisles, you can see the criticism which the later artists passed
on the old work. They found it too refined, too brilliant, too jewel-like
for the size of the new cathedral; the play of light and colour allowed
the eye too little repose; indeed, the eye could not see their whole
beauty, and half their value was thrown away in this huge stone setting. At best they must have seemed astray on the bleak, cold, windy
plain of Beauce,—homesick for Palestine or Cairo,—yearning for
Monreale or Venice,—but this is not our affair, and, under the protection of the Empress Virgin, Saint Bernard himself could have
afforded to sin even to drunkenness of colour. With trifling expense of
imagination one can still catch a glimpse of the crusades in the glory
of the glass. The longer one looks into it, the more overpowering it
becomes, until one begins almost to feel an echo of what our two
hundred and fifty million arithmetical ancestors, drunk with the
passion of youth and the splendour of the Virgin, have been calling to
us from Mont-Saint-Michel and Chartres. No words and no wine
could revive their emotions so vividly as they glow in the purity of the
colours; the limpidity of the blues; the depth of the red; the intensity
of the green; the complicated harmonies; the sparkle and splendour of
the light; and the quiet and certain strength of the mass.

   With too strong direct sun the windows are said to suffer, and become a cluster of jewels—a delirium of coloured light. The lines, too,
have different degrees of merit. These criticisms seldom strike a
chance traveller, but he invariably makes the discovery that the designs within the medallions are childish. He may easily correct them,
if he likes, and see what would happen to the window; but although
this is the alphabet of art, and we are past spelling words of one sylla-
ble, the criticism teaches at least one lesson. Primitive man seems to
have had a natural colour-sense, instinctive like the scent of a dog.
Society has no right to feel it as a moral reproach to be told that it has
reached an age when it can no longer depend, as in childhood, on its
taste, or smell, or sight, or hearing, or memory; the fact seems likely
enough, and in no way sinful; yet society always denies it, and is
invariably angry about it; and, therefore, one had better not say it.
On the other hand, we can leave Delacroix and his school to fight out
the battle they began against Ingres and his school, in French art,
nearly a hundred years ago, which turned in substance on the same
point. Ingres held that the first motive in colour-decoration was line,
and that a picture which was well drawn was well enough coloured.
Society seemed, on the whole, to agree with him. Society in the
twelfth century agreed with Delacroix. The French held then that the
first point in colour-decoration was colour, and they never hesitated

to put their colour where they wanted it, or cared whether a green camel or a pink lion looked like a dog or a donkey provided they got their harmony or value. Everything except colour was sacrificed to line in the large sense, but details of drawing were conventional and subordinate. So we laugh to see a knight with a blue face, on a green horse, that looks as though drawn by a four-year-old child, and probably the artist laughed, too; but he was a colourist, and never sacrificed his colour for a laugh.

We tourists assume commonly that he knew no better. In our simple faith in ourselves, great hope abides, for it shows an earnestness hardly less than that of the crusaders; but in the matter of colour one is perhaps less convinced, or more open to curiosity. No school of colour exists in our world to-day, while the Middle Ages had a dozen; but it is certainly true that these twelfth-century windows break the French tradition. They had no antecedent, and no fit succession. All the authorities dwell on their exceptional character. One is sorely tempted to suspect that they were in some way an accident; that such an art could not have sprung, in such perfection, out of nothing, had it been really French; that it must have had its home elsewhere—on the Rhine—in Italy—in Byzantium—or in Bagdad.

The same controversy has raged for near two hundred years over the Gothic arch, and everything else mediæval, down to the philosophy of the schools. The generation that lived during the first and second crusades tried a number of original experiments, besides capturing Jerusalem. Among other things, it produced the western portal of Chartres, with its statuary, its glass, and its flèche, as a by-play; as it produced Abélard, Saint Bernard, and Christian of Troyes, whose acquaintance we have still to make. It took ideas wherever it found them;—from Germany, Italy, Spain, Constantinople, Palestine, or from the source which has always attracted the French mind like a magnet—from ancient Greece. That it actually did take the ideas, no one disputes, except perhaps patriots who hold that even the ideas were original; but to most students the ideas need to be accounted for less than the taste with which they were handled, and the quickness with which they were developed. That the taste was French, you can see in the architecture, or you will see if ever you meet the Gothic elsewhere; that it seized and developed an idea quickly, you have seen in the arch, the flèche, the porch, and the windows, as well as in the glass; but what we do not comprehend, and never shall, is the appetite behind all this; the greed for novelty: the fun of life. Every one who has lived since the sixteenth century has felt deep distrust for every one who lived before it, and of every one who believed in the Middle Ages. True it is that the last thirteenth-century artist died a long time before our planet began its present rate of revolution; it had to come to rest, and begin again; but this does not prevent astonishment that the twelfth-century planet revolved so fast. The pointed arch not only came as an idea into France, but it was developed into a system of architecture and covered the country with buildings on a scale of height never before attempted except by the dome, with an expenditure of wealth that would make a railway system look cheap, all in a space of about fifty years; the glass came with it, and went with it, at least as far as concerns us; but, if you need other evidence, you can consult Renan, who is the highest authority: "One of the most singular phenomena of the literary history of the Middle Ages," says Renan of Averroës, "is the activity of the intellectual commerce, and the rapidity with which books were spread from one end of Europe to the other. The philosophy of Abélard during his lifetime (1100–42) had penetrated to the ends of Italy. The French poetry of the trouvères counted within less than a century translations into German, Swedish, Norwegian, Icelandic, Flemish, Dutch, Bohemian, Italian, Spanish"; and he might have added that England needed no translation, but helped to compose the poetry, not being at that time so insular as she afterwards became. "Such or such a work, composed in Morocco or in Cairo, was known at Paris and at Cologne in less time than it would need in our days for a German book of capital importance to pass the Rhine"; and Renan wrote this in 1852 when German books of capital importance were revolutionizing the literary world.

One is apt to forget the smallness of Europe, and how quickly it could always be crossed. In summer weather, with fair winds, one can sail from Alexandria or from Syria, to Sicily, or even to Spain and France, in perfect safety and with ample room for freight, as easily now as one could do it then, without the aid of steam; but one does not now carry freight of philosophy, poetry, or art. The world still struggles for unity, but by different methods, weapons, and thought. The mercantile exchanges which surprised Renan, and which have puzzled historians, were in ideas. The twelfth century was as greedy for them in one shape as the nineteenth century in another. France paid for them dearly, and repented for centuries; but what creates surprise to the point of incredulity is her hunger for them, the youthful gluttony with which she devoured them, the infallible taste with which she dressed them out. The restless appetite that snatched at the pointed arch, the stone flèche, the coloured glass, the illuminated missal, the chanson and roman and pastorelle, the fragments of Aristotle, the glosses of Avicenne, was nothing compared with the genius which instantly gave form and flower to them all.

This episode merely means that the French twelfth-century artist may be supposed to have known his business, and if he produced a grotesque, or a green-faced Saint, or a blue castle, or a syllogism, or a song, that he did it with a notion of the effect he had in mind. The glass window was to him a whole,—a mass,—and its details were his amusement; for the twelfth-century Frenchman enjoyed his fun, though it was sometimes rather heavy for modern French taste, and less refined than the Church liked. These three twelfth-century windows, like their contemporary portal outside, and the flèche that goes with them, are the ideals of enthusiasts of mediæval art; they are above the level of all known art, in religious form; they are inspired; they are divine! This is the claim of Chartres and its Virgin. Actually, the French artist, whether architect, sculptor, or painter in glass, did rise here above his usual level. He knew it when he did it, and probably he attributed it, as we do, to the Virgin; for these works of his were hardly fifty years old when the rest of the old church was burned; and already the artist felt the virtue gone out of him. He could not do so well in 1200 as he did in 1150; and the Virgin was not so near.

The proof of it—or, if you prefer to think so, the proof against it— is before our eyes on the wall above the lancet windows. When Villard de Honnecourt came to Chartres, he seized at once on the western rose as his study, although the two other roses were probably there, in all their beauty and lightness. He saw in the western rose some quality of construction which interested him; and, in fact, the western rose is one of the flowers of architecture which reveals its beauties slowly without end; but its chief beauty is the feeling which unites it with the portal, the lancets, and the flèche. The glassworker here in the interior had the same task to perform. The glass of the lancets was fifty years old when the glass for the rose was planned; perhaps it was seventy, for the exact dates are unknown, but it does not matter, for the greater the interval, the more interesting is the treatment. Whatever the date, the glass of the western rose cannot be much earlier or much later than that of the other roses, or that of the choir, and yet you see at a glance that it is quite differently treated. On such matters one must, of course, submit to the opinion of artists, which one does the more readily because they always disagree; but until the artists tell us better, we may please ourselves by fancying that the glass of the rose was intended to harmonize with that of the lancets, and unite it with the thirteenth-century glass of the nave and transepts. Among all the thirteenth-century windows the western rose alone seems to affect a rivalry in brilliancy with the lancets, and carries it so far that the separate medallions and pictures are quite lost,—especially in direct sunshine,—blending in a confused effect of opals, in a delirium of colour and light, with a result like a cluster of stones in jewelry. Assuming as one must, in want of the artist's instruction, that he knew what he wanted to do, and did it, one must take for granted that he treated the rose as a whole, and aimed at giving it harmony with the three precious windows beneath. The effect is that of a single large ornament; a round breastpin, or what is now called a sunburst, of jewels, with three large pendants beneath.

We are ignorant tourists, liable to much error in trying to seek motives in artists who worked seven hundred years ago for a society which thought and felt in forms quite unlike ours, but the mediæval pilgrim was more ignorant than we, and much simpler in mind; if the idea of an ornament occurs to us, it certainly occurred to him, and still more to the glassworker whose business was to excite his illusions. An artist, if good for anything, foresees what his public will see; and what his public will see is what he ought to have intended—the measure of his genius. If the public sees more than he himself did, this is his credit; if less, this is his fault. No matter how simple or ignorant we are, we ought to feel a discord or a harmony where the artist meant us to feel it, and when we see a motive, we conclude that other people have seen it before us, and that it must, therefore, have been intended. Neither of the transept roses is treated like this one; neither has the effect of a personal ornament; neither is treated as a jewel. No one knew so well as the artist that such treatment must give the effect of a jewel. The Roses of France and of Dreux bear indelibly and flagrantly the character of France and Dreux; on the western rose is stamped with greater refinement but equal decision the character of a much greater power than either of them.

No artist would have ventured to put up, before the eyes of Mary in Majesty, above the windows so dear to her, any object that she had not herself commanded. Whether a miracle was necessary, or whether genius was enough, is a point of casuistry which you can settle with Albertus Magnus or Saint Bernard, and which you will understand as little when settled as before; but for us, beyond the futilities of unnecessary doubt, the Virgin designed this rose; not perhaps in quite the same perfect spirit in which she designed the lancets, but still wholly for her own pleasure and as her own idea. She placed upon the breast of her Church—which symbolized herself—a jewel so gorgeous that no earthly majesty could bear comparison with it, and which no other heavenly majesty has rivalled. As one watches the light play on it, one is still overcome by the glories of the jewelled rose and its three gemmed pendants; one feels a little of the effect she meant it to produce even on infidels, Moors, and heretics, but infinitely more on the men who feared and the women who adored her;—not to dwell

too long upon it, one admits that hers is the only Church. One
would admit anything that she should require. If you had only the
soul of a shrimp, you would crawl, like the Abbé Suger, to kiss her
feet.

Unfortunately she is gone, or comes here now so very rarely that we
never shall see her; but her genius remains as individual here as the
genius of Blanche of Castile and Pierre de Dreux in the transepts.
That the three lancets were her own taste, as distinctly as the Trianon
was the taste of Louis XIV, is self-evident. They represent all that
was dearest to her; her Son's glory on her right; her own beautiful
life in the middle; her royal ancestry on her left: the story of her
divine right, thrice-told. The pictures are all personal, like family portraits. Above them the man who worked in 1200 to carry out the
harmony, and to satisfy the Virgin's wishes, has filled his rose with a
dozen or two little compositions in glass, which reveal their subjects
only to the best powers of a binocle. Looking carefully, one discovers
at last that his gorgeous combination of all the hues of Paradise contains or hides a Last Judgment—the one subject carefully excluded
from the old work, and probably not existing on the south portal for
another twenty years. If the scheme of the western rose dates from
1200, as is reasonable to suppose, this Last Judgment is the oldest in
the church, and makes a link between the theology of the first crusade,
beneath, and the theology of Pierre Mauclerc in the south porch. The
churchman is the only true and final judge on his own doctrine, and we
neither know nor care to know the facts; but we are as good judges as
he of the feeling, and we are at full liberty to feel that such a Last
Judgment as this was never seen before or since by churchman or here-
tic, unless by virtue of the heresy which held that the true Christian
must be happy in being damned since such is the will of God. That
this blaze of heavenly light was intended, either by the Virgin or by
her workmen, to convey ideas of terror or pain, is a notion which the
Church might possibly preach, but which we sinners knew to be false
in the thirteenth century as well as we know it now. Never in all these
seven hundred years has one of us looked up at this rose without feeling it to be Our Lady's promise of Paradise.

Here as everywhere else throughout the church, one feels the Virgin's presence, with no other thought than her majesty and grace. To
the Virgin and to her suppliants, as to us, who though outcasts in other
churches can still hope in hers, the Last Judgment was not a symbol
of God's justice or man's corruption, but of her own infinite mercy.
The Trinity judged, through Christ;—Christ loved and pardoned,
through her. She wielded the last and highest power on earth and in
hell. In the glow and beauty of her nature, the light of her Son's

infinite love shone as the sunlight through the glass, turning the Last
Judgment itself into the highest proof of her divine and supreme
authority. The rudest ruffian of the Middle Ages, when he looked at
this Last Judgment, laughed; for what was the Last Judgment to her!
An ornament, a plaything, a pleasure! a jewelled decoration which she
wore on her breast! Her chief joy was to pardon; her eternal instinct
was to love; her deepest passion was pity! On her imperial heart the
flames of hell showed only the opaline colours of heaven. Christ the
Trinity might judge as much as He pleased, but Christ the Mother
would rescue; and her servants could look boldly into the flames.

If you, or even our friends the priests who still serve Mary's
shrine, suspect that there is some exaggeration in this language, it will
only oblige you to admit presently that there is none; but for the moment we are busy with glass rather than with faith, and there is a world
of glass here still to study. Technically, we are done with it. The
technique of the thirteenth century comes naturally and only too
easily out of that of the twelfth. Artistically, the motive remains the
same, since it is always the Virgin; but although the Virgin of Chartres
is always the Virgin of Majesty, there are degrees in the assertion of
her majesty even here, which affect the art, and qualify its feeling.
Before stepping down to the thirteenth century, one should look at
these changes of the Virgin's royal presence.

First and most important as record is the stone Virgin on the south
door of the western portal, which we studied, with her Byzantine
Court; and the second, also in stone, is of the same period, on one of the
carved capitals of the portal, representing the Adoration of the Magi.
The third is the glass Virgin at the top of the central lancet. All three
are undoubted twelfth-century work; and you can see another at Paris,
on the same door of Notre Dame, and still more on Abbé Suger's
window at Saint-Denis, and, later, within a beautiful grisaille at
Auxerre; but all represent the same figure; a Queen, enthroned,
crowned, with the symbols of royal power, holding in her lap the infant King whose guardian she is. Without pretending to know what
special crown she bears, we can assume, till corrected, that it is the
Carlovingian imperial, not the Byzantine. The Trinity nowhere appears except as implied in the Christ. At the utmost, a mystic hand
may symbolize the Father. The Virgin as represented by the artists of
the twelfth century in the Ile de France and at Chartres seems to be
wholly French in spite of the Greek atmosphere of her workmanship.
One might almost insist that she is blonde, full in face, large in figure,
dazzlingly beautiful, and not more than thirty years of age. The Child
never seems to be more than five.

You are equally free to see a Southern or Eastern type in her face, and perhaps the glass suggests a dark type, but the face of the Virgin on the central lancet is a fourteenth-century restoration which may or may not reproduce the original, while all the other Virgins represented in glass, except one, belong to the thirteenth century. The possible exception is a well-known figure called Notre-Dame-de-la-Belle-Verrière in the choir next the south transept [fig. 109]. A strange, almost uncanny feeling seems to haunt this window, heightened by the veneration in which it was long held as a shrine, though it is now deserted for Notre-Dame-du-Pilier on the opposite side of the choir. The charm is partly due to the beauty of the scheme of the angels, supporting, saluting, and incensing the Virgin and Child with singular grace and exquisite feeling, but rather that of the thirteenth than of the twelfth century. Here, too, the face of the Virgin is not ancient. Apparently the original glass was injured by time or accident, and the colours were covered or renewed by a simple drawing in oil. Elsewhere the colour is thought to be particularly good, and the window is a favourite mine of motives for artists to exploit, but to us its chief interest is its singular depth of feeling. The Empress Mother sits full-face, on a rich throne and dais, with the Child on her lap, repeating her attitude except that her hands support His shoulders. She wears her crown; her feet rest on a stool, and both stool, rug, robe, and throne are as rich as colour and decoration can make them. At last a dove appears, with the rays of the Holy Ghost. Imperial as the Virgin is, it is no longer quite the unlimited empire of the western lancet. The aureole encircles her head only; she holds no sceptre; the Holy Ghost seems to give her support which she did not need before, while Saint Gabriel and Saint Michael, her archangels, with their symbols of power, have disappeared. Exquisite as the angels are who surround and bear up her throne, they assert no authority. The window itself is not a single composition; the panels below seem inserted later merely to fill up the space; six represent the Marriage of Cana, and the three at the bottom show a grotesque little demon tempting Christ in the Desert. The effect of the whole, in this angle which is almost always dark or filled with shadow, is deep and sad, as though the Empress felt her authority fail, and had come down from the western portal to reproach us for neglect. The face is haunting. Perhaps its force may be due to nearness, for this is the only instance in glass of her descending so low that we can almost touch her, and see what the twelfth century instinctively felt in the features which, even in their beatitude, were serious and almost sad under the austere responsibilities of infinite pity and power.

No doubt the window is very old, or perhaps an imitation or reproduction of one which was much older, but to the pilgrim its interest lies mostly in its personality, and there it stands alone. Although the Virgin reappears again and again in the lower windows,—as in those on either side of the Belle-Verrière; in the remnant of window representing her miracles at Chartres, in the south aisle next the transept; in the fifteenth-century window of the chapel of Vendôme which follows; and in the third window which follows that of Vendôme and represents her coronation,—she does not show herself again in all her majesty till we look up to the high windows above. There we shall find her in her splendour on her throne, above the high altar, and still more conspicuously in the Rose of France in the north transept. Still again she is enthroned in the first window of the choir next the north transept. Elsewhere we can see her standing, but never does she come down to us in the full splendour of her presence. Yet wherever we find her at Chartres, and whatever period, she is always Queen. Her expression and attitude are always calm and commanding. She never calls for sympathy by hysterical appeals to our feelings; she does not even altogether command, but rather accepts the voluntary, unquestioning, unhesitating, instinctive faith, love, and devotion of mankind. She will accept ours, and we have not the heart to refuse it; we have not even the right, for we are her guests.

The Legendary Windows

One's first visit to a great cathedral is like one's first visit to the British Museum; the only intelligent idea is to follow the order of time, but the museum is a chaos in time, and the cathedral is generally all of one and the same time. At Chartres, after finishing with the twelfth century, everything is of the thirteenth. To catch even an order in time, one must first know what part of the thirteenth-century church was oldest. The books say it was the choir. After the fire of 1194, the pilgrims used the great crypt as a church where services were maintained; but the builders must have begun with the central piers and the choir, because the choir was the only essential part of the church. Nave and transepts might be suppressed, but without a choir the church was useless, and in a shrine, such as Chartres, the choir was the whole church. Toward the choir, then, the priest or artist looks first; and, since dates are useful, the choir must be dated. The same popular enthusiasm, which had broken out in 1145, revived in 1195 to help the rebuilding; and the work was pressed forward with the same feverish haste, so that ten years should have been ample to provide for the choir, if for nothing more; and services may have been resumed there as early as the year 1206; certainly in 1210. Probably the windows were designed and put in hand as soon as the architect gave the measurements, and any one who intended to give a window would have been apt to choose one of the spaces in the apse, in Mary's own presence, next the sanctuary.

The first of the choir windows to demand a date is the Belle-Verrière, which is commonly classed as early thirteenth-century, and may go with the two windows next it, one of which—the so-called Zodiac window—bears a singularly interesting inscription: "Comes Teobaldus dat . . . ad preces Comitis Pticensis" [Count Thibaut gives . . . at the behest of the Count of Le Perche]. If Shakespeare could write the tragedy of *King John*, we cannot admit ourselves not to have read it, and this inscription might be a part of the play. The "pagus perticensis" lies a short drive to the west, some fifteen or twenty miles on the road to Le Mans, and in history is known as the Comté du Perche, although its memory is now preserved chiefly by its famous breed of Percheron horses. Probably the horse also dates from the crusades, and may have carried Richard Cœur-de-Lion, but in any case the count of that day was a vassal of Richard, and one of his intimate friends, whose memory is preserved forever by a single line in Richard's prison-song:—

> Mes compaignons cui j'amoie et cui j'aim,
> Ces dou Caheu et ces dou Percherain.[2]

In 1194, when Richard Cœur-de-Lion wrote these verses, the Comte du Perche was Geoffroy III, who had been a companion of Richard on his crusade in 1192, where, according to the Chronicle, "he shewed himself but a timid man"; which seems scarcely likely in a companion of Richard; but it is not of him that the Chartres window speaks, except as the son of Mahaut or Matilda of Champagne who was a sister of Alix of Champagne, Queen of France. The Table shows, therefore, that Geoffroy's son and successor as the Comte du Perche—Thomas—was second cousin of Louis the Lion, known as King Louis VIII of France. They were probably of much the same age.

If this were all, one might carry it in one's head for a while, but the relationship which dominates the history of this period was that of all these great ruling families with Richard Cœur-de-Lion and his brother John, nicknamed Lackland, both of whom in succession were the most powerful Frenchmen in France. The Table shows that their mother Eleanor of Guienne, the first Queen of Louis VII, bore him two daughters, one of whom, Alix, married, about 1164, the Count Thibaut of Chartres and Blois, while the other, Mary, married the great Count

2 "My friends whom I loved and whom I love, Those gentle men of Caheu and of Perche" [Ed.].

of Champagne. Both of them being half-sisters of Cœur-de-Lion and John, their children were nephews or half-nephews, indiscriminately, of all the reigning monarchs, and Cœur-de-Lion immortalized one of them by a line in his prison-song, as he immortalized Le Perche:—

> Je nel di pas de celi de Chartain,
> La mere Loeis.[3]

"Loeis," therefore, or Count Louis of Chartres, was not only nephew of Cœur-de-Lion and John Lackland, but was also, like Count Thomas of Le Perche, a second cousin of Louis VIII. Feudally and personally he was directly attached to Cœur-de-Lion rather than to Philip Augustus.

If society in the twelfth century could follow the effects of these relationships, personal and feudal, it was cleverer than society in the twentieth; but so much is simple: Louis of France, Thibaut of Chartres, and Thomas of Le Perche, were cousins and close friends in the year 1215, and all were devoted to the Virgin of Chartres. Judging from the character of Louis's future queen, Blanche of Castile, their wives were, if possible, more devoted still; and in that year Blanche gave birth to Saint Louis, who seems to have been the most devoted of all.

Meanwhile their favourite uncle, Cœur-de-Lion, had died in the year 1199. Thibaut's great-grandmother, Eleanor of Guienne, died in 1202. King John, left to himself, rapidly accumulated enemies innumerable, abroad and at home. In 1203, Philip Augustus confiscated all the fiefs he held from the French Crown, and in 1204 seized Normandy. John sank rapidly from worse to worst, until at last the English barons rose and forced him to grant their Magna Carta at Runnimede in 1215.

The year 1215 was, therefore, a year to be remembered at Chartres, as at Mont-Saint-Michel; one of the most convenient dates in history. Every one is supposed, even now, to know what happened then, to give another violent wrench to society, like the Norman Conquest in 1066. John turned on the barons and broke them down; they sent to France for help, and offered the crown of England to young Louis, whose father, Philip Augustus, called a council which pledged support to Louis. Naturally the Comte du Perche and the Comte de Chartres must have pledged their support, among the foremost, to go with Louis to England. He was then twenty-nine years old; they were probably somewhat younger.

The Zodiac window, with its inscription, was the immediate result.

---

[3] "I do not say it of the one of Chartres, The mother of Louis" [Ed.].

The usual authority that figures in the histories is Roger of Wendover, but much the more amusing for our purpose is a garrulous Frenchman known as the Ménestrel de Rheims who wrote some fifty years later. After telling in his delightful thirteenth-century French, how the English barons sent hostages to Louis, "et mes sires Loueys les fit bien gardeir et honourablement," the Ménestrel continued:—

> Et assembla granz genz par amours, et par deniers, et par lignage. Et fu avec lui li cuens dou Perche, et li cuens de Montfort, et li cuens de Chartres, et li cuens de Monbleart, et mes sires Enjorrans de Couci, et mout d'autre grant seigneur dont je ne parole mie.[4]

The Comte de Chartres, therefore, may be supposed to have gone with the Comte du Perche, and to have witnessed the disaster at Lincoln which took place May 20, 1217, after King John's death:—

> Et li cuens dou Perche faisait l'avantgarde, et courut tout leiz des portes; et la garnisons de laienz issi hors et leur coururent sus; et i ot asseiz trait et lancié; et chevaus morz et chevaliers abatuz, et gent à pié morz et navreiz. Et li cuens dou Perche i fu morz par un ribaut qui li leva le pan dou hauberc, et l'ocist d'un coutel; et fu desconfite l'avantgarde par la mort le conte. Et quant mes sires Loueys le sot, si ot graigneur duel qu'il eust onques, car il estoit ses prochains ami de char.[5]

Such language would be spoiled by translation. For us it is enough to know that the "ribaut" who lifted the "pan," or skirt, of the Count's "hauberc" or coat-of-mail, as he sat on his horse refusing to surrender to English traitors, and stabbed him from below with a knife, may have been an invention of the Ménestrel; or the knight who pierced with his lance through the visor to the brain, may have been an invention of Roger of Wendover; but in either case, Count Thomas du Perche lost his life at Lincoln, May 20, 1217, to the deepest

[4] "And there assembled people great by their loves, their riches, and their blood. And with them were the Count of Parche, and the Count of Montfort, and the Count of Chartres, and the Count of Montbléart, and my lord Enjorrans of Coucy, and many another great lord, of whom I will not speak" [Ed.].
[5] "The Count of Perche had the advance guard and ran around the gates; and the garrison issued forth and fell upon him; and there the bow and the lance were used a great deal; and there were dead horses and wounded knights, and footsoldiers dead and wounded. And the Count of Perche was killed by a lowly pillager, who lifted the visor of his helmet an slew him with a knife; and at the death of the count the advance guard was routed. And when my lord Louis heard of it, he was sadder than he had ever been, for he had been his close friend and relative" [Ed.].

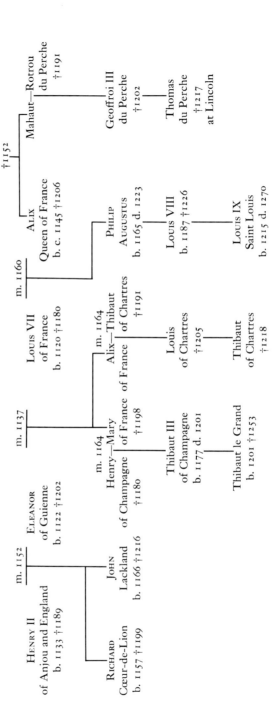

Thibaut II
of Champagne
†1152

Mahaut—Rotrou
du Perche
†1191

Geoffroi III
du Perche
†1202

Thomas
du Perche
†1217
at Lincoln

Alix
Queen of France
b. c. 1145 †1206

Philip
Augustus
b. 1165, d. 1223

Louis VIII
b. 1187 †1226

Louis IX
Saint Louis
b. 1215, d. 1270

m. 1160

Louis VII
of France
b. 1120 †1180

m. 1164
Alix—Thibaut
of France of Chartres
†1191

Louis
of Chartres
†1205

Thibaut
of Chartres
†1218

m. 1137

m. 1164
Henry—Mary
of Champagne of France
†1180 b. 1145 d. 1198

Thibaut III
of Champagne
b. 1177 d. 1201

Thibaut le Grand
b. 1201 †1253

Eleanor
of Guienne
b. 1122 †1202

John
Lackland
b. 1166 †1216

m. 1152

Henry II
of Anjou and England
b. 1133 †1189

Richard
Cœur-de-Lion
b. 1157 †1199

regret of his cousin Louis the Lion as well as of the Count Thibaut of Chartres, whom he charged to put up a window for him in honour of the Virgin.

The window must have been ordered at once, because Count Thibaut, "le Jeune ou le Lépreux," died himself within a year, April 22, 1218, thus giving an exact date for one of the choir windows. Probably it was one of the latest, because the earliest to be provided would have been certainly those of the central apsidal chapel. According to the rule laid down by Viollet-le-Duc, the windows in which blue strongly predominates, like the Saint Sylvester, are likely to be earlier than those with a prevailing tone of red. We must take for granted that some of these great legendary windows were in place as early as 1210, because, in October of that year, Philip Augustus attended mass here. There are some two dozen of these windows in the choir alone, each of which may well have represented a year's work in the slow processes of that day, and we can hardly suppose that the workshops of 1200 were on a scale such as to allow of more than two to have been in hand at once. Thirty or forty years later, when the Sainte Chapelle was built, the workshops must have been vastly enlarged, but with the enlargement, the glass deteriorated. Therefore, if the architecture were so far advanced in the year 1200 as to allow of beginning work on the glass, in the apse, the year 1225 is none too late to allow for its completion in the choir.

Dates are stupidly annoying;—what we want is not dates but taste;—yet we are uncomfortable without them. Except the Perche window, none of the lower ones in the choir helps at all; but the clerestory is more useful. There they run in pairs, each pair surmounted by a rose. The first pair (numbers 27 and 28) next the north transept, shows the Virgin of France, supported, according to the Abbés Bulteau and Clerval, by the arms of Bishop Reynault de Mouçon, who was Bishop of Chartres at the time of the great fire in 1194 and died in 1217. The window number 28 shows two groups of peasants on pilgrimage; below, on his knees, Robert of Berou, as donor: "ROBERTUS DE BEROU: CARN. CANCELLARIUS" [Robert of Berou, Chancellor of Chartres] [fig. 113]. The Cartulary of the Cathedral contains an entry (Buletau, i, 123): "The 26th February, 1216, died Robert de Berou, Chancellor, who has given us a window." The Cartulary mentions several previous gifts of windows by canons or other dignitaries of the Church in the year 1215.

Next follow, or once followed, a pair of windows (numbers 29 and 30) which were removed by the sculptor Bridan, in 1788, in order to obtain light for his statuary below. The donor was "DOMINA JOHANNES BAPTISTA," who, we are told, was Jeanne de Dammartin; and the window was given in memory, or in honour, of her marriage to Ferdinand of Castile in 1237. Jeanne was a very great lady, daughter of the comte d'Aumale and Marie de Ponthieu. Her father affianced her in 1235 to the King of England, Henry III, and even caused the marriage to be celebrated by proxy, but Queen Blanche broke it off, as she had forbidden, in 1231, that of Yolande of Britanny. She relented so far as to allow Jeanne in 1237 to marry Ferdinand of Castile, who still sits on horseback in the next rose: "Rex Castillæ." He won the crown of Castile in 1217 and died in 1252, when Queen Jeanne returned to Abbéville and then, at latest, put up this window at Chartres in memory of her husband.

The windows numbers 31 and 32 are the subject of much dispute, but whether the donors were Jean de Chatillon or the three children of Thibaut le Grand of Champagne, they must equally belong to the later series of 1260–70, rather than to the earlier of 1210–20. The same thing is or was true of the next pair, numbers 33 and 34, which were removed in 1773, but the record says that at the bottom of number 34 was the figure of Saint Louis's son, Louis of France, who died in 1260, before his father, who still rides in the rose above.

Thus the north side of the choir shows a series of windows that precisely cover the lifetime of Saint Louis (1215–70). The south side begins, next the apse, with windows numbers 35 and 36, which belong, according to the Comte d'Armancourt, to the family of Montfort, whose ruined castle crowns the hill of Montfort l'Amaury, on the road to Paris, some forty kilometres northeast of Chartres. Every one is supposed to know the story of Simon de Montfort who was killed before Toulouse in 1218. Simon left two sons, Amaury and Simon. The sculptor Bridan put an end also to the window of Amaury, but in the rose, Amaury, according to the Abbés, still rides on a white horse. Amaury's history is well known. He was made Constable of France by Queen Blanche in 1231; went on crusade in 1239; was captured by the infidels, taken to Babylon, ransomed, and in returning to France, died at Otranto in 1241. For that age Amaury was but a commonplace person, totally overshadowed by his brother Simon, who went to England, married King John's daughter Eleanor, and became almost king himself as Earl of Leicester. At your leisure you can read Matthew Paris's dramatic account of him and of his death at the battle of Evesham, August 5, 1265. He was perhaps the last of the very great men of the thirteenth century, excepting Saint Louis himself, who lived a few years longer. M. d'Armancourt insists that it is the great Earl of Leicester who rides with his visor up, in full armour, on a brown horse, in the rose above the windows numbers 37 and 38. In any case, the windows would be later than 1240.

The next pair of windows, numbers 39 and 40, also removed in 1788, still offer, in their rose, the figure of a member of the Courtenay family. Gibbon was so much attracted by the romance of the Courtenays as to make an amusing digression on the subject which does not concern us or the cathedral except so far as it tells us that the Courtenays, like so many other benefactors of Chartres Cathedral, belonged to the royal blood. Louis-le-Gros, who died in 1137, besides his son Louis-le-Jeune, who married Eleanor of Guienne in that year, had a younger son, Pierre, whom he married to Isabel de Courtenay, and who, like Philip Hurepel, took the title of his wife. Pierre had a son, Pierre II, who was a cousin of Philip Augustus, and became the hero of the most lurid tragedy of the time. Chosen Emperor of Constantinople in 1216, to succeed his brothers-in-law Henry and Baldwin, he tried to march across Illyria and Macedonia, from Durazzo opposite Brindisi, with a little army of five thousand men, and instantly disappeared forever. The Epirotes captured him in the summer of 1217, and from that moment nothing is known of his fate.

On the whole, this catastrophe was perhaps the grimmest of all the Shakespearean tragedies of the thirteenth century; and one would like to think that the Chartres window was a memorial of this Pierre, who was a cousin of France and an emperor without empire; but M. d'Armancourt insists that the window was given in memory not of this Pierre, but of his nephew, another Pierre de Courtenay, Seigneur de Conches, who went on crusade with Saint Louis in 1249 to Egypt, and died shortly before the defeat and captivity of the King, on February 8, 1250. His brother Raoul, Seigneur d'Illiers, who died in 1271, is said to be donor of the next window, number 40. The date of the Courtenay windows should therefore be no earlier than the death of Saint Louis in 1270; yet one would like to know what has become of another Courtenay window left by the first Pierre's son-in-law, Gaucher or Gaultier of Bar-sur-Seine, who seems to have been Vicomte de Chartres, and who, dying before Damietta in 1218, made a will leaving to Notre Dame de Chartres thirty silver marks, "de quibus fieri debet miles montatus super equum suum" [and from these there shall be paid a soldier mounted upon his own horse]. Not only would this mounted knight on horseback supply an early date for these interesting figures, but would fix also the cost, for a mark contained eight ounces of silver, and was worth ten sous, or half a livre. We shall presently see that Aucassins gave twenty sous, or a livre, for a strong ox, so that the "miles montatus super equum suum" in glass was equivalent to fifteen oxen if it were money of Paris, which is far from certain.

This is an economical problem which belongs to experts, but the historical value of these early evidences is still something,—perhaps still as much as ten sous. All the windows tend to the same conclusion. Even the last pair, numbers 41 and 42, offer three personal clues which lead to the same result:—the arms of Bouchard de Marly who died in 1226, almost at the same time as Louis VIII; a certain Colinus or Colin, "de camera Regis," who was alive in 1225; and Robert of Beaumont in the rose, who seems to be a Beaumont of Le Perche, of whom little or nothing is as yet certainly known. As a general rule, there are two series of windows, one figuring the companions or followers of Louis VIII (1215–26); the other, friends or companions of Saint Louis (1226–70), Queen Blanche uniting both. What helps to hold the sequences in a certain order, is that the choir was complete, and services regularly resumed there, in 1210, while in 1220 the transept and nave were finished and vaulted. For the apside windows, therefore, we will assume, subject to correction, a date from 1200 to 1225 for their design and workmanship; for the transept, 1220 to 1236; and for the nave a general tendency to the actual reign of Saint Louis from 1236 to 1270. Since there is a deal of later glass scattered everywhere among the earlier, the margin of error is great; but by keeping the reign of Louis VIII and its personages distinct from that of Louis IX and his generation, we can be fairly sure of our main facts. Meanwhile the Sainte Chapelle in Paris, wholly built and completed between 1240 and 1248, offers a standard of comparison for the legendary windows.

The choir of Chartres is as long as the nave, and much broader, besides that the apse was planned with seven circular projections which greatly increased the window space, so that the guidebook reckons thirty-seven windows. A number of these are grisailles, and the true amateur of glass considers the grisailles to be as well worth study as the legendary windows. They are a decoration which has no particular concern with churches, and no distinct religious meaning, but, it seems, a religious value which Viollet-le-Duc is at some trouble to explain; and, since his explanation is not very technical, we can look at it, before looking at the legends:—

> The colouration of the windows had the advantage of throwing on the opaque walls a veil, or coloured glazing, of extreme delicacy, always assuming that the coloured windows themselves were harmoniously toned. Whether their resources did not permit the artists to adopt a complete system of coloured glass, or whether they wanted to get daylight in purer quality into their interiors,—whatever may have been their reasons,—they resorted to this beautiful grisaille decoration which is also a colouring harmony obtained by

the aid of a long experience in the effects of light on translucent surfaces. Many of our churches retain grisaille windows filling either all, or only a part, of their bays. In the latter case, the grisailles are reserved for the side windows which are meant to be seen obliquely, and in that case the coloured glass fills the bays of the fond, the apsidal openings which are meant to be seen in face from a distance. These lateral grisailles are still opaque enough to prevent the solar rays which pass through them from lighting the coloured windows on the reverse side; yet, at certain hours of the day, these solar rays throw a pearly light on the coloured windows which gives them indescribable transparence and refinement of tones. The lateral windows in the choir of the Auxerre Cathedral, half-grisaille, half-coloured, throw on the wholly coloured apsidal window, by this means, a glazing the softness of which one can hardly conceive. The opaline light which comes through these lateral bays, and makes a sort of veil, transparent in the extreme, under the lofty vaulting, is crossed by the brilliant tones of the windows behind, which give the play of precious stones. The solid outlines then seem to waver like objects seen through a sheet of clear water. Distances change their values, and take depths in which the eye gets lost. With every hour of the day these effects are altered, and always with new harmonies which one never tires of trying to understand; but the deeper one's study goes, the more astounded one becomes before the experience acquired by these artists, whose theories on the effects of colour, assuming that they had any, are unknown to us and whom the most kindly-disposed among us treat as simple children.

You can read the rest for yourselves. Grisaille is a separate branch of colour-decoration which belongs with the whole system of lighting and fenêtrage, and will have to remain a closed book because the feeling and experience which explained it once are lost, and we cannot recover either. Such things must have been always felt rather than reasoned, like the irregularities in plan of the builders; the best work of the best times shows the same subtlety of sense as the dog shows in retrieving, or the bee in flying, but which tourists have lost. All we can do is to note that the grisailles were intended to have values. They were among the definements of light and colour with which the apse of Chartres is so crowded that one must be content to feel what one can, and let the rest go.

Understand, we cannot! nothing proves that the greatest artists who ever lived have, in a logical sense, understood! or that omnipotence has ever understood! or that the utmost power of expression has ever been capable of expressing more than the reaction of one energy on another, but not of two on two; and when one sits here, in the central axis of this complicated apse, one sees, in mere light alone, the reaction of hundreds of energies, although time has left only a wreck of what the artist put here. One of the best window spaces is wholly filled up by the fourteenth-century doorway to the chapel of Saint Piat, and only by looking at the two windows which correspond on the north does a curious inquirer get a notion of the probable loss. The same chapel more or less blocks the light of three other principal windows. The sun, the dust, the acids of dripping water, and the other works of time, have in seven hundred years corroded or worn away or altered the glass, especially on the south side. Windows have been darkened by time and mutilated by wilful injury. Scores of the panels are wholly restored, modern reproductions or imitations. Even after all this loss, the glass is probably the best-preserved, or perhaps the only preserved part of the decoration in colour, for we never shall know the colour-decoration of the vaults, the walls, the columns, or the floors. Only one point is fairly sure;—that on festivals, if not at other times, every foot of space was covered in some way or another, throughout the apse, with colour; either paint or tapestry or embroidery or Byzantine brocades and Oriental stuffs or rugs, lining the walls, covering the altars, and hiding the floor. Occasionally you happen upon illuminated manuscripts showing the interiors of chapels with their colour-decoration; but everything has perished here except the glass.

If one may judge from the glass of later centuries, the first impression from the thirteenth-century windows ought to be disappointment. You should find them too effeminate, too soft, too small, and above all not particularly religious. Indeed, except for the nominal subjects of the legends, one sees nothing religious about them; the medallions, when studied with the binocle, turn out to be less religious than decorative. Saint Michael would not have felt at home here, and Saint Bernard would have turned from them with disapproval; but when they were put up, Saint Bernard was long dead, and Saint Michael had yielded his place to the Virgin. This apse is all for her. At its entrance she sat, on either side, in the Belle-Verrière or as Our Lady of the Pillar, to receive the secrets and the prayers of suppliants who wished to address her directly in person; there she bent down to our level, resumed her humanity, and felt our griefs and passions. Within, where the cross-lights fell through the wide columned space behind the high altar, was her withdrawing room, where the decorator and builder thought only of pleasing her. The very faults of the architecture and effeminacy of taste witness the artists' object. If the glassworkers had thought of themselves or of the public or even of the priests, they would have strained for effects, strong masses of colour, and striking subjects to impress the imagination. Nothing of the sort is even suggested. The great, awe-inspiring mosaic figure of the Byzantine half-dome was a splendid religious effect, but this artist had in his mind an altogether different thought. He was in the Virgin's employ; he was decorating her own chamber in her own palace; he wanted to please her; and he knew her tastes, even when she did not give him her personal orders. To him, a dream would have been an order. The salary of the twelfth-century artist was out of all relation with the percentage of a twentieth-century decorator. The artist of 1200 was probably the last who cared little for the baron, not very much for the priest, and nothing for the public, unless he happened to be paid by the guild, and then he cared just to the extent of his hire, or, if he was himself a priest, not even for that. His pay was mostly of a different kind, and was the same as that of the peasants who were hauling the stone from the quarry at Berchères while he was firing his ovens. His reward was to come when he should be promoted to decorate the Queen of Heaven's palace in the New Jerusalem, and he served a mistress who knew better than he did what work was good and what was bad, and how to give him his right place. Mary's taste was infallible; her knowledge like her power had no limits; she knew men's thoughts as well as acts, and could not be deceived. Probably, even in our own time, an artist might find his imagination considerably stimulated and his work powerfully improved if he knew that anything short of his best would bring him to the gallows, with or without trial by jury; but in the twelfth century the gallows was a trifle; the Queen hardly considered it a punishment for an offence to her dignity. The artist was vividly aware that Mary disposed of hell.

All this is written in full, on every stone and window of this apse, as legible as the legends to any one who cares to read. The artists were doing their best, not to please a swarm of flat-eared peasants or slow-witted barons, but to satisfy Mary, the Queen of Heaven, to whom the Kings and Queens of France were coming constantly for help, and whose absolute power was almost the only restraint recognized by Emperor, Pope, and clown. The colour-decoration is hers, and hers alone. For her the lights are subdued, the tones softened, the subjects selected, the feminine taste preserved. That other great ladies interested themselves in the matter, even down to its technical refinements, is more than likely; indeed, in the central apside chapel, suggesting the Auxerre grisaille that Viollet-le-Duc mentioned, is a grisaille which bears the arms of Castile and Queen Blanche; further on, three other grisailles bear also the famous castles, but this is by no means the strongest proof of feminine taste. The difficulty would be rather to find a touch of certainly masculine taste in the whole apse.

Since the central apside chapel is the most important, we can begin with the windows there, bearing in mind that the subject of the central window was the Life of Christ, dictated by rule or custom. On Christ's left hand is the window of Saint Peter; next him is Saint Paul. All are much restored; thirty-three of the medallions are wholly new. Opposite Saint Peter, at Christ's right hand, is the window of Saint Simon and Saint Jude; and next is the grisaille with the arms of Castile. If these windows were ordered between 1205 and 1210, Blanche, who was born in 1187, and married in 1200, would have been a young princess of twenty or twenty-five when she gave this window in grisaille to regulate and harmonize and soften the lighting of the Virgin's boudoir. The central chapel must be taken to be the most serious, the most studied, and the oldest of the chapels in the church, above the crypt. The windows here should rank in importance next to the lancets of the west front which are only about sixty years earlier. They show fully that difference.

Here one must see for one's self. Few artists know much about it, and still fewer care for an art which has been quite dead these four hundred years. The ruins of Nippur would hardly be more intelligible to the ordinary architect of English tradition than these twelfth-century efforts of the builders of Chartres. Even the learning of Viollet-le-Duc was at fault in dealing with a building so personal as this, the history of which is almost wholly lost. This central chapel must have been meant to give tone to the apse, and it shows with the colour-decoration of a queen's salon, a subject-decoration too serious for the amusement of heretics. One sees at a glance that the subject-decoration was inspired by church-custom, while colour was an experiment and the decorators of this enormous window space were at liberty as colourists to please the Countess of Chartres and the Princess Blanche and the Duchess of Brittany, without much regarding the opinions of the late Bernard of Clairvaux or even Augustine of Hippo, since the great ladies of the Court knew better than the Saints what would suit the Virgin.

The subject of the central window was prescribed by tradition. Christ is the Church, and in this church he and his Mother are one; therefore the life of Christ is the subject of the central window, but the treatment is the Virgin's, as the colours show, and as the absence of every influence but hers, including the Crucifixion, proves officially. Saint Peter and Saint Paul are in their proper place as the two great ministers of the throne who represent the two great parties in western religion, the Jewish and the Gentile. Opposite them, balancing by their family influence the weight of delegated power, are two of Mary's nephews, Simon and Jude; but this subject branches off again into matters so personal to Mary that Simon and Jude require closer acquaintance. One must study a new guidebook—the *Golden Legend*, by the blessed James, Bishop of Genoa and member of the order of Dominic, who was born at Varazze or Voragio in almost the same year that Thomas was born at Aquino, and whose *Legenda Aurea*, written about the middle of the thirteenth century, was more popular history than the Bible itself, and more generally consulted as authority. The decorators of the thirteenth century got their motives quite outside the Bible, in sources that James of Genoa compiled into a volume almost as fascinating as the *Fioretti of Saint Francis*.

According to the *Golden Legend* and the tradition accepted in Jerusalem by pilgrims and crusaders, Mary's family connection was large. It appears that her mother Anne was three times married, and by each husband had a daughter Mary, so that there were three Marys, half-sisters.

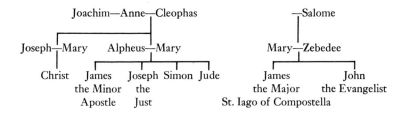

Simon and Jude were, therefore, nephews of Mary and cousins of Christ, whose lives were evidence of the truth not merely of Scripture, but specially of the private and family distinction of their aunt, the Virgin Mother of Christ. They were selected, rather than their brothers, or cousins James and John, for the conspicuous honour of standing opposite Peter and Paul, doubtless by reason of some merit of their own, but perhaps also because in art the two counted as one, and therefore the one window offered two witnesses, which allowed the artist to insert a grisaille in place of another legendary window to complete the chapel on their right. According to Viollet-le-Duc, the grisaille in this position regulates the light and so completes the effect.

If custom prescribed a general rule for the central chapel, it seems to have left great freedom in the windows near by. At Chartres the curved projection that contains the next two windows was not a chapel, but only a window-bay, for the sake of the windows, and, if the artists aimed at pleasing the Virgin, they would put their best work there. At Bourges in the same relative place are three of the best windows in the building:—the Prodigal Son, the New Alliance and the Good Samaritan; all of them full of life, story, and colour, with little reference to a worship or a saint. At Chartres the choice is still more striking, and the windows are also the best in the building, after the twelfth-century glass of the west front. The first, which comes next to Blanche's grisaille in the central chapel, is given to another nephew of Mary and apostle of Christ, Saint James the Major, whose life is recorded in the proper Bible Dictionaries, with a terminal remark as follows:—

> For legends respecting his death and his connections with Spain, see the Roman Breviary, in which the healing of a paralytic and the conversion of Hermogenes are attributed to him, and where it is asserted that he preached the Gospel in Spain, and that his remains were translated to Compostella. . . . As there is no shadow of foundation for any of the legends here referred to, we pass them by without further notice. Even Baronius shows himself ashamed of them. . . .

If the learned Baronius thought himself required to show shame for all the legends that pass as history, he must have suffered cruelly durin his laborious life, and his sufferings would not have been confined to the annals of the Church; but the historical accuracy of the glass windows is not our affair, nor are historians especially concerned in the events of the Virgin's life, whether recorded or legendary. Religion is, or ought to be, a feeling, and the thirteenth-century windows are original documents, much more historical than any recorded in the Bible, since their inspiration is a different thing from their authority. The true life of Saint James or Saint Jude or any other of the apostles, did not, in the opinion of the ladies in the Court of France, furnish subjects agreeable enough to decorate the palace of the Queen of Heaven; and that they were right, any one must feel, who compares these two windows with subjects of dogma. Saint James, better known as Santiago of Compostella, was a compliment to the young Dauphine— before Dauphines existed—the Princess Blanche of Castile, whose arms, or castles, are on the grisaille window next to it. Perhaps she chose him to stand there. Certainly her hand as seen plainly enough throughout the church to warrant suspecting it here. As a nephew, Saint James was dear to the Virgin, but, as a friend to Spain, still more dear to Blanche, and it is not likely that pure accident caused three adjacent windows to take a Spanish tone.

The Saint James in whom the thirteenth century delighted, and whose windows one sees at Bourges, Tours, and wherever the scallop-shell tells of the pilgrim, belongs not to the Bible but to the *Golden Legend*. This window was given by the Merchant Tailors whose signature appears at the bottom, in the corners, in two pictures that paint the tailor's shop of Chartres in the first quarter of the thirteenth century. The shop-boy takes cloth from chests for his master to show to customers, and to measure off by his ell. The story of Saint James begins in the lower panel, where he receives his mission from Christ. Above, on the right, he seems to be preaching. On the left appears a figure which tells the reason for the popularity of the story. It is Almogenes, or in the Latin, Hermogenes, a famous magician in great credit among the Pharisees, who has the command of demons, as you see, for behind his shoulder, standing, a little demon is perched, while he orders his pupil Filetus to convert James. Next, James is shown in discussion with a group of listeners. Filetus gives him a volume of false doctrine. Almogenes then further instructs Filetus. James is led away by a rope, curing a paralytic as he goes. He sends his cloak to Filetus to drive away the demon. Filetus receives the cloak, and the droll little demon departs in tears. Almogenes, losing his temper, sends two demons, with horns on their heads and clubs in their hands, to reason with James; who sends them back to remonstrate with Almogenes. The demons then bind Almogenes and bring him before James, who discusses differences with him until Almogenes burns his books of magic and prostrates himself before the Saint. Both are then brought before Herod, and Almogenes breaks a pretty heathen idol, while James goes to prison. A panel comes in here, out of place, showing Almogenes enchanting Filetus, and the demon entering into possession of him. Then Almogenes is seen being very roughly handled by a young Jew, while the bystanders seem to approve. James next makes Almogenes throw his books of magic into the sea; both are led away to execution, curing the infirm on their way; their heads are cut off; and, at the top, God blesses the orb of the world.

That this window was intended to amuse the Virgin seems quite as reasonable an idea as that it should have been made to instruct the people, or us. Its humour was as humorous then as now, for the French of the thirteenth century loved humour even in churches, as their grotesques proclaim. The Saint James window is a tale of magic, told with the vivacity of a fabliau; but if its motive of amusement seems still a forced idea, we can pass on, at once, to the companion window which holds the best position in the church, where, in the usual cathedral, one expects to find Saint John or some other apostle; or Saint Joseph; or a doctrinal lesson such as that called the New

Alliance where the Old and New Testament are united. The window which the artists have set up here is regarded as the best of the thirteenth-century windows, and is the least religious.

The subject is nothing less than the *Chanson de Roland* in pictures of coloured glass, set in a border worth comparing at leisure with the twelfth-century borders of the western lancets. Even at Chartres, the artists could not risk displeasing the Virgin and the Church by following a wholly profane work like the *Chanson* itself, and Roland had no place in religion. He could be introduced only through Charlemagne, who had almost as little right there as he. The twelfth century had made persistent efforts to get Charlemagne into the Church, and the Church had made very little effort to keep him out; yet by the year 1200, Charlemagne had not been sainted except by the anti-Pope Pascal III in 1165, although there was a popular belief, supported in Spain by the necessary documents, that Pope Calixtus II in 1122 had declared the so-called Chronicle of Archbishop Turpin to be authentic. The Bishop of Chartres in 1200 was very much too enlightened a prelate to accept the Chronicle or Turpin or Charlemagne himself, still less Roland and Thierry, as authentic in sanctity; but if the young and beautful Dauphine of France, and her cousins of Chartres, and their artists, warmly believed that the Virgin would be pleased by the story of Charlemagne and Roland, the Bishop might have let them have their way in spite of the irregularity. That the window was an irregularity, is plain; that it has always been immensely admired, is certain; and that Bishop Renaud must have given his assent to it, is not to be denied.

The most elaborate account of this window can be found in Mâle's *Art Religieux* (pp. 444–50). Its feeling or motive is quite another matter, as it is with the statuary on the north porch. The Furriers or Fur Merchants paid for the Charlemagne window, and their signature stands at the bottom, where a merchant shows a fur-lined cloak to his customer. That Mary was personally interested in furs, no authority seems to affirm, but that Blanche and Isabel and every lady of the Court, as well as every king and every count, in that day, took keen interest in the subject, is proved by the prices they paid, and the quantities they wore. Not even the Merchant Tailors had a better standing at Court than the Furriers, which may account for their standing so near the Virgin. Whatever the cause, the Furriers were allowed to put their signature here, side by side with the Tailors, and next to the Princess Blanche. Their gift warranted it. Above the signature, in the first panel, the Emperor Constantine is seen, asleep, in Constantinople, on an elaborate bed, while an angel is giving him the order to seek aid from Charlemagne against the Saracens. Charlemagne appears, in full armour of the year 1200, on horseback. Then Charlemagne, sainted, wearing his halo, converses with two bishops on the subject of a crusade for the rescue of Constantine. In the next scene, he arrives at the gates of Constantinople where Constantine receives him. The fifth picture is most interesting; Charlemagne has advanced with his knights and attacks the Saracens; the Franks wear coats-of-mail, and carry long, pointed shields; the infidels carry round shields; Charlemagne, wearing a crown, strikes off with one blow of his sword the head of a Saracen emir; but the battle is desperate; the chargers are at full gallop, and a Saracen is striking at Charlemagne with his battle-axe. After the victory has been won, the Emperor Constantine rewards Charlemagne by the priceless gift of three chasses or reliquaries, containing a piece of the true Cross; the Suaire or grave-cloth of the Saviour; and a tunic of the Virgin. Charlemagne then returns to France, and in the next medallion presents the three chasses and the crown of the Saracen king to the church at Aix, which to a French audience meant the Abbey of Saint-Denis. This scene closes the first volume of the story.

The second part opens on Charlemagne, seated between two persons, looking up to heaven at the Milky Way, called then the Way of Saint James, which directs him to the grave of Saint James in Spain. Saint James himself appears to Charlemagne in a dream, and orders him to redeem the tomb from the infidels. Then Charlemagne sets out, with Archbishop Turpin of Rheims and knights. In presence of his army he dismounts and implores the aid of God. Then he arrives before Pampeluna and transfixes with his lance the Saracen chief as he flies into the city. Mounted, he directs workmen to construct a church in honour of Saint James; a little cloud figures the hand of God. Next is shown the miracle of the lances; stuck in the ground at night, they are found in the morning to have burst into foliage, prefiguring martyrdom. Two thousand people perish in battle. Then begins the story of Roland which the artists and donors are so eager to tell, knowing, as they do, that what has so deeply interested men and women on earth, must interest Mary who loves them. You see Archbishop Turpin celebrating mass when an angel appears, to warn him of Roland's fate. Then Roland himself, also wearing a halo, is introduced, in the act of killing the giant Ferragus. The combat of Roland and Ferragus is at the top, out of sequence, as often happens in the legendary windows. Charlemagne and his army are seen marching homeward through the Pyrenees, while Roland winds his horn and splits the rock without being able to break Durendal. Thierry, likewise sainted,

brings water to Roland in a helmet. At last Thierry announces
Roland's death. At the top, on either side of Roland and Ferragus, is
an angel with incense.

The execution of this window is said to be superb. Of the colour,
and its relations with that of the Saint James, one needs time and long
acquaintance to learn the value. In the feeling, compared with that of
the twelfth century, one needs no time in order to see a change. These
two windows are as French and as modern as a picture of Lancret; they
are pure art, as simply decorative as the decorations of the Grand
Opera. The thirteenth century knew more about religion and decoration than the twentieth century will ever learn. The windows were
neither symbolic nor mystical, nor more religious than they pre-
tended to be. That they are more intelligent or more costly or more
effective is nothing to the purpose, so long as one grants that the combat of Roland and Ferragus, or Roland winding his olifant, or Charlemagne cutting off heads and transfixing Moors, were subjects never
intended to teach religion or instruct the ignorant, but to please the
Queen of Heaven as they pleased the queens of earth with a roman, not
in verse but in colour, as near as possible to decorative perfection.
Instinctively one looks to the corresponding bay, opposite, to see what
the artists could have done to balance these two great efforts of their
art; but the bay opposite is now occupied by the entrance to Saint
Piat's chapel and one does not know what changes may have been
made in the fourteenth century to rearrange the glass; yet, even as it
now stands, the Sylvester window which corresponds to the Charlemagne is, as glass, the strongest in the whole cathedral. In the next
chapel, on our left, comes the martyrs, with Saint Stephen, the first
martyr, in the middle window. Naturally the subject is more serious,
but the colour is not differently treated. A step further, and you see
the artists returning to their lighter subjects. The stories of Saint
Julian and Saint Thomas are more amusing than the plots of half
the thirteenth-century romances, and not very much more religious.
The subject of Saint Thomas is a pendant to that of Saint James, for
Saint Thomas was a great traveller and an architect, who carried
Mary's worship to India as Saint James carried it to Spain. Here is
the amusement of many days in studying the stories, the colour and
the execution of these windows, with the help of the *Monographs* of
Chartres and Bourges or the *Golden Legend* and occasional visits
to Le Mans, Tours, Clermont Ferrand, and other cathedrals; but, in
passing, one has to note that the window of Saint Thomas was given
by France, and bears the royal arms, perhaps for Philip Augustus the
King; while the window of Saint Julian was given by the Carpenters
and Coopers. One feels no need to explain how it happens that the

taste of the royal family, and of their tailors, furriers, carpenters, and
coopers, should fit so marvellously, one with another, and with that of
the Virgin; but one can compare with theirs the taste of the Stone-
workers opposite, in the window of Saint Sylvester and Saint Melchi-
ades, whose blues almost kill the Charlemagne itself, and of the
Tanners in that of Saint Thomas of Canterbury; or, in the last chapel
on the south side, with that of the Shoemakers in the window to Saint
Martin, attributed for some reason to a certain Clemens vitrearius
Carnutensis, whose name is on a window in the cathedral of Rouen.
The name tells nothing, even if the identity could be proved. Clement
the glassmaker may have worked on his own account, or for others;
the glass differs only in refinements of taste or perhaps of cost. Nicolas
Lescine, the canon, or Geoffroi Chardonnel, may have been less rich
than the Bakers, and even the Furriers may have not had the revenues
of the King; but some controlling hand has given more or less identical taste to all.

What one can least explain is the reason why some windows, that
should be here, are elsewhere. In most churches, one finds in the choir
a window of doctrine, such as the so-called New Alliance, but here the
New Alliance is banished to the nave. Besides the costly Charlemagne
and Saint James windows in the apse, the Furriers and Drapers gave
several others, and one of these seems particularly suited to serve as
companion to Saint Thomas, Saint James, and Saint Julian, so that it
is best taken with these while comparing them. It is in the nave, the
third window from the new tower, in the north aisle,—the window of
Saint Eustace. The story and treatment and beauty of the work would
have warranted making it a pendant to Almogenes, in the bay now
serving as the door to Saint Piat's chapel, which should have been the
most effective of all the positions in the church for a legendary story.
Saint Eustace, whose name was Placidas, commanded the guards of
the Emperor Trajan. One day he went out hunting with huntsmen
and hounds, as the legend in the lower panel of the window begins; a
pretty picture of a stag hunt about the year 1200; followed by one still
prettier, where the stag, after leaping upon a rock, has turned, and
shows a crucifix between his horns, the stag on one side balancing the
horse on the other, while Placidas on his knees yields to the miracle of
Christ. Then Placidas is baptized as Eustace; and in the centre, you
see him with his wife and two children—another charming composition—leaving the city. Four small panels in the corners are said to
contain the signatures of the Drapers and Furriers. Above, the story
of adventure goes on, showing Eustace bargaining with a shipmaster
for his passage; his embarcation with wife and children, and their
arrival at some shore, where the two children have landed, and the

master drives Eustace after them while he detains the wife. Four small panels here have not been identified, but the legend was no doubt familiar to the Middle Ages, and they knew how Eustace and the children came to a river, where you can see a pink lion carrying off one child, while a wolf, which has seized the other, is attacked by shepherds and dogs. The children are rescued, and the wife reappears, on her knees before her lord, telling of her escape from the shipmaster, while the children stand behind; and then the reunited family, restored to the Emperor's favour, is seen feasting and happy. At last Eustace refuses to offer a sacrifice to a graceful antique idol, and is then shut up, with all his family, in a brazen bull; a fire is kindled beneath it; and, from above, a hand confers the crown of martyrdom.

Another subject, which should have been placed in the apse, stands in a singular isolation which has struck many of the students in this branch of church learning. At Sens, Saint Eustace is in the choir, and by his side is the Prodigal Son. At Bourges also the Prodigal Son is in the choir. At Chartres, he is banished to the north transept, where you will find him in the window next the nave, almost as though he were in disgrace; yet the glass is said to be very fine, among the best in the church, while the story is told with rather more vivacity than usual; and as far as colour and execution go, the window has an air of age and quality higher than the average. At the bottom you see the signature of the corporation of Butchers [fig. 114]. The window at Bourges was given by the Tanners. The story begins with the picture showing the younger son asking the father for his share of the inheritance, which he receives in the next panel, and proceeds, on horseback, to spend, as one cannot help suspecting, at Paris, in the Latin Quarter, where he is seen arriving, welcomed by two ladies. No one has offered to explain why Chartres should consider two ladies theologically more correct than one; or why Sens should fix on three, or why Bourges should require six. Perhaps this was left to the artist's fancy; but, before quitting the twelfth century, we shall see that the usual young man who took his share of patrimony and went up to study in the Latin Quarter, found two schools of scholastic teaching, one called Realism, the other Nominalism, each of which in turn the Church had been obliged to condemn. Meanwhile the Prodigal Son is seen feasting with them, and is crowned with flowers, like a new Abélard, singing his songs to Héloïse, until his religious capital is exhausted, and he is dragged out of bed, to be driven naked from the house with sticks, in this also resembling Abélard. At Bourges he is gently turned out; at Sens he is dragged away by three devils. Then he seeks service, and is seen knocking acorns from boughs, to feed his employer's swine; but, among the thousands of young men who must have come here directly from the schools, nine in every ten said that he was teaching letters to his employer's children or lecturing to the students of the Latin Quarter. At last he decides to return to his father,—possibly the Archbishop of Paris or the Abbot of Saint-Denis, —who receives him with open arms, and gives him a new robe, which to the ribald student would mean a church living—an abbey, perhaps Saint-Gildas-de-Rhuys in Brittany, or elsewhere. The fatted calf is killed, the feast is begun, and the elder son, whom the malicious student would name Bernard, appears in order to make protest. Above, God, on His throne, blesses the globe of the world.

The original symbol of the Prodigal Son was a rather different form of prodigality. According to the Church interpretation, the Father had two sons; the older was the people of the Jews; the younger, the Gentiles. The Father divided his substance between them, giving to the older the divine law, to the younger, the law of nature. The younger went off and dissipated his substance, as one must believe, on Aristotle; but repented and returned when the Father sacrificed the victim—Christ—as the symbol of reunion. That the Synagogue also accepts the sacrifice is not so clear; but the Church clung to the idea of converting the Synagogue as a necessary proof of Christ's divine character. Not until about the time when this window may have been made, did the new Church, under the influence of Saint Dominic, abandon the Jews and turn in despair to the Gentiles alone.

The old symbolism belonged to the fourth and fifth centuries, and, as told by the Jesuit fathers Martin and Cahier in their *Monograph* of Bourges, it should have pleased the Virgin who was particularly loved by the young, and habitually showed her attachment to them. At Bourges the window stands next the central chapel of the apse, where at Chartres is the entrance to Saint Piat's chapel; but Bourges did not belong to Notre Dame, nor did Sens. The story of the prodigal sons of these years from 1200 to 1230 lends the window a little personal interest that the Prodigal Son of Saint Luke's Gospel could hardly have had even to thirteenth-century penitents. Neither the Church nor the Crown loved prodigal sons. So far from killing fatted calves for them, the bishop in 1209 burned no less than ten in Paris for too great intimacy with Arab and Jew disciples of Aristotle. The position of the Bishop of Chartres between the schools had been always awkward. As for Blanche of Castile, her first son, afterwards Saint Louis, was born in 1215; and after that time no Prodigal Son was likely to be welcomed in any society which she frequented. For her, above all other women on earth or in heaven, prodigal sons felt most antipathy, until, in 1229, the quarrel became so violent that she turned her police on them and beat a number to death in the streets. They retaliated without regard for loyalty or decency, being far from model youth and prone to relapses from virtue, even when forgiven and beneficed.

The Virgin Mary, Queen of Heaven, showed no prejudice against prodigal sons, or even prodigal daughters. She would hardly, of her own accord, have ordered such persons out of her apse, when Saint Stephen at Bourges and Sens showed no such puritanism; yet the Chartres window is put away in the north transept. Even there it still stands opposite the Virgin of the Pillar, on the women's and Queen Blanche's side of the church, and in an excellent position, better seen from the choir than some of the windows in the choir itself, because the late summer sun shines full upon it, and carries its colours far into the apse. This may have been one of the many instances of tastes in the Virgin which were almost too imperial for her official court. Omniscient as Mary was, she knew no difference between the Blanches of Castile and the students of the Latin Quarter. She was rather fond of prodigals, and gentle toward the ladies who consumed the prodigal's substance. She admitted Mary Magdalen and Mary the Gipsy to her society. She fretted little about Aristotle so long as the prodigal adored her, and naturally the prodigal adored her almost to the exclusion of the Trinity. She always cared less for her dignity than was to be wished. Especially in the nave and on the porch, among the peasants, she liked to appear as one of themselves; she insisted on lying in bed, in a stable, with the cows and asses about her, and her baby in a cradle by the bedside, as though she had suffered like other women, though the Church insisted she had not. Her husband, Saint Joseph, was notoriously uncomfortable in her Court, and always preferred to get as near to the door as he could. The choir at Chartres, on the contrary, was aristocratic; every window there had a court quality, even down to the contemporary Thomas A'Becket, the fashionable martyr of good society. Theology was put into the transepts or still further away in the nave where the window of the New Alliance elbows the Prodigal Son. Even to Blanche of Castile, Mary was neither a philanthropist nor theologist nor merely a mother,— she was an absolute Empress, and whatever she said was obeyed, but sometimes she seems to have willed an order that worried some of her most powerful servants.

Mary chose to put her Prodigal into the transept, and one would like to know the reason. Was it a concession to the Bishop or the Queen? Or was it to please the common people that these familiar picture-books, with their popular interest, like the Good Samaritan and the Prodigal Son, were put on the walls of the great public hall? This can hardly be, since the people would surely have preferred the Charlemagne and Saint James to any other. We shall never know; but sitting here in the subdued afternoon light of the apse, one goes on for hours reading the open volumes of colour, and listening to the steady discussion by the architects, artists, priests, princes, and princesses of the thirteenth century about the arrangements of this apse. However strong-willed they might be, each in turn whether priest, or noble, or glassworker, would have certainly appealed to the Virgin and one can imagine the architect still beside us, in the growing dusk of evening, mentally praying, as he looked at the work of a finished day: "Lady Virgin, show me what you like best! The central chapel is correct, I know. The Lady Blanche's grisaille veils the rather strong blue tone nicely, and I am confident it will suit you. The Charlemagne window seems to me very successful, but the Bishop feels not at all easy about it, and I should never have dared put it here if the Lady Blanche had not insisted on a Spanish bay. To balance at once both the subjects and the colour, we have tried the Stephen window in the next chapel, with more red; but if Saint Stephen is not good enough to satisfy you, we have tried again with Saint Julian, whose story is really worth telling you as we can tell it; and with him we have put Saint Thomas because you loved him and gave him your girdle. I do not myself care so very much for Saint Thomas of Canterbury opposite, though the Count is wild about it, and the Bishop wants it; but the Sylvester is stupendous in the morning sun. What troubles me most is the first right-hand bay. The princesses would not have let me put the Prodigal Son there, even if it were made for the place. I've nothing else good enough to balance the Charlemagne unless it be the Eustace. Gracious Lady, what ought I to do? Forgive me my blunders, my stupidity, my wretched want of taste and feeling! I love and adore you! All that I am, I am for you! If I cannot please you, I care not for Heaven! but without your help, I am lost!"

Upon my word, you may sit here forever imagining such appeals, and the endless discussions and criticisms that were heard every day, under these vaults, seven hundred years ago. That the Virgin answered the questions is my firm belief, just as it is my conviction that she did not answer them elsewhere. One sees her personal presence on every side. Any one can feel it who will only consent to feel like a child. Sitting here any Sunday afternoon, while the voices of the children of the maîtrise are chanting in the choir,—your mind held in the grasp of the strong lines and shadows of the architecture; your eyes flooded with the autumn tones of the glass; your ears drowned with the purity of the voices; one sense reacting upon another until sensation reaches the limit of its range,—you, or any other lost soul, could, if you cared to look and listen, feel a sense beyond the human ready to reveal a sense divine that would make that world once more intelligible, and would bring the Virgin to life again, in all the depths of feeling which she shows here,—in lines, vaults, chapels, colours, legends, chants,—more eloquent than the prayer-book, and more beautiful than the autumn sunlight; and any one willing to try could feel it like the child, reading new thought without end into the art he has studied a hundred times; but what is still more convincing, he could, at will, in an instant, shatter the whole art by calling into it a single motive of his own.

BRIEF GLOSSARY OF
ARCHITECTURAL TERMS

Aedicula: a canopy-like structure.

Ambulatory: an aisle curving around the apse or hemicycle.

Apse: the chapellike sanctuary of the church; usually semicircular.

Arcade: a row of arches on piers or columns, separating one aisle from another.

Archivolt: a wedge-shaped stone forming part of the arch over a portal; usually sculpted.

Barrel vault: a continuous semicircular or pointed vault resting on walls.

Bay: in Gothic architecture, the design unit of the wall, extending from the pavement to the peak of the vault.

Choir: the area preceding the sanctuary; originally architectural as well as liturgical; in the Gothic period, the straight bays preceding the hemicycle.

Clearstory: the top story, with windows.

Corbel: a projecting support.

Cornice: a projecting moulding at the top of a wall, from which the roof springs.

Crossing: the intersection of nave and transept.

Crypt: the semisubterranean story of a church where relics were usually kept.

Dado: the lower portion of a wall, directly above the pavement; usually ornamented.

Embrasure: the oblique walls leading out from the jambs of a portal.

Façade: a front or face, generally on the west.

Flying buttress: an arch rising from a wall buttress to rest against the clearstory at the point where the vault begins.

Formeret: a vault rib lying against the wall.

Gantry: a frame structure resting on side supports so as to reach over an open central space.

Groined vault: a vault covering one bay in stair, with ridges connecting the supports.

Hemicycle: the curved eastern termination of the church; a Gothic "apse."

Jambs: the posts at the sides of a portal and, by extension, the oblique walls leading out from them.

Lintel: a horizontal beam, usually decorated.

Nave: the central aisle of a church.

Pier: a support flanked by voids.

Pilaster: a rectangular projection in masonry, usually for decorative effect.

Plinth: in medieval architecture, the lowest element in the pedestal of a pier; usually with a moulding in the upper part.

Porch: a covered, projecting structure, usually open on the front and sides.

Quadripartite vault: a ribbed vault formed by two intersecting ribs.

Radiating chapel: a chapel "radiating" off an ambulatory.

Respond: a column or group of columns on a wall, supporting a member of the vaulting.

Ribbed vault: a vault with ribs connecting the supports.

Rinceau: a decorative, vine-like form.

Sexpartite vault: a ribbed vault having, in plan, three ribs that intersect in a common point.

Socle: in medieval architecture, the element directly below the base moulding of a pier.

Statue-column: a relief sculpture in which the support is a column.

String course: a horizontal decorative element.

Tas-de-charge: the construction of the vault springer in horizontal layers.

Tenon: a projecting member meant to be inserted into a hole (the mortise).

Transept: the cross arms of a church.

Tribune: a gallery in the second story, the full width of the aisle below it.

Triforium: a narrow, bandlike zone somewhere above the main arcade; often containing a longitudinal passage in the thickness of the wall.

Trumeau: the post in the center of a medieval portal.

Thrust: the direction in which the weight of a vault pushes.

Turret: a "small tower," generally used as part of the decorative ensemble at the spire-level of a Gothic tower.

Tympanum: the field, semicircular or pointed, above a doorway; usually sculpted.

Vault: a covering, usually of stone.

Voussoir: a wedge-shaped stone forming part of an arch.

Webbing: the thin cover laid over the ribs of a ribbed vault.

SELECTED BIBLIOGRAPHY

(Asterisks indicate those books which are available in paperback editions.)

S. Abdul-Hak, *La sculpture des porches du transept de la cathédrale de Chartres*, Paris, 1942.

*Henry Adams, *Mont-Saint-Michel and Chartres*, American Institute of Architects, 1904 (often reprinted).

J. Bony, "The Resistance to Chartres in Early Thirteenth-Century Architecture," *Journal of the British Archaeological Association*, ser. 3, vols. 20–21, 1957–1958, pp. 35–52.

M. J. Bulteau, *Monographie de la cathédrale de Chartres*, 3 vols., Chartres, 1887–1892.

Y. Delaporte, *Les vitraux de la cathédrale de Chartres*, 3 vols., Chartres, 1926.

P. Durand, *Monographie de Notre-Dame de Chartres*, Paris, 1881; atlas of drawings, Paris, 1867.

E. Fels, "Die Grabung an der Fassade der Kathedrale von Chartres," *Kunstchronik*, vol. 8, 1955, pp. 149–151.

H. Focillon, *The Art of the West in the Middle Ages*, 2 vols., London and New York, 1963; first published as *Art d'occident*, Paris, 1938.

L. Grodecki, "The Transept Portals of Chartres Cathedral," *Art Bulletin*, vol. 33, 1951, pp. 156–164.

*H. Jantzen, *The High Gothic: The Classic Cathedrals of Chartres, Reims and Amiens*, New York, 1962.

H. H. Hilberry, "The Cathedral of Chartres in 1030," *Speculum*, vol. 34, 1959, pp. 561–572.

J. R. Johnson, "The Tree of Jesse Window of Chartres: Laudes Regiae," *Speculum*, vol. 36, 1961, pp. 1–22.

J. R. Johnson, *The Radiance of Chartres*, New York, 1965.

*A. Katzenellenbogen, *The Sculptural Programs of Chartres Cathedral*, Baltimore, 1959, and New York, 1964.

P. Kidson, *Sculpture at Chartres*, London, 1958, and New York, 1959.

A. Lapeyre, *Des façades occidentales de Saint-Denis et de Chartres aux portails de Laon*, Paris, 1960.

*E. Mâle, *The Gothic Image: Religious Art in France of the Thirteenth Century*, New York, 1958.

J. Mallion, *Le jubé de la cathédrale de Chartres*, Chartres, 1964.

*E. Panofsky, *Gothic Architecture and Scholasticism*, New York, 1967.

A. Priest, "The Masters of the West Façade of Chartres," *Art Studies*, vol. 1, 1923, pp. 28–44.

G. Richter, *Chartres: Idee und Gestalt der Kathedrale*, Stuttgart, 1958.

W. Sauerländer, "Zu den Westportale von Chartres," *Kunstchronik*, vol. 9, 1956, pp. 155–156.

W. Sauerländer, "Tombeaux chartrains du premier quart du XIIIᵉ siècle," *Information d'histoire de l'art*, vol. 9, 1964, pp. 47–59.

W. Sauerländer, *Von Sens bis Strassburg*, Berlin, 1966.

O. G. von Simson, *The Cathedral of Chartres*, New York, 1956.

*——, *The Gothic Cathedral: Origins of Gothic Architecture and the Medieval Concept of Order*, New York, 1964.

W. Stoddard, *The West Portals of Saint-Denis and Chartres*, Cambridge, Mass., 1952.

K. M. Swoboda, "Zur Frage dem Anteil des führenden Meisters am Gesamtkunstwerk der Kathedrale von Chartres," *Festschrift Hans R. Hahnloser*, Basel, 1961, pp. 37–46.

J. van der Meulen, "Histoire de la construction de la cathédrale Notre-Dame de Chartres après 1194," *Bulletin, Société archéologique d'Eure-et-Loir*, (Mémoires), vol. 23, 1965, pp. 79–126.

J. van der Meulen, "Recent Literature on the Chronology of Chartres Cathedral," *Art Bulletin*, vol. 49, 1967, pp. 152–172.

W. Vöge, *Die Anfänge des monumentalen Stiles im Mittelalter*, Strasbourg, 1894.

W. Vöge, "Die Bahnbrecher des Naturstudiums," *Zeitschrift für bildende Kunst*, n.f., vol. 25, 1914, pp. 193–216.

Picture and Guide Books

M. Aubert, *La cathédrale de Chartres*, Paris, 1952.

Y. Delaporte, *Chartres*, Paris, 1939.

Y. Delaporte, *Notre-Dame de Chartres*, Paris, 1957.

L. Grodecki, *Chartres*, Paris, 1963.

E. Houvet, *Cathédrale de Chartres*, 5 vols. in 7, Chelles, 1919.

E. Mâle, *La cathédrale de Chartres*, Paris, 1948.

J. Maunoury, *Chartres*, Paris, 1959.

R. Merlet, *La cathédrale de Chartres*, Paris 1909, and (in English) 1939.

W. Sauerländer, *Die Kathedrale von Chartres*, Stuttgart, 1954.

A. Vigneau, *La cathédrale de Chartres*, Paris, 1935.

J. Villette, *Chartres et sa cathédrale*, Paris, 1962.

ROBERT BRANNER is Professor and Chairman of Art
History and Archaeology at Columbia University. In
1963 his *La cathédrale de Bourges* won the Alice Davis
Hitchcock Award as the most distinguished book
that year on architectural history by an American
author. His other books include *Gothic Architecture*
and *Burgundian Gothic Architecture*. Professor Branner holds the doctorate from Yale University and has
been awarded a Guggenheim Fellowship. He was
formerly editor of the *Journal of the Society of
Architectural Historians*.